More Acclaim for *Decoding Liberation*

As Open Source software continues its successful penetration of mainstream business practice and economic thought, we're at risk of losing sight of a critical part of what Richard Stallman meant when he said the 'free' part of free software is like free speech, not free beer. In *Decoding Liberalism*, Samir Chopra and Scott Dexter recapture and extend a part of the conversation that will ultimately be much more important than business models, patent and copyright law, or total cost of ownership for a piece of software. What does the open source model offer to political, artistic, and scientific freedom, and thus to the human enterprise of creativity beyond the guts of a computing machine? Their book is an eloquent, thoughtful, adventurous, and exciting dive into what really matters about changing the rules of code.
—**Steven Weber**, author of *The Success of Open Source*

An exceptionally well-written and conceptualized work on an underexplored area of computer science. Summing Up: Highly recommended.
—*Choice*

[A] unique, important, and sympathetic examination ... *Decoding Liberation* unpacks the history, ethics, political economy, and aesthetic practice of free software production. Chopra and Dexter examine FOSS as a philosophically inspired social movement built by hackers and wrought through the creation of technology. There is a philosophy and politics to all technology, as the authors repeatedly point out, but FOSS practice makes these more explicit and more visible in ways that make it an ideal target for their interdisciplinary analysis. A technologically grounded and philosophical evaluation of technical practice and artifacts, Chopra and Dexter's approach is an effective and deeply appropriate fit for FOSS.
—*Minds and Machines*

This would be a very useful text for students looking to cover the literature on FLOSS, particularly those from a science background who wish to know more about the social and philosophical side of software development.
—*Theory, Culture & Society*

It is the rare work in this space that I can recommend equally to the novice and expert, but *Decoding Liberation* is one. Additionally, individuals from a broad range of disciplines will be able to find something that resonates here. This is perhaps the work's chief value: because it is accessible to so many, it has the potential to spur further discussion on these issues in a way that many works could never expect. *Decoding Liberation* is a remarkable collaboration that invites further debate.
—*Resource Center for Cyberculture Studies*

As the first sustained philosophical treatment of the Free and Open Source Software movements, *Decoding Liberation* achieves one thing for certain. By covering broad areas of the philosophical landscape—political philosophy, aesthetics, ethics, and philosophy of science—Chopra and Dexter have shown the range of FOSS issues that can be informed by philosophy. In opting to paint with a broad brush, they have, I believe, opened many spaces for critical dialog.
—*APA Newsletter on Philosophy and Computers*

Routledge Studies in New Media and Cyberculture:

Routledge Studies in New Media and Cyberculture is dedicated to furthering original research in new media and cyberculture studies. International in scope, the series places an emphasis on cutting edge scholarship and interdisciplinary methodology. Topics explored in the series will include comparative and cultural studies of video games, blogs, online communities, digital music, new media art, cyberactivism, open source, mobile communications technologies, new information technologies, and the myriad intersections of race, gender, ethnicity, nationality, class, and sexuality with cyberculture.

Series Titles

Cyberpop: Digital Lifestyles and Commodity Culture
Sidney Eve Matrix, University of Winnipeg

The Internet in China: Cyberspace and Civil Society
Zixue Tai, Southern Illinois University

Racing Cyberculture: Minoritarian Internet Art
Chris McGahan, Yeshiva University

Decoding Liberation: The Promise of Free and Open Source Software
Samir Chopra and Scott Dexter, Brooklyn College of the City University of New York

Forthcoming Titles

Virtual English: Internet Use, Language, and Global Subjects
Jillian Enteen, Northwestern University

Decoding Liberation

The Promise of Free and Open Source Software

Samir Chopra and
Scott D. Dexter

Routledge
Taylor & Francis Group
New York   London

First published in 2008
by Routledge
711 Third Avenue, New York, NY 10017, USA

Simultaneously published in the UK
by Routledge
2 Park Square, Milton Park, Abingdon, Oxon OX14 4RN

This edition first published in paperback in 2010

Routledge is an imprint of the Taylor & Francis Group,
an informa business

© 2008, 2010 Taylor & Francis

Typeset in Times Light Standard by Taylor & Francis.

Trademark Notice: Product or corporate names may be trademarks or
registered trademarks, and are used only for identification and
explanation without intent to infringe.

Library of Congress Cataloging in Publication Data
Chopra, Samir.
  Decoding liberation : the promise of free and open source software /
Samir Chopra, Scott D. Dexter.
    p. cm. – (Routledge studies in new media and cyberculture)
  Includes bibliographical references and index.
  1. Open source software. 2. Computer software – Development –
Social aspects. I. Dexter, Scott. II. Title.
  QA76.76.S46C56 2007
  005.3 – dc22
                          2007004119

ISBN10: 0-415-97893-9 (hbk)
ISBN10: 0-415-87678-8 (pbk)
ISBN10: 0-203-94214-0 (ebk)

ISBN13: 978-0-415-97893-4 (hbk)
ISBN13: 978-0-415-87678-0 (pbk)
ISBN13: 978-0-203-94214-7 (ebk)

Dedication

To Noor, light of my life.

S. C.

To Jill, because she hates being the center of attention.

S. D.

Contents

Acknowledgments

A number of our colleagues and friends helped us get this project off the ground. Timothy Shortell, one of the 101 Most Dangerous Academics in America, loaned us his copy of Steven Weber's *The Success of Open Source*; Corey Robin and Sharon Zukin both read and provided advice on the book proposal; Robert Tempio expertly guided our proposal into the right hands. Our editor, Matthew Byrnie, demonstrated faith in this project from very early on. For their comments on early versions of two chapters, we thank the members of the Faculty Fellowship Publications Program at the CUNY Graduate Center during the Spring 2005 semester: Jordi Getman-Eraso, Janet Johnson, Anru Lee, Costas Panayotakis, Fredrick Wasser, and Sharon Zukin. We also thank Lee Quinby and the Zicklin Seminar at Brooklyn College for their support during the Fall 2006 semester.

Richard Stallman provided extraordinarily timely and constructive feedback on versions of Chapters 1, 2, and 4. We owe him another intellectual debt, in that much of this book is directly inspired by his writings.

David Arnow, Carolina Bank-Muñoz, David Berry, Matt Butcher, Fernando Cassia, Chris Cardona, Thomas Chance, Marvin Croy, John Frohnmeyer, Benjamin Mako Hill, James "JD" Howell, Aaron Kozbelt, Lee Quinby, George Thiruvathukal, Saam Trivedi, Robert Viscusi, Donna Wilson, and Thomas Wren provided intellectual support, critique, and encouragement. Portions of some chapters were presented at the International Conference on Knowledge, Technology and Society 2005; Computer Ethics and Philosophical Enquiry 2005; North American Computers and Philosophy Conference 2005; and the American Philosophical Association's Central Division Meeting 2006. We thank audiences at these meetings for their comments and discussion.

Noor Alam, Jill Cirasella, Dayton Clark, David Coady, Gabriella Coleman, David Dexter, Sharon Dexter, Virginia Held, Jelena Karanovic, Chandra Kumar, Edward Levine, Sean Sullivan, John Sutton, and Katherine Willis were dedicated readers of different versions of the chapters; we thank them all for their graceful handling of anxious authors.

Jill Cirasella and Katherine Willis performed astonishing feats of librarianship; Camille Martin helped dissolve bureaucratic obstacles; a PSC-CUNY research award helped in the procurement of books and supplies; Aaron Tenenbaum continues to be a sensitive and accommodating chair.

Pilon Coffee, Rasily Supari, International Food Store, John's Bakery and Cafe, the MTA, Yo in Midtown, Dogfish Head Craft Brewery, Chris Parnell, Andy Samberg, Mark Feuerstein, Sam Friedlander, Adam Stein, VoxPop, Prospect Park, Transportation Alternatives, Ali Mohammed Grocery, Yahoo! Groups, and Gmail facilitated the long hours of writing.

S. C.

S. D.

I owe multifarious intellectual and personal debts: Jim Whitescarver, for dazzling me with his regular expressions and his spirit of constant inquiry; Rakesh Kushwaha, for the companionship, and for help with my struggles with coding; Gurinder Johar, for showing me work on computers could be playful; my brother, Ashutosh Chopra, for being the first hacker I knew; Devendra Vamathevan, for the first beautiful algorithm I had ever seen; the Computerized Conferencing and Communications Center, for teaching me most of the computer science I know; Thomas Meyer, for discussions about the philosophy of science; Norman Foo, for providing a great research environment in Sydney; JD Howell, for making GNU/Linux installs fun; Rohit Parikh, for teaching me much about mathematics, philosophy and computer science; Murray Turoff and Roxanne Hiltz, for introducing me to a study of technology's social and political implications; the UNIX community, for putting on many, many brilliant performances; all those in the free software and open source communities that keep their code free in all the ways they know.

My families continue to provide the emotional sustenance that lifts me each day. I am thankful for their love and support to the Chopras, the Sabharwals, the Tulis, the Sens, the Alams, and the Ahujas. A special thanks to Ashu, Ritu and Akul for keeping a home for me in India.

No expression of my gratitude to my wife, partner, and best friend, Noor Alam, would do justice to all she does for me. But I'll go ahead and thank her anyway.

I was fortunate in this project to have the perfect coauthor: Scott Dexter. I grew in many ways —intellectually and personally—while working with him on this book. We started talking about politics and technology years ago, and have not stopped yet. I look forward to many more conversations with *mi buen amigo*.

S. C.

I wouldn't have been able to imagine participating in a project like this had I not stumbled into a community of scholars and activists during graduate school. Most especially, Rachel Barish, Jon Curtiss, Tamara Joseph, and Karen Miller opened the possibility of finding an intersection between the academy and a vision of the world as it ought to be. Alejandra Marchevsky and Jeanne Theoharis aided in my search for that intersection while also demonstrating the intense intellectual satisfaction that comes of writing with four hands on one keyboard.

Many friends provided intellectual, emotional, and gastronomic support before and during this project; I am especially thankful for Noor Alam, Carolina Bank-Muñoz, Patrick Doyle, Mikael Elsila, Teresa Hill, Christina Ingoglia, Shira Kamm, Gloria Karimian, Ted Levine, Nikki McDaniel, Jack Shuler, and George Theoharis.

Frank Hughes and Fran Anastasi Darge brought their prodigious intuitions to my pursuit of harmonious relationships within and between body and mind. The musical community created by Raquy Danziger, the Cavemen, and my fellow Messengers continues to be an unexpectedly important source of and outlet for creative energy.

My parents, David and Sharon Dexter, and my sister and brother-in-law, Katherine Dexter Willis and Richard Willis, have shared all my anticipations and anxieties; their steady enthusiasm and delight in my endeavors sustains me.

My discovery of Jill Cirasella in the library is the single most valuable result of this project.

My gratitude to Samir Chopra goes well beyond that I would accord any ordinary coauthor. I am unutterably fortunate to have in him not only an ideal writing partner but also a traveling companion, an ally in the topsy-turvy arena of academic politics, and a true friend.

S. D.

Introduction

Technological artifacts of the past consisted only of hardware: engines, motors, pumps, levers, switches, gears. To control the hardware was to control the technology. Hardware is expensive to acquire and maintain, so technology was invariably controlled by large economic entities — states, then corporations. Concerns about social control invariably addressed control of technology; Marx's concerns about the control of the means of production were focused on the hardware that both crystallized and generated capitalist power.

The twentieth century brought a new form of technology, one in which hardware and control are explicitly separated. The means of production no longer inhere solely in hardware; control is transferable, distributable, plastic, and reproducible, all with minimal cost. Control of technology may be democratized, its advantages spread more broadly than ever before. The reactionary response to this promise is an attempt to embrace and co-opt this control to advance entrenched social, economic, and political power. It is this reaction that free software resists.

* * *

The software that runs on our computers is a sequence of instructions for the computer to execute; these instructions are represented, in a fashion directly understood by the computer's hardware, as 0s and 1s. Programs in this form, called *binaries* or *executables*, are extraordinarily difficult for humans to understand. While it is theoretically possible to determine the purpose and function of a program in binary form through *reverse engineering*, it is exceedingly time-consuming and only rarely attempted. Similarly, it might be possible to modify the function of a program by modifying its binary representation, but this, too, is unsustainably expensive. Instead, the vast majority of modern software is written using a variety of *high-level languages*. Automated translation programs (*compilers*) then convert these high-level programs (*source code*) into executable binary code. Programs in high-level languages, while difficult to interpret without training, enable programmers to communicate their design logic to other programmers using language and symbols intentionally based on natural language (usually English) and mathematics. Thus, it is reasonably straightforward for one programmer to read another's work and understand not only the function of the program but the manner in which that functionality is achieved.

In the past few decades, most commercial software has been distributed in binary form only, thereby providing users with usable programs but concealing the techniques by which these programs achieve their purposes. Source code for such proprietary programs is regarded as a trade secret, the revelation of which supposedly has disastrous economic effects for its corporate creator.

But there is an alternative: to distribute software *with* its source code. This is the guiding principle of free and open source software (FOSS). At various points in the history of software development, in particular communities of programmers and enthusiasts, and among some modern software corporations, distribution of source code has been and continues to be a fundamental practice. This distribution creates several potentials for users: to inspect the code of the software they use, to modify it if they are so inclined, and to send the modifications back to the originator for incorporation in future versions of the software. The core distinction between FOSS and proprietary software is that FOSS makes available to its users the knowledge and innovation contributed by the creator(s) of the software, in the form of the created source code. This permits, even encourages, interested programmers to become involved with the ongoing development of the software, disseminates knowledge about the inner workings of computing artifacts, and sustains autonomy among the community of software users. Allowing this form of user participation in the evolution of software has created vast and sophisticated networks of programmers, software of amazingly high quality, and an eructation of new business practices.

The terms *free software* and *open source software* are nearly synonymous terms for a particular approach to developing and distributing software. We use the phrase *free and open source software*, or FOSS, to include both notions explicitly. There are important distinctions to be made, however, between the open source and free software movements; we will refer to them individually when the difference is crucial.

* * *

The FOSS phenomenon is the subject of numerous political, economic, and sociological studies, all reacting to the potential for radical change it embodies. These studies focus mainly on four claims.

First, FOSS is a novel technology for producing software: it "represent[s] a new mode of production — commons-based peer production" (Benkler 2002) and is "a critique of existing laws, contracts, and business practices . . . [with] the potential to explicitly change the 'political-economic structure of society'" (Kelty 2002). Therefore, it is supported by new microeconomic, political, and personal dynamics that may shed light on other areas of economic productivity and modes of collaboration. This new mode of production serves as the basis for examinations of its historical antecedents, parallels from other (sub)cultures, and potential application to other domains of inquiry and cultural and scientific production (Ghosh 2005). The novelty of FOSS, for these investigations, is that it contrasts with the economies of exclusionary property relations, supported by weighty legal structures, which characterized the preexisting software industry. From the perspective of software engineering, FOSS's proponents tout the superiority of its bazaarlike development model over the rigid cathedrals of proprietary-software houses (Raymond 2000). Economists, in turn, are concerned with how this method of production functions, examining the personal motivations and microeconomics of its workforce (Lerner and Tirole 2001), and political scientists investigate the governance schemes that support successful FOSS projects (Weber 2004). Inevitably, some of these claims of novelty are also the subject of critique (Fitzgerald 2005; Glass 2005; Rusovan, Lawford, and Parnas 2005).

Second, FOSS provides a social good that proprietary software cannot; for example, FOSS may be the only viable source of software in developing nations, where programming talent is abundant but prices for proprietary-software licenses are prohibitive. Countries such as China and India have seen in FOSS an opportunity to draw on their wealth of programming talent to provide the technological infrastructure for their rapidly expanding economies. Microsoft's substantial investments in Indian education initiatives may be prompted by worries that free software might fill indigenous needs instead (Chandrasekhar 2002). FOSS has been cited by Venezuelan President Hugo Chavez as a key element of achieving economic independence from the global North (Leonard 2006). At the 2005 World Social Forum in Porto Allegre, the Youth Camp focused largely on FOSS issues (Juris 2005). This enthusiasm for FOSS extends to the industrialized First World as well, as many members of the European Union adopt it for governmental administration (Europa 2003).

Third, FOSS challenges many central concepts of intellectual property. Its novel copyright-licensing schemes have prompted much debate about the foundations, both ethical and economic, of apparently well-established notions such as property and ownership (Dixon 2003; St. Laurent 2004). The emphasis on continual innovation — hailed as the key to FOSS's superior software engineering — puts it into direct conflict with the ideologies of patenting. FOSS forces debate on the distinction between ideas and their expressions that is fundamental to patent and copyright law (Davis et al. 1996; Swann and Turner 2004). Indeed, a new cottage industry of legal analysis and application has sprung up to deal with the questions evoked by FOSS's licensing schemes and its opposition to software patents. This is in no small part driven by corporate concern about whether FOSS can coexist with existing business practices.

Finally, FOSS is a threat to the corporate status quo. This facet of FOSS has been trumpeted vigorously by open source advocates, who argue that open source software is a new and better way of doing business: one that should, as a result of free-market competition, supplant much (though not all) of the proprietarily licensed software produced and sold today (Dibona, Cooper, and Stone 2005;

DiBona, Ockman, and Stone 1999; Raymond 2000). Such advocacy reflects a broader optimism about the ability of FOSS, with other novel modes of industrial organization, to subvert dominant industrial structures. Stakeholders in the status quo are demonstrably aware of this threat, as the leaked "Halloween Papers," revealing Microsoft's sense of the threat of free software, dramatically show (Raymod 1998). To most outsiders, the FOSS community seems remarkably hostile to proprietary-software giants. But this adversarial position is fragmented: while some developers indeed hope fervently for the downfall of Microsoft, many seek only for it to show us the code.

* * *

In this book we take free software to be a liberatory enterprise in several dimensions. While the freedom to inspect source code is most commonly associated with FOSS, of more interest to us are the political, artistic, and scientific freedoms it brings in its wake. The title of this book reflects this promise: in a world that is increasingly encoded, our free software carries much potential for liberation. Granted, claims about technology and freedom are nothing new; much of the early hype about the Internet was rhetoric of this kind. But what is important about the recurrence of such hyperbolic enthusiasm is that it is clearly articulated evidence of a desire for technology to live up to its potential as a liberatory force.

With this book, the investigation of free software becomes broader than those conducted by lawyers, economists, businessmen, and cultural theorists: FOSS carries many philosophical implications that must be carefully explored and explicated. FOSS, most important, focuses attention on that often-misunderstood creature: software. To understand it as mere machine instructions, to ignore its creative potential and its power to enforce political and social control, is to indulge in a problematic blindness.

We do not contend that "knowledge [or information] just wants to be free," that this is a fait accompli. But we do want to understand what this freedom might be and how we might go about achieving it. While the potential of free software is often alluded to, it is not fully understood. This book is partly an expression of a utopian hope, partly an expression of the fear that a liberatory moment is slipping away.

* * *

In the first chapter, we begin with a history of software development as an industrial process, characterizing the emergence of the GNU free software project in the 1980s as a natural step in the evolution of software, one that challenged the anomalous proprietary-software regimes that had taken hold in the late 1970s. We show how this history reflects the value of cooperative work, and track the slow move toward the eventual commodification of software; while free software is legitimately regarded as a radical intervention in the software industry, it may also be thought of as a return to software's roots. We investigate the political economies of software, examining the extent to which FOSS invokes or revises traditional notions of property and production. In our narrative, the 1998 schism between the free software and open source movements — where a faction within the free software community changed tactics and language to court commercial interests — is a crucial event. We examine the potential for co-optation that the open source movement has created, drawing it apart from the free software moment, which remains committed to an antitechnocratic, emancipatory, yet pragmatic vision.

In Chapter Two, we examine the ethical positions enshrined in the constitutive documents of the free and open source movements. The freedoms enumerated in the Free Software Definition and Open Source Definition provide normative ethical guidance to the FOSS community. Building on these definitions, free software licensing schemes grant a suite of rights and freedoms, to programmers and users alike, that are much broader than those granted by proprietary-software licensing schemes. At a finer granularity, the particular licenses take different approaches to protecting these rights and freedoms; hence, choosing a license is an important responsibility of the free software developer. The discussion in this chapter is intended both to support this decision making and to assess the ethical implications of the rhetorical character of these documents.

Chapter Three addresses the FOSS creative process, which facilitates group collaboration and innovation through unique organizational structures. This examination relies on an analysis of the aesthetics of software in general, invoking notions of beauty in science, and uncovering the meaning of "beautiful code" through the testimonials of programmers themselves. FOSS's social and technical organization carries the greatest potential to produce such beautiful code by affording programmers' artistic freedoms.

Building on the previous chapter, in Chapter Four we argue that both the creative possibilities and the scientific objectivity of computing are compromised by proprietary software and the closed standards it proliferates. One necessary condition for the objectivity of science is that its practices and products remain public, open for mutual critique within the scientific community. But the industrialization of computer science and the application of "intellectual property" that is its natural consequence prevent the public practice of computer science. Defenses of commercial computer science on grounds of economic expediency ring hollow when we realize that these have never distinguished science from pseudoscience. We speculate on the shape of computing practices in a world in which all code is free, and show that it leads to a radically different conception of computing as a science.

In the final chapter, we address the role of free software in a world infused with code. In this world, distinctions between human and machine evanesce: personal and social freedoms in this domain are precisely the freedoms granted or restricted by software. In the cyborg world, software will retain its regulatory role, but it will also become a language of interaction with our extended cyborg selves. We point out that questions about the cyborg world's polity are essential questions of technology; the language of the cyborg world must be free, as natural languages are, in order to protect the liberties of our cyborg selves. We argue for transparency in governmentality in the information age and show that free software embodies the anarchist ideal of eliminating the indiscriminate, opaque application of power.

1

Free Software and Political Economy

"For us, open source is capitalism and a business opportunity at its very best."

—Jonathan Schwartz, president and chief operating officer,
Sun Microsystems (Galli 2005)

"The narrative of the programmer is not that of the worker who is gradually given control; it is that of the craftsperson from whom control and autonomy were taken away."

—Steven Weber (Weber 2004, 25)

Free software, in its modern incarnation, was founded largely on an ideology of "freedom, community, and principle," with little regard for the profit motive (Stallman 1999, 70). Yet today FOSS makes headlines daily[1] as corporations relying on "open source development" demonstrate remarkable financial success (Vaughan-Nichols 2005; Brown 2006); those that before hewed to closed-source development and distribution now open significant parts of their code repositories (Farrell 2006) and develop partnerships with open source firms (Haskins 2006; Krill 2006); and free and open source software–licensing schemes become challenges to be tackled by legal departments of software firms keen to draw on FOSS's unique resources (Lindquist 2006).

FOSS incorporates a complex of political ideologies, economic practices, and models of governance that sustain it and uphold its production of value. It is a political economy whose cultural logic cannot be understood without reference to the history of computing and software development, the arc of which traverses some of the most vigorous technological innovation in history, a political economy heavily reliant on the marriage of industry and science. This historical context provides a framework both for placing FOSS's salient characteristics and ideologies in dialogue with theories of political economy and for examining the import of the distinction between the free and open source movements. In particular, political economy provides a useful lens through which to understand the ways in which free and open source software invoke and revise traditional notions of property and production. While the principles of the free software movement were originally orthogonal to proprietary software and its attendant capitalist culture, the recent Open Source Initiative seeks greater resonance between them. Examining the process of this convergence enables an understanding of how capitalism is able to coexist with, and possibly co-opt, putative challenges to its dominance of the industrial and technological realms.

A Brief History of Computing and Software Development

The term "software" encompasses many modalities of conveying instruction to a computing device, marking out a continuum between programming the computer and using it, from microcode and firmware — "close to the metal" — to the mouse clicks of a gamer. Our contemporary interactions with computers, whether punching digits into cell phones or writing books on word processors, would be unrecognizable to users of fifty years ago. Then, computers were conceived as highly specialized machines for tasks beyond human capacity; visions of widespread computer use facilitating human creativity were purest speculation. This conception was changed by successive waves of user movements that radically reconfigured notions of computing and its presence in everyday life.

The postwar history of computing is marked by steady technological advance punctuated by critical social and economic interventions. In the 1950s, IBM introduced computing to American business; in the late 1950s, at MIT, the hacker movement established the first cultural counterweight to corporate computing; in the 1970s, personal computers demonstrated a new breadth of applications, attracting a more diverse population of users; and in the 1990s, the Internet became a truly global information network, sparking intense speculation about its political, cultural, and, indeed, metaphysical implications.

The history of software is intermingled with that of hardware; innovations in software had little effect on the practice of computing unless they were in sync with innovations in hardware.[2] In particular, much of computing's early technical history concerns hardware innovations that removed bottlenecks in computational performance. Software and programming emerged as a separate concern parallel to these developments in hardware. During the Second World War, J. Presper Eckert and John W. Mauchly designed and built the Electronic Numerical Integrator and Computer (ENIAC) at the University of Pennsylvania for the purpose of calculating artillery ballistic trajectories for the U.S. Army (Weik 1961). The first electronic general-purpose computer, the ENIAC, which became operational in 1946, would soon replace Herman Hollerith's tabulating and calculating punch-card machines, then made popular by IBM. But it was Eckert and Mauchly's next invention, the Electronic Discrete Variable Automatic Computer (EDVAC), designed with the significant collaboration of the prodigious mathematician John von Neumann, that represented true innovation (Kempf 1961). It was one of the first machines designed according to the "stored program" principle developed by von Neumann in 1945. Before stored-program computing, "programming" the computer amounted to a radical reconstruction of the machine, essentially hardwiring the program instructions directly into the machine's internals. But with the stored-program principle, which allowed programs to be represented and manipulated as data, humans could interact with the machine purely through software without needing to change its hardware: as the physical hardware became a platform on which any program could be run, the computer became a truly general-purpose machine.

The term "programming a computer" originated around this time, though the relatively mundane "setting up" was a more common term (Ceruzzi 2003, 20). The task of programming in its early days bore little resemblance to today's textual manipulations and drag-and-drop visual development environments. The electromechanical programmable calculator Harvard Mark I, designed by Howard Aiken, accepted instructions in the form of a row of punched holes on paper tape; Grace Murray Hopper, who joined the Mark I project in 1944, was history's first programmer. The Mark I was not a stored-program computer, so repeated sequences of instructions had to be individually coded on successive tape segments. Later, Aiken would modify the Mark I's circuitry by hardwiring some of the more commonly used sequences of instructions. Based on this successful technique, Aiken's design for the Mark III incorporated a device, similar to Konrad Zuse's "Programmator," that enabled the translation of programmer commands into the numerical codes understood by the Mark III processor.

With the advent of the stored-program computer, general-purpose computers became their own programmators. The first software libraries consisted of program sequences stored on tape for subsequent repeated use in user programs. This facilitated the construction, from reusable components, of special-purpose programs to solve specific problems. To some observers, this project promised to do for programming what Henry Ford had done for automobile manufacturing: to systematize production, based on components that could be used in many different programs (Mahoney 1990). Von Neumann's sorting program for the EDVAC was probably the first program for a stored-program computer; Frances Holberton wrote similar sorting routines for UNIVAC data tapes.

In 1946, the University of Pennsylvania, striving to eliminate all commercial interests from the university, pressured Eckert and Mauchly to relinquish patent royalties from their inventions. The pair resigned, taking the computer industry with them, and founded the company that developed the UNIVAC. In the early days of commercial computing, software innovations were typically directed toward making usable machines for the small user community that constituted the embryonic computer market. The U.S. Census Bureau was one of Eckert and Mauchly's first customers; Eckert and Mauchly's machines found application in inventory management, logistics, and election prediction. In an early acknowledgement that computing cultures, such as they were, were different in universities, Eckert and Mauchly's first corporate customer, General Electric, had to convince its stockholders that it had not come under the sway of "longhaired academics" (Ceruzzi 2003, 33).

In May 1952, IBM ended UNIVAC's monopoly, joining the business of making and marketing computers by introducing the IBM 701. Thus began the epic cycle, part and parcel of the computing industry's mythology, of dominant players upstaged by nimble upstarts. By 1956, IBM had shot past UNIVAC on the basis of its technical superiority and refined marketing techniques, with other corporate players such as Honeywell, GE, and RCA fueling the competition. IBM had become the dominant player in the computing sector by 1960,[3] to the extent that the Justice Department, suspecting antitrust violations, began to show an interest in the company's business practices[4] that would culminate in the longest running antitrust case of all time, starting in 1969. As curiosity grew about its internal governance techniques, IBM was investigated by the media as well; the magazine *Datamation,* for example, extensively covered IBM's internal affairs. Not all this media attention was uncritical: IBM was accused of being a poor technical innovator, of taking over projects brought to maturity by others, of lagging behind others in technical advances (Ceruzzi 2003). These charges would echo in the 1990s as Microsoft achieved similar dominance over the software world.

IBM's classic mainframes, such as the 7090, were first installed in the late 1950s. Used in scientific, technical, and military applications, they came complete with lab-coated attendants, whirring tape drives, sterile white-walled data centers, and highly restricted access for both machine operators (responsible, for example, for the logistics of loading programs) and programmers. While the real control lay in the hands of the programmers, few were ever allowed in the computer room. Given the high costs of computing time, no programmer ever interacted with a machine directly. All jobs were run in batches, groups of jobs clustered together to minimize idle processor time. Programmers developed their work on decks of punched cards that were transferred to a reel of tape mounted by the operators onto a tape drive connected to the mainframe. Many programmers never saw the machines that ran their programs. The operators performed the tasks of mounting and unmounting tapes, reading status information and delivering output. Contrary to appearances, the work was not intellectually challenging: indeed, most operator tasks were later relegated to collections of software known as "operating systems." In case of system malfunctions, however, operators were able to load programs by flipping switches to alter the bits of machine registers directly. Though tedious, this manipulation gave the operators an intimate relationship with the machine.

The advent of transistorized circuits brought increased power efficiency and circuit miniaturization; computers became smaller and cheaper, making their way to universities. While these machines were intended for use in data processing courses — that is, for strictly pedagogical purposes — at university computer centers students began a pattern of "playing with computers." Users were envisioning applications for computers that went beyond their intended purposes.

By 1960, the structures of commercial and academic computing were much the same, organized around computing centers that separated programmers from the machines they programmed. The drawbacks of the batch-processing model were first noticed in universities when the discipline of computer programming was initially taught: batch processing greatly constrained the amount of iterative feedback available to the student programmers. Thus the needs of the university, and the breadth of its user base, began to manifest themselves in academic requirements for computing. In a foreshadowing of contemporary university–corporate relations, IBM offered its 650 system to universities at massively discounted rates under the condition that they would offer computing courses. This strategy marked the beginning of direct corporate influence on the curricula of academic computing departments, one of the many not-so-benign relationships between university and corporation that contributed to the industrialization of the sciences (Noble 1979).

Programming Languages

The first programming languages, called "assembly languages," simply provided mnemonics for machine instructions, with "macros" corresponding to longer sequences of instructions; large libraries of such macros were maintained by each user site. These languages used named variables for numeric memory addresses to enhance human readability; "assembler" programs managed these variable names and oversaw memory allocation. Given their utility to programmers, it is no surprise that the first assembler for the IBM 704 was developed in collaboration with the SHARE user group (see below). Computing pioneers had not foreseen the widespread nature of the activity of programming: it developed in response to user needs and was largely driven by them.

Even early in the development of the programming discipline, the cohort of programmers was regarded as a priesthood, largely because of the apparent obscurity of the code they manipulated. This obscurity was a primary motivation for J. H. Laning and N. Zierler's development of the first "compiler," a program that automatically translated programming commands entered by users into machine code. But this compiler was significantly slower than other methods for performing such translations. The continuing desire for efficient automatic translation led to the development of high-level programming languages, which also promised to dispel some of the mystery surrounding the practice of programming.

This phase of software's history was one of heavy experimentation in programming-language design. The design of FORTRAN (FORmula TRANSlation) — developed in 1957 for the IBM 704 — made it possible to control a computer without direct knowledge of its internal mechanisms. COBOL (COmmon Business Oriented Language), a self-documenting language with descriptive variable names, was designed to make programming more accessible to a wider user base. More languages were developed — ALGOL (ALGOrithmic Language) and SNOBOL

(StriNg Oriented symBOlic Language) among them — each promising ease of use combined with technical power. These developments defined the trajectory of programming languages toward greater abstraction at the programmer level. While programmers still had to master the syntax of these languages, their design allowed programmers to focus more exclusively on the logic of their programs.

In 1954, a cooperative effort to build a compiler for the IBM 701 was organized by four of IBM's customers (Douglas Aircraft, North American Aviation, Ramo-Wooldridge, and The RAND Corporation) and IBM. Known as the Project for the Advancement of Coding Techniques (PACT), this group wrote a working compiler that went on to be released for the IBM 704 as well (Kim 2006). In 1955, a group of IBM 701 users located in Los Angeles, each faced with the unappealing prospect of upgrading their installations to the new 704, banded together in a similar belief that sharing skills and experiences was better than going it alone. The group, called Society to Help Alleviate Redundant Effort (SHARE), grew rapidly — to sixty-two member organizations members in the first year — and developed an impressive library of routines that each member could use. The founding of SHARE — today still a vibrant association of IBM users with over twenty thousand members[5] — was a blessing for IBM, as it accelerated the acceptance of its equipment and likely helped sales of the 704. As it grew, the group developed strong opinions about IBM's technical agenda; IBM had little choice but to acknowledge SHARE's direct influence on its decisions. SHARE also contributed significant software for IBM products, ranging from libraries for scientific computing to the SHARE Operating System (SOS).

It became increasingly common for the collaborative effort among corporations and users to produce vital technical components such as operating systems, as important to system usability as high-level programming languages: the FORTRAN Monitor System for the IBM 7090 was developed by a user group, while, in 1956, another group at the GM Research Laboratories developed routines for memory handling and allocation. In 1959, Bernie Galler, Bob Graham, and Bruce Arden at the University of Michigan, in order to meet the pedagogical needs of the student population, developed the Michigan Algorithmic Decoder (MAD), a programming language used in the development of RUNOFF, the first widely used text-processing system. In the fledgling world of computing, user cooperation and sharing was necessary; thus, the utility of collaborative work in managing the complexity of a technology was established early.

Though IBM developed system software for its legendary 360 series, it was only made usable through such user efforts. So onerous were the difficulties experienced by IBM in producing the 360 that software engineer Frederick Brooks was inspired to set out a systematic approach to software design based on division of labor in the programming process. Championed first by Harlan Mills in a sequence of articles written in the late 1960s (Mills 1983), these ideas about software design were presented by Brooks in his groundbreaking 1975 text on software engineering, *The Mythical Man-Month* (Brooks 1995). Mills and

Brooks, acknowledging that the software industry was engaged in a "manufacturing process" like no other, laid out principles by which the labor of creating source code might be divided among groups of programmers to facilitate the efficient development of high-quality code. This industrial move introduced division of labor to emphasize efficiency: from the beginning, industrialization was pushed onto computer science, with long-term implications for the practice of the science.[6] The complexity of software that Brooks described was recognized throughout the industry by 1968, when NATO's Science Committee convened the first conference on software engineering at Garmisch-Partenkirchen, Germany. Concurrently, pioneering computer scientist Edsger Djikstra published his influential letter, "Go-To Statement Considered Harmful" (Djikstra 1968), in an attempt to move programming to a more theoretical basis on which his new paradigm of "structured programming" could rest.

The year 1968 also saw a significant discussion unfold on the pages of the *Communications of the Association of Computing Machinery* (CACM), the flagship journal of the primary society for computing professionals. In a policy paper published by the Rockford Research Institute, Calvin Mooers had argued for trademark protection for his TRAC language to prevent its modification by users. University of Michigan professor Bernie Galler responded in a letter to the CACM, arguing that that the best and most successful programming languages benefited from the input of users who could change them, noting in particular the success of SNOBOL, which he suggested had "benefited from 'meritorious extensions' by 'irrepressible young people' at universities" (Galler 1968). Mooers responded:

> The visible and recognized TRAC trademark informs this public . . . that the language or computer capability identified by this trademark adheres authentically and exactly to a carefully drawn Rockford Research standard. . . . An adequate basis for proprietary software development and marketing is urgently needed particularly in view of the doubtful capabilities of copyright, patent or "trade secret" methods when applied to software. (Mooers 1968)

While most computer science professionals acknowledged the need for some protection in order to maintain compatibility among different versions of a language, Galler's views had been borne out by the successful examples of collaborative development by the SHARE and MAD user groups. Significantly, Mooers's communiqué had noted the inapplicability of extant legal protections to software, which would continue to be a point of contention as the software industry grew. As it turned out, Galler's analysis was correct, and the trademarked TRAC language never became popular.

Pressure from the U.S. government, and IBM's competitors, soon led to the phenomenon of "unbundling," a significant step toward the commodification of software. In 1968, responding to IBM's domination of the market, Control Data Corporation filed an antitrust suit against IBM. Anticipating a similar suit by the Department of Justice, IBM began to sell software and support services separately from its mainframes (though it preferred to lease its machines rather than sell them, maintaining nominal control over its products). IBM's Customer Information Control System (CICS) was its first software "product"; IBM's competitors were now able to sell software to customers who used IBM's hardware.

Digital Equipment Corporation (DEC) adopted a different business model with the PDP-1 minicomputer, the first model in what would become the very successful PDP line. The name, Programmed Data Processor, was deliberately chosen to avoid some of the connotations of "computers" as unwieldy and over-priced.[7] DEC sold the PDP-1 complete with system software, and, like IBM, encouraged user modifications to the system. DEC's policy, because it did not have the internal resources to develop software to enhance the PDP-1's function-ality and user-friendliness, was to encourage its customers to participate in the ongoing development of its products. DEC thereby explicitly acknowledged the value that customers' knowledge added. To further support this approach, DEC adopted a laissez-faire attitude toward its copyrightable material, going so far as to provide copies of its technical manuals, on cheap newsprint, to its customers.

Hacker Cultures

DEC's close relationship with one class of customer, the university, enabled it to stay at the cutting edge of innovation. Universities were attracted to the openness and flexible power of the PDP-1, which became an integral part of the hacker cultures that emerged on campuses nationwide. In 1961, MIT acquired the PDP-1, and the Signal Committee's Tech Models and Railroad Club (TMRC) adopted it as their plaything, using it to create games, music programs, and other diver-sions. The complex culture that grew up around this machine rejected the corpo-rate, high-priest-run, batch-processing style of operation that characterized IBM's products (the TMRC coined the pejorative "coolie" to describe the industrial-style writing of code [Levy 1994, 57]), valuing instead inquiry, interaction with tech-nology, and community governance. It introduced a distinctive lexicon, social conventions, and community ethic: in short, a new and thriving subculture.

In *Hackers*, his history of computing pioneers, Steven Levy (Levy 1994, 40–45) enumerates the tenets of the new community's "hacker ethic" as follows:

1. Access to computers — and anything which might teach you something about the way the world works — should be unlimited and total. Always yield to the Hands-On Imperative!!
2. All information should be free.
3. Mistrust authority — promote decentralization.
4. Hackers should be judged by their hacking, not bogus criteria such as age, race, class or position.
5. You can create art and beauty on a computer.
6. Computers can change your life for the better.

The hacker ethic contains the seeds of many defining characteristics of the culture of free software: resistance to the domination of technical standards and code by one central authority, the belief in a meritocracy underwritten by technical competence, the fierce protection of the freedom of information, and the belief in the social and personal transformative potential of computing. What we now think of as the "free software sensibility" is easily discerned in stories like that of TMRC hacker Stewart Nelson, who began hacking by disassembling telephones to understand their functioning. This in turn led to an understanding of how the telephone system worked, how telephones interacted with other devices; he saw no legitimate reason why these explorations should be subject to technical or sociopolitical constraints. The road from these investigative actions to modifying the code of an operating system so that it works correctly with a new printer is a straight one: each action pushes the limits of understanding through independent experimentation and "tinkering." Early hacker culture and the contemporary free software movement are thus part of a narrative continuum about taking control of technology and preserving user autonomy.

A few hardware generations after the PDP-1, DEC's PDP-10 became the locus of several sites of hacker culture, such as MIT's AI Lab and Project MAC, Stanford's Artificial Intelligence Laboratory, and Carnegie Mellon University. Programmers nourished by these rich hacker cultures went on to do seminal work in operating systems, artificial intelligence, and theoretical computer science. Xerox's Palo Alto Research Center (PARC), arguably the single largest producer of technical innovation[8] in the post-mainframe era, also supported a thriving hacker community. Stanford and PARC would later become focal points of the entrepreneurial frenzy that transformed California's Santa Clara Valley into Silicon Valley (O'Mara 2005). The PDP-10 was also the dominant machine on the early ARPANET, a tiny assemblage of university and government computers that would become the Internet. Back at MIT, researchers had rejected the system software provided by DEC for the PDP-6 and instead developed their legendary operating system, the Incompatible Time-sharing System (ITS), which became the longest running time-sharing system[9] of all time. The language, humor, and values developed by the ITS hackers form the foundation of our contemporary understanding of hacker culture.

Another hacker's delight was just around the corner: 1969 witnessed the birth of not just ARPANET but also Unix. Designed and written by Ken Thompson and Dennis Ritchie at AT&T Bell Labs on a DEC PDP-7, it was the first operating system to be written in a machine-independent medium, the high-level language called C (though it was initially implemented in assembly language). As a consequence, it was easily ported to other hardware platforms. Its popularity was largely due to its provision of a common software environment across a diverse range of hardware. The marriage of Unix and C created a new variation of hacker culture, centered on the extraordinarily rich and flexible Unix programming environment that supported intercommunicating programs and networking.

Significantly, because U.S. Department of Justice antitrust provisions kept communications companies out of the computing business, Unix was not sold by AT&T but licensed at no charge, with source code included.[10] The first operating system to include core Internet software like the TCP/IP networking protocols, Unix provided substantial nourishment to the communication culture, fueled by e-mail and bulletin boards, which had sprung up around the ARPANET and its backbone PDP-10 sites. Typically, the use of these computing facilities for personal communication was unauthorized, but funding agencies were more than willing to pay this price for fostering a brilliantly innovative community of collaboration. This networking culture culminated in the 1980s in the Usenet, the premier meeting ground and information exchange for an entire generation of Internet users (Hauben, Hauben, and Truscott 1997).

Parallel to these developments in institutional sectors, a thriving community of hobbyists, enthusiasts, and entrepreneurs was experimenting with the implications of new developments in microprocessors, in what would become known as personal computing. As they explored, well before the advent of the IBM PC, what could be accomplished with hardware of limited computational power, they believed software should be shared freely both to further innovation and to spread the word about the growing power of personal computing. These computing enthusiasts bought and used computing kits consisting of hardware components and instructions for their assembly; they wrote fledgling operating systems and utility programs; they met frequently to discuss problems, solutions, and computing experiences. Alternative economies of exchange in an environment where knowledge was a valuable commodity did not take long to emerge: the expertise of each was available to all, and remuneration simply meant having a solution provided in exchange for another (Levy 1994). In the April 12, 1975, issue (the second) of the Homebrew Computing Club's newsletter, the cover editorial enumerates some members' ideas for the club's activities and mission:

> Perhaps the club can be a central REPRO & dissemination point for hard-to-otherwise-get listings & schematics, paper tape sources and binaries AS WELL AS a place where software written in PL/M be compiled, simulated. etc., for creating working or usable binaries. . . . [M]eet to exchange ideas, share skills, problems and solutions. . . . Particularly maintain a local resource file with reciprocal arrangements with contiguous groups. . . . Exchange information. . . . mostly an information and learning center. . . . to offer a chance to get together and exchange ideas on software and hardware. . . . serve as information exchange medium; run technical discussion & education sessions. . . . share skills. . . . perform want-ad matching so that people can find what they want to have. Generally useful software, individual specific routines people have written. . . . share ideas and stop trying to have so many small business men trying to make a few dollars. (Moore 1975)

By 1975, three separate hacker cultures were thriving: the ITS community at MIT, the Unix/C networked crowd, and the personal computing enthusiasts, located largely on the West Coast. Although each group had its favorite hardware and programming languages, they jointly subscribed to the hacker ethic with its love of sharing and the belief that computing was a Good Thing. These cultures suffered blows: DEC terminated its support of the PDP-10, and the ITS system, weakened by its lack of portability, soon died out. In the early 1980s, Unix workstations, especially those designed by Sun Microsystems (founded by Unix hackers from Stanford), became wildly popular. These relied on graphical windowing systems. The most popular, the X Window System, continued to rely on the cultural standards of sharing code: its code was given away, and users fine-tuned their versions for the local environment before releasing patches back to the X Consortium.[11]

By 1984, around the time of the divestiture and breakup (enforced by the U.S. Department of Justice) of AT&T, two communities of hackers remained: the Unix community — which had largely absorbed the ITS community — and the PC community. But Unix became a proprietary system; as each vendor added its own proprietary features, customers and vendors alike squabbled over which version would be the One True Unix. Most significant, its flourishing culture of networked innovation on a common platform began to dissolve. As the hardware compatibility that was Unix's main strength vanished, vendors tried unsuccessfully to tap into the PC market by offering Unix-like systems for personal computers, though without the access to source code that the original Unix systems provided. Vendors' failures to understand the importance of providing source code to the creation of an independent and empowered user group meant that no hacker culture grew in the Unix/PC environment. The Unix community would continue to flounder till the coupling, in the early 1990s, of the GNU utilities with the Linux kernel.

The Continuing Commodification of Software

Mainframe vendors, and their customers, treated software as purely ancillary to the "real" product: the hardware (IBM's unbundling, under duress, was more the exception than the rule). In the nascent communities of hackers, PC enthusiasts, and university researchers, the notion of software as a good that could be sold — or property that could be stolen — was an alien one, until Bill Gates's 1976 open letter to the Homebrew Computer Club, in which he accused its members of stealing his software. With Microsoft still in its infancy, Gates was only the coauthor of a small (if important) program, a translator for the BASIC programming language, which allowed most hobbyists to experiment effectively with their Altair computers. In his letter, he notes the laissez-faire attitude of hobbyists toward software ownership, makes several crucial claims about the economic structure of the emerging software market, and concludes by accusing the community of widespread theft:[12]

To me, the most critical thing in the hobby market right now is the lack of good software courses, books and software itself. Without good software . . . will quality software be written for the hobby market? . . . Paul Allen and myself . . . developed Altair BASIC. The value of the computer time we have used exceeds $40,000. Two surprising things are apparent: 1) Most of these "users" never bought BASIC (less than 10% of all Altair owners have bought BASIC), and 2) The amount of royalties we have received from sales to hobbyists makes the time spent on Altair BASIC worth less than $2 an hour. Why is this? As the majority of hobbyists must be aware, most of you steal your software. Hardware must be paid for, but software is something to share. Who cares if the people who worked on it get paid? Is this fair? One thing you do do is prevent good software from being written. Who can afford to do professional work for nothing? What hobbyist can put 3-man years into programming, finding all bugs, documenting his product and distribute for free? The fact is, no one besides us has invested a lot of money in hobby software . . . there is very little incentive to make this software available to hobbyists. Most directly, the thing you do is theft . . . Nothing would please me more than being able to hire ten programmers and deluge the hobby market with good software. (Gates 1976)

This conflict between Gates and the Homebrew Computing Club's members was indicative of an emerging tension in the hacker community (Levy 1994). Some simply wanted to use machines for the sake of using machines (embodying the "tools-to-make-tools" philosophy), some saw computing technology as carrying political and normative implications, and some were especially sensitive to the commercial possibilities of this technology. This divergence would also underwrite the schism, in the 1990s, between the free software and open source movements.

These tensions in the hacker community were manifested most notably in the conflict among MIT, Lisp Machines, Inc. (LMI), and Symbolics, Inc., a conflict that indirectly resulted in the birth of the GNU free software project. In the late 1970s, members of MIT's Artificial Intelligence laboratory had developed a prototype computer, the "Lisp Machine," specially optimized for programs written in the Lisp programming language. Sensing commercial potential for this machine, lab members began discussing possible commercialization. After strong disagreement within the lab over business tactics, Symbolics and LMI were spun off, both staffed by former lab members and hackers. The Lisp Machine system software was copyrighted by MIT, used by Symbolics under license, and also shared with LMI. The actual source code was kept on an MIT server, where both Symbolics and MIT staff could make changes, though changes and improvements were openly available to all three parties. This system persisted until 1981, when, in a dispute with MIT, Symbolics began to insist that MIT's improvements be made available only to Symbolics, effectively stifling LMI, which was unable to maintain its own version of the software. Richard Stallman, one of the only members remaining in the AI lab, described the impact of Symbolics's decision:

> [T]hey demanded that we had to choose a side, and use either the MIT version . . . or the Symbolics version. . . . If we worked on and improved the Symbolics version, we would be supporting Symbolics alone. If we used and improved the MIT version . . . we would be doing work available to both companies, but Symbolics saw that we would be supporting LMI because we would be helping them continue to exist. . . . Up until that point, I hadn't taken the side of either company, although it made me miserable to see what had happened to our community and the software. But now, Symbolics had forced the issue. So, in an effort to help keep Lisp Machines going — I began duplicating all of the improvements Symbolics had made to the Lisp machine system. I wrote the equivalent improvements again myself. . . . [F]or two years, I prevented them from wiping out Lisp Machines Incorporated, and the two companies went on. . . . Meanwhile, it was time to start building a new community to replace the one that their actions and others had wiped out. (Stallman 2002)

Stallman had already experienced the technical frustrations of having code closed off:

> The . . . AI Lab received a graphics printer as a gift from Xerox around 1977. It was run by free software to which we added many convenient features. For example, the software would notify a user immediately on completion of a print job. Whenever the printer had trouble, such as a paper jam or running out of paper, the software would immediately notify all users who had print jobs queued. . . . Later Xerox gave the AI Lab a newer, faster printer, one of the first laser printers. It was driven by proprietary software that ran in a separate dedicated computer, so we couldn't add any of our favorite features . . . no one was informed when there was a paper jam, so the printer often went for an hour without being fixed. The system programmers at the AI Lab were capable of fixing such problems. . . . Xerox was uninterested in fixing them, and chose to prevent us, so we were forced to accept the problems. (Stallman 1992)

Stallman's response to this state of affairs was a radical plan to develop an entire system built of free software and, further, to think about how a hacker's software could remain free software. Symbolics had shown it was possible to close freely available code, to build on the efforts of others but not give back in turn. Stallman's system, dubbed GNU (for the recursive acronym "GNU's Not Unix"), while clearly pragmatic from a technical perspective, embodied a broader philosophical and social goal: to replicate and disseminate the ideals of freedom and cooperation that characterized much of hacker culture, particularly that of the golden days of the MIT AI lab.

Stallman's original newsgroup announcement of his intention to develop a system built exclusively from free software did not distinguish between "free" as in liberty and "free" as in price, though it does acknowledge the existence of a community with shared values:

FromCSvax:pur-ee:inuxc!ixn5c!ihnp4!houxm!mhuxi!eagle!mit-vax!mit-eddie!RMS@MIT-OZ

From: RMS%MIT-OZ@mit-eddie

Newsgroups: net.Unix-wizards,net.usoft

Subject: new Unix implementation

Date: Tue, 27-Sep-83 12:35:59 EST

Organization: MIT AI Lab, Cambridge, MA

Free Unix!

Starting this Thanksgiving I am going to write a complete Unix-compatible software system called GNU (for Gnu's Not Unix), and give it away free to everyone who can use it. . . .

Why I Must Write GNU

I consider that the golden rule requires that if I like a program I must share it with other people who like it. I cannot in good conscience sign a nondisclosure agreement or a software license agreement. So that I can continue to use computers without violating my principles, I have decided to put together a sufficient body of free software so that I will be able to get along without any software that is not free. (Stallman 1983)

These values, Stallman perceived, were being steadily eroded by the increasingly proprietary nature of commercial software. Central to GNU's objective was the practice, known as "copyleft," of providing source code so users could modify, enhance, and customize their software without restriction, as long as any distribution of a modified version also included the source code (Moody 2002). Stallman began implementing large parts of a Unix-like operating system, including development tools such as the *gcc* compiler and the *gdb* debugger, shell environments such as *bash*, the editor *emacs*, and a host of utilities. To provide organizational structure and ongoing support for these efforts, Stallman founded the Free Software Foundation (FSF) in 1985.

  Stallman's announcement was also a call for help and mutual aid, both of which he would receive in good measure and which would serve as the model for the development of the most identifiable symbol of the free software movement: the GNU/Linux system.

The Rise of Free Software and the "Open Source" Schism

The Internet introduced a mode of information transfer that facilitated something near and dear to hackers: open and easy sharing of knowledge. Without the Internet, Stallman could neither have made his announcement public, nor have called upon, or expected, the kind of collaboration he received. Similarly, the development of the Linux kernel began, in 1991, with Linus Torvalds obtaining POSIX standards[13] documents electronically; posting his first release to an FTP site; and announcing the code, asking for help, and receiving bug fixes by e-mail. Torvalds chose to release Linux source code under the GNU General Public License (GPL) (written by Stallman), which ensured that any changes to the kernel code, if included in a subsequent distribution, would have to be released back to the Linux development community.

The Linux project shared with GNU the practice of distributing source code, though largely for the pragmatic value of having as wide a range as possible of talented programmers making improvements for incorporation in the "central" version. GNU/Linux became the latest in a long line of software systems, from the SOS, through much of DEC's system and applications software, to the ITS system at MIT, which were developed and maintained through collective effort. The Linux development process, further amplified both by the growing population of competent programmers on the Internet and by the combination of the Linux kernel with the GNU project's software, saw the quality and popularity of the system increase to the point that by the late 1990s, several corporations, such as IBM, announced support for GNU/Linux. A growing collection of powerful free software, such as Apache, BIND, and Sendmail, which powered the Internet, as well as GNU/Linux, had begun to demonstrate their superiority to proprietary commercial software.

In 1998, a group of respected free software developers, seeking a higher profile and greater corporate acceptance for the free software development model, launched the "Open Source Initiative" (OSI).[14] The initiative followed a successful campaign to persuade Netscape, on technical and business grounds, to open the source code for its popular Communicator suite. This commercially oriented drive required a significant change in free software rhetoric and tactics, which quickly developed into a full-blown philosophical and tactical schism among free software adherents. Spearheaded by free software developers Eric Raymond and Bruce Perens, the OSI claimed the term "free software" was too confusing for business leaders (who apparently do not understand the difference between free speech and free beer[15]) and chose the term "open source" to increase the attractiveness of the free software development model to the business community.

Starting with this break, the free software community has been confronted with the question of how much to compromise its original ideals in the name of widespread acceptance and success of its products. While the OSI and the FSF share many philosophical and pragmatic positions, their views on the rights and responsibilities of users, their relative tolerance of proprietary software, and their relationship with the world of corporate software production are subtly but significantly different. As an example, the Free Software Foundation actively encourages the use of software licenses that ensure the freedom of the licensed software in perpetuity, while the Open Source Initiative takes no position on which of many FOSS licenses most effectively protects the movement's commitment to the availability of source code. These differences are a particular expression of a fundamental division among FOSS developers over the relative valuation of technical pragmatism and the idealism of open information exchange and dissemination.

The FOSS world's relationship with the corporate world has always been an uneasy one. While many FOSS licensing schemes embody a laissez-faire attitude toward the commercialization of code, many developers still identify sufficiently with the old university-centric hacker ethic to feel uncomfortable about the possibility of corporate co-optation. This was evident in the reaction of the Unix community in 1982 when Bill Joy, a programmer working on Unix at Berkeley, moved to the fledgling Sun Microsystems, taking the Unix codebase with him. Even though this code was licensed as free software, and his action did not restrict the freedom of other programmers to work on the Unix code, his move was nonetheless perceived as traitorous by the community (Weber 2004, 181). This tension continues to be a significant determinant of the internal debate and future direction of the free and open source software communities.

The history of software development thus chronicles a complicated relationship among three groups often in conflict: large corporations engaged in the manufacture of valuable technical goods, scientific researchers working in university labs, and a loose coalition of technology enthusiasts. It is a history of the growth of one of the largest, most innovative, and most valuable industries on the planet, one whose products continue to reshape our political and economic realities. This history, inseparable from a larger history of computer science and technology, is one of a deep and ongoing struggle to determine how software should be made, used, and understood, and is therefore critical to our analysis of its political economy.

Political Economy and Software Production

Understanding the political economy of a system requires an inquiry into both its creation of value and its organizational principles: How does it operationalize concepts such as labor, value, property, and production? What are its regulative principles? How is it governed, and how are conflicts resolved? Thus, analyses of the political economy of FOSS seek to understand the roots of its economic and political viability. Steve Weber's seminal analysis of the FOSS community includes an examination of the processes by which the "management" or the "people" of free software enable internal resolution of technical or political conflicts (Weber 2004). This study has the sort of anthropological or ethnographic flavor also found in Eric Raymond's *The Cathedral and the Bazaar* (Raymond 2001). Others have studied the incentive schemes — such as shared sociocultural norms, rational choice incentives, or reputation enhancement — that motivate developers to contribute their labor to projects without direct financial recompense (Gallaway and Kinnear 2004; Benkler 2002; Boston Consulting Group

2002; Ghosh and Glott 2002; Cusumano et al. 2005; Ghosh 1998; Himanen 2002; Weber 2004; Kollock 1997; Benkler 2006; Hippel and Krogh 2003; Lancashire 2001; Lerner and Tirole 2001). These studies are an unassailable argument that the free software phenomenon challenges traditional assumptions about organized intellectual and economic activity. When intangible nonrival goods alter modes of production and make possible economic exchanges reliant not only on monetary incentive schemes, classical political economy fails.

Classical Analysis of Software Production

Viewed through the lens of Karl Marx's and Adam Smith's commodity-centric theories, the software industry is based on the production, consumption, and exchange of a good bought and sold in accordance with the value placed on it by the market. This scarcity-based analysis necessarily assumes limited amounts of software can be produced and suggests the price of the good is a function of market pressures.

Such analysis, under the further assumption of society's increasing need for information-related goods, predicts the demand for programming skills will constantly expand, with the price paid for these skills also determined by the market. This determination takes into account programmer skill, education, and market forces such as capacity, supply, and demand. The interactions between sellers and buyers determine the wages of software workers. Programmers strive to find the highest possible price for their skills in the market, while prices paid for programming capability reflect market demand as it responds to the expressed need of its consumers. With these conditions in place, Marx would predict, the software market, driven by the irresistible energy of capitalist enterprise, would expand to global scope.

In this classical politico-economic picture, Marxist analysis claims workers are deprived of the surplus value associated with a product. The capitalist owns the means of production, pays the worker a wage that undervalues her labor, and sells the goods at a profitable margin. The labor value provided by the worker is denied her. Further, because the worker sells her labor power to earn a living, and the capitalist owns the manufacturing process, the product of her labor is alien to the worker. This analysis would see in industrialized software production the same control and exploitation of labor. In such a system, over a period of time, software production will move to regions of low-cost labor, or, alternatively, low-cost labor will be imported to areas in which it is required. Consequently, the price paid for software labor power will diminish to the minimum necessary to maintain the class of programmers. These predictions are confirmed by recent practices ranging from outsourcing to software parks in India to U.S. immigration policies that allot specialty worker visas to hire computer scientists at below-market rates.

The Creation of Value by Proprietary Software

In the nascent computing industry, when the provision and maintenance of hardware was the main cost of computing systems and customer bases were tiny, hardware vendors made their source code freely available, encouraging customers to modify it and develop their own. No independent market for software existed; it was subsidiary to the primary commodity, hardware. Thus, control of the means of production of computing systems stayed with the corporate owner. IBM's move to unbundle its software from its hardware introduced software as a new commodity, necessitating the creation of new controls of the means of production of this knowledge-based commodity.

Bill Gates's intervention with the Homebrew Computer Club was a move toward creating scarcity in the ballooning software market for personal computers, with his letter suggesting software could be a marketable commodity only if the prevalent practices of shared development and unrestrained code sharing were squashed. Ignoring what had been demonstrated in the corporate sector by SHARE and in the academic sector by MAD, Gates's letter asserts that personal-computing user groups organized around such practices would be unable to produce high-quality software and would render the software economy unviable. That the scarcity of software is maintained by the questionable application of copyright and trade secret law[16] suggests that alternative political economies, ones that acknowledge the plenitude of software, are not implausible.

Gates's claims are merely the latest restatement of the "techno-economic determinist" story, a mythology that suggests economically successful technologies are selected through the interaction of three filters (Noble 1991). First, scientists and engineers, with their dedication to rationality and efficiency, methodically subject technological possibilities to objective scrutiny. Second, practical businessmen and financiers develop and deploy only the most economically viable technologies. Finally, the anonymous operation of the self-regulating market ensures only the most socially beneficial technologies survive the rigors of competition. Such a story has neither the space nor the need for the self-governing technological communities typified by the FOSS movement.

Once both hardware and software were commodified, the new software capitalists needed to, and indeed did, retain control of the means of production. For a knowledge-based commodity like software, the knowledge and skills of the worker are an integral component of the means of production. These are controlled, for example, through nondisclosure agreements — gag orders that prohibit workers from revealing details of their work to entities external to their employer both during and, in some cases, after employment (Radack 1994). Other knowledge is carried not only by the workers themselves but also by the source code they create; because source code is the key to software's inherent modifiability, restricting access to source code is a crucial component of the control of the means of production.

Control over the source code is established by a twofold regime that places restrictions on the copying of the executable (by employing copyright law) and on availability of source code (treated as a trade secret). Thus, the means of production remain with the corporate owner of the software. The lack of knowledge of the code alienates users from the product as they are unable to modify the code, while the inability of the worker to receive full value for his skills alienates him from his knowledge, as he is not permitted to discuss it, let alone make it available to a larger set of potential employers.

Because proprietary software is written for profit, it must create a commercial advantage. But software has the serious disadvantage that competitors could replicate its functionality, which would rapidly destroy profits. Therefore, proprietary software, in order to meet its profit imperative, must build in technical barriers to competition (Levien 1998). Most software is inherently dependent on other components of the system in which it operates; often the usefulness of the software depends on how well it interoperates with its environment. Thus, one approach to creating value is to create an environment in which competitors would be unlikely to succeed. Proprietary-software vendors are thus driven to monopolistic practices — like imposing technical barriers to interoperability with competitors' products — as they attempt to control the environment in which their programs run. Microsoft, for instance, does not just write proprietary applications; it also produces the operating system that provides the environment for those applications. This bundling of operating system and application is an integral part of its competitive strategy. While the operating system is nominally open to rivals for Microsoft's applications, they cannot use its resources as effectively, for Microsoft "allows Microsoft applications to cheat, and call directly into the undocumented . . . system call interface to provide services that competing applications cannot" (Allison 2005). Thus control over source code, programmers' knowledge, and the details of the relationship between software and its environment all contribute to creating value in proprietary software.

"Late Capitalism"

The distributed, asynchronous process of software production that led to GNU/ Linux has many features in common with the globalized economy. These features are often understood as characteristic of a particular stage in the evolution of capitalism (Harvey 1989, Jameson 1991). Most histories of capitalism identify three stages in its evolution: the classical nineteenth-century capitalism that was the concern of Smith and Marx, the early-twentieth-century monopoly capitalism predicted by Marx, and the twenty-first century's distributed, multinational, global or "late" capitalism, a cluster of notions related to a global change in industrial practices and concerns, including "the new international division of labor, a vertiginous new dynamic in international banking and the stock exchanges . . . new forms of media interrelationship . . . computers and automation, [and] the flight of production to advanced Third World areas" (Jameson 1991, xix).

Late capitalism, then, incorporates the globalization of capital, the movement from manufacturing to service-based economies in the First World, the dispersion of labor due to porous borders and networked command and control, the imposed flexibility of labor (long working days, twenty-four-hour factories), the increasing interconnectedness of world economies, the classification of knowledge as a commodity, and the displacement of the marginal cost model of production: "[T]he informational revolution will transform industry by redefining and rejuvenating manufacturing processes. . . . Just as through the process of modernization all production tended to become industrialized, so too through the process of postmodernization all production tends toward the production of services, toward becoming informationalized" (Harvey 1989, 120).

Many programmers participate in FOSS communities in order to trade on their knowledge and skills (Lakhani and Wolf 2005; Ghosh and Glott 2002; Boston Consulting Group 2002; Lerner and Tirole 2001; Raymond 2000). FOSS programmers can support themselves by selling their expertise in programming by offering postsale services and customizations, rather than relying, however indirectly, on sales of the products they develop. The willingness of programmers to share their code demonstrates their understanding that knowledge is the truly valuable commodity, not the ephemeral products they make. This understanding of commodity and compensation is summed up in Raymond's formula for economic success: "Give away the recipe, open a restaurant."

As an international community, FOSS employs the characteristic logic of late capitalism: decentralized power, distributed sovereignty, and a reworked concept of commodity that stresses the provision of services rather than the accumulation of physical goods (Harvey 1989, 159). Its labor force, consisting of a vast pool of highly contingent labor, is dispersed across all time zones, as workers write new code or search for flaws in others' code before sending suggested modifications to a central assembly point. These projects employ powerful code-management systems: while there is a flurry of fixes, what is actually admitted to the codebase is strictly controlled by social and technical constraints (Weber 2004). FOSS development, with its flexible labor force, global extent, reliance on technological advances, valuation of knowledge, and production of intangibles, has fully embraced the modern knowledge economy.

This largely monolithic treatment of FOSS is inaccurate in a number of ways. Individual developers bring a broad diversity of techniques, knowledge, and ideologies to the community, and attempts to place them into well-defined categories are destined to fail. But there is an unmistakable division, closely related to considerations of political economy, between the open-source movement (specifically, the OSI) and the free software movement (specifically, the FSF). As we have seen, the free software movement was founded on a perspective of software as a social good; the open source movement exists to make the case that open source software is more technically efficient and therefore could create more value for commercial software enterprises. That is, the free software movement is committed to the freedom of software regardless of any constraints that this stance may impose on the accumulation of wealth, while the open source movement is more open to occasional compromises to the freedom of software when required by the commercial imperative. This distinction is not simply a theoretical one; it fuels vigorous debates about FOSS philosophy (Stallman 1992), licensing terms (The Free Software Foundation 2006), and the role of proprietary software in FOSS development (Laffoon 2005; Stallman 2000; Sweet 2001).

Despite these differences, the broad FOSS community continues to thrive, maintaining creativity and producing software with both technical and economic value. The question of how FOSS manages to deviate from traditional political economy, yet continue to produce value, remains one of deep interest.

FOSS and the Creation of Value

OSI founder Eric Raymond, in addition to being a veteran FOSS developer, is one of the first, and most widely read, observers of the FOSS political economy. In a series of essays written in the late 1990s, he offers analyses of the distinguishing features of the FOSS development model ("The Cathedral and the Bazaar" [Raymond 2001]), its unique treatment of property ("Homesteading the Noosphere" [Raymond 2000]), and its internal economic logic ("The Magic Cauldron" [Raymond 2004]).

In "The Magic Cauldron," Raymond asserts that FOSS produces value because it views the software industry as one based on service rather than manufacturing. For Raymond, a software good has both use-value and sale-value. The former is its value as a productivity multiplier; the latter is its value as a salable commodity. Traditional analyses of software, using a manufacturing model, make two key assumptions: that software development time is paid for by sale-value, and that the sale-value of software is directly proportional to development costs and use-value. Thus, this model assumes that software is like any other manufactured good. Raymond suggests, however, that this characterization is inaccurate. Most software, perhaps as much as 90 to 95 percent,[17] is not written for retail sale; this includes in-house customization, hardware-specific device drivers, and "embedded" code such as that found in cell phones, cars, and microwave ovens. Most programmers' time is spent on the maintenance of code; these development costs are not part of sale-value. Moreover, the value of software rapidly diminishes when its manufacturer no longer supports it: consumers' expectations of support have a direct impact on the software's sale-value.

Thus, Raymond argues, if most of software's total costs are in its maintenance, debugging, and support, then charging a high price for sale and very little for subsequent service does not serve anyone well. Software vendors will concentrate on hasty releases of new products, to the detriment of after-sales service, and increasing customer bases mean more demands on service, which is too expensive for software vendors to provide. Such a state of affairs is conducive to the creation of a monopoly: most vendors will fail as they discontinue services, driving their customers to the few remaining competitors. Lowering the price of a desirable good, however, and thereby increasing its sales, will increase the cost of the support infrastructure, pushing vendors toward a service-driven model, one based on a *"continuing* exchange of value between the vendor and the customer," (Raymond 2000, emphasis in original) that mitigates against monopoly.

When software becomes free or open source, however, only its sale-value is threatened. FOSS makes it difficult to capture sale-value because its licenses allow unlimited copying: the first copy may be sold, but it is hard to sell future copies. But Raymond provides two examples in which developer salaries are paid for by use-value. In Cisco's risk-spreading model, an inversion of the nondisclosure agreement model, the software that operates Cisco products is given away as a hedge against the departure of the developers — and the specialized knowledge they carry — and to ensure continued and future support. In the consortium-funded Apache Project, a form of precompetitive collaboration, member organizations willingly fund the development of the FOSS licensed Apache server, recognizing that a secure scalable webserver is a crucial part of the technical and economic infrastructure of the Internet, one which supports the economic viability of anyone reliant on Internet-based business. The creation and funding of the Mozilla Foundation's Firefox project is similarly motivated by the universal desire for users/consumers to have access to a high-quality browser (Baker 2005).

Proprietary alternatives to FOSS licensing are incompatible, both economically and technically, with the FOSS community's perspectives on value creation through software development. First, "no party (with the possible exception of the originator of a piece of code) [should] be in a *privileged* position to extract profits" (Raymond 2000, emphasis in original). Second, such licenses, with their restrictions on redistribution, introduce legal enforcement costs that must be passed on to customers. Finally, these restrictions on redistribution prevent further development of the software in different directions, which acts as a damper on both economic and technical innovation. Thus, despite licenses that fail to capture sale-value, FOSS continues to produce value via the "inverse commons": due to network effects, the value of the software in the commons increases as more people use it and contribute to its further development. Here, the antirival nature of software commodities becomes apparent: the most valuable code in the commons is that which is most heavily used.

The feature of open source software (Raymond particularly cites the Linux kernel) that most directly enables continuing value creation is not technical but sociological: it is easy to submit changes to the codebase — the only barrier to entry is intimate technical knowledge of the code. The number of contributors to a project, and hence its chance of success, is inversely proportional to the number of obstacles to active participation faced by a potential contributor.

Ultimately, it is the governance of the FOSS community that enables this continual production of value. In "Homesteading the Noosphere" (Raymond 2000), Raymond distinguishes hacker pragmatism from the "zealotry" and "anticommercialism" of the FSF, a reflection of the historical differences in motivations among hackers. These differences are bridged by the taboos of the culture, such as those against unauthorized distribution of changes to a project or removing a developer's name from project credits, which Raymond argues are essential to community governance. In this context, choosing a licensing scheme is a decision of political economy, one that not only creates value by attracting developers and users but also facilitates governance by making public a set of assumptions about acceptable behavior.

Recognizing that notions of property and ownership have limited applicability in domains where "property is infinitely reduplicable, highly malleable, and the surrounding culture has neither coercive power relationships nor material scarcity economics" (Raymond 2000), Raymond suggests that software ownership is properly understood as the exclusive right to redistribute modified versions of software: ownership happens when someone founds a project, inherits the original, or takes over an orphaned project. Understood this way, the FOSS notion of property is akin to that of the Anglo-American common-law theory of land tenure, which allows for ownership through homesteading, transfer of title and adverse possession, respectively. Raymond asserts similar systems of ownership emerge when "property has high economic or survival value and no single authority is powerful enough to force central allocation of goods" (Raymond 2000).

The FOSS economy's abundance of storage space, network bandwidth, and computing power, rather than yielding the power and wealth typically associated with physical property, gives rise instead to a gift economy like those found in cultures without "significant material-scarcity problems with survival goods. . . . In gift cultures social status is determined not by what you control but by what you give away" (Raymond 2000). In these cultures, the only available measure of competitive success is reputation; governance structures exist primarily to maximize and protect reputation incentives.

FOSS Governance

Political scientist Steven Weber, in *The Success of Open Source,* argues that FOSS creates value through a distinctive model for the facilitation and distribution of innovation. As illustrated by the FOSS development process, this model rests on four principles: "Empower people to experiment," "Enable bits of information to find each other," "Structure information so it can recombine with other pieces of information," and "Create a governance system that sustains this process" (Weber 2004, 234). Effective FOSS governance, "setting parameters for voluntary relationships among autonomous parties" (Weber 2004, 172), solves problems of coordination and incentivization to support the kinds of innovation that create value.

The most dramatic manifestation of the failure of coordination in a FOSS project is the phenomenon of forking. Under most circumstances, developers agree that the most effective way to exploit the openness of source is to work in coordinated fashion toward some shared goal of functionality. Any of them is free, however, to break away with a copy of the code and start developing the software toward another set of goals; this may be motivated by disagreements about, for example, licensing terms, the technical direction of the project, or the effectiveness of project leadership. The software's production tree splits — "forks" — at this point; the original development proceeds along one branch, the breakaway programmer's version develops along another. Most developers see the right to fork both as one fundamental to the FOSS enterprise and as one that should be exercised exceptionally rarely as it consumes many resources and can generate gross inefficiencies. Given the tendency of FOSS developers to disagree frequently and vigorously, forking is a surprisingly rare occurrence. But the rarity of forking is also attributable to effective governance, particularly "individual incentives, cultural norms, and leadership practices" (Weber 2004, 159).

These individual incentives apply to the FOSS developer as a rational actor in a marketplace of innovation: traders who hope to offer arbitrarily many copies of their own innovation in return for individual copies of many others' innovations rely on an interoperability among items for trade, which would be diminished by forking just as the proliferation of proprietary versions of Unix diminished the market value of a Unix programmer's skills. Similarly, a developer's concern for the long-term health of his reputation mitigates against many potential forks: while initiating a fork may bring a short-term gain in authority and reputation, setting a precedent of forking may make the new branch, and the developer's reputation, similarly vulnerable. Moreover, a new fork would need to attract "followers" to enable any significant development; a developer who does not already have a substantial reputation would have difficulty successfully forking an established project.

Cultural norms inform the governance of which code is actually included in a FOSS project's codebase. The fundamental question here is one of who "owns" the project (Raymond 2000); subordinate to this is the question of precisely how ownership, or authority in general, relates to the process by which code submissions are accepted or rejected. In small projects, these decisions are one of the many responsibilities of the individual owner; larger projects such as Linux, Apache, and mozilla.org exemplify a variety of collective decision-making strategies and techniques. Orthogonal to the structural considerations of how decisions are made is "technical rationality," a norm that values dispute resolution based on "engineering culture . . . bottom up, pragmatic, and grounded heavily in experience rather than theory" (Weber 2004, 164). This mitigates against disagreements manifesting on a personal level: projects are held together by the mutual understanding that disagreements reveal intellectual and technical differences, not personal ones.

The leaders of successful large projects understand the importance of arguments based on technical rationality; they are committed to "documenting the reasons for design choices and code changes in the language of technical rationality that is the currency for this community" (Weber 2004, 167). Failures of leadership most often arise from abandoning this currency: failing to support even those contributors whose work is rejected while allowing "ego-based conflict" to persist, or making technical decisions without incorporating feedback from other developers. Linus Torvalds's success as the leader of Linux, exemplifying the best aspects of technical rationality and minimizing personal disagreement, relies in part on his ability to communicate the joy and satisfaction of programming.

FOSS governance relies on a mixture of social and technical strategies. As Torvalds learned as the Linux kernel and its development group grew rapidly, "engineering principles are important because they reduce organizational demands on the social and political structure for managing people" (Weber 2004, 173). This growth presented several technical and governance challenges. As the number of new developers grew, bringing new and diverse ideas for the direction of the kernel's development, Torvalds's original design of the kernel as one large interrelated piece of code became unmanageable. The kernel was therefore redesigned as a cluster of smaller, more independent, modules of code.

A similar crisis, demonstrating the challenge of forking and the role of technical solutions in solving governance problems, arose in 1998, when Torvalds began to ignore important contributions to the Linux kernel. At that time, Linux kernel developer Dave Miller maintained a "mirror" site called VGER, at Rutgers University, to make access to Linux kernel source more convenient for North American developers. Miller started accepting contributions to the kernel that Torvalds did not, which rapidly led to a de facto fork in the kernel's development. This fork rapidly became a rift in the entire community, as Torvalds lashed out against Miller's actions even as developers increasingly complained about Torvalds's unresponsiveness. The healing of this rift required a twofold solution: an organizational solution, in which leading Linux developers, with Torvalds, agreed on a new hierarchical scheme for handling incoming code, and a technical solution, in which veteran developer Larry McVoy offered to create new source-management software, specifically designed for use in open source projects, which would greatly ease the demands on Torvalds and his lieutenants.

Governance, Labor, and Co-optation

FOSS development projects, organized under a multiplicity of governance schemes, may differ in the kinds of leadership qualities they value, their shared cultural norms, project teleology, the structure of incentives, and decision-making processes. The *BSD groups[18] have a common cultural norm of valuing technological problem-solving as much as, or more than, profit or the promulgation of political ideologies (Coleman 2005). Others, such as the FSF, have broad sociotechnological goals in mind.[19] The Debian group's developers have "cobbled a hybrid organizational structure that integrates three different modes of governance — democratic majoritarian rule, a guild-like meritocracy, and an ad-hoc process of rough consensus" (Coleman 2005). These glimpses of governance schemes, in the context of political economy, expose to us an eclectic mix of labor organization and management structures.

The FOSS practice of distributing source code and accreting changes submitted by user-programmers is a form of production where the traditional practice of dividing labor among a pool of programmers is enhanced, expanded, and rendered radically flexible. The labor pool for a FOSS project is not limited to a small group of workers, but is expanded, exploiting the Internet, so that the cycle of distribution and accumulation of modifications is orders of magnitude more efficient and effective than the code-sharing of the past.

FOSS, that is, relies on "distribution of labor," an enhanced form of division of labor, by opening the gates of the virtual factory. The organization of this "factory" can be hierarchical, but this governance does not imply a hierarchical imposition of work assignments. The development of the Linux kernel is controlled by one man, Linus Torvalds, sitting astride its mountain of code. He and his lieutenants maintain control over the product through a rigorous system of quality control[20] while leaving individual developers free to pursue their chosen tasks within the kernel project. To make an industrial analogy, while senior developers often act somewhat like foremen, workers are not told where to go or what to do. Instead, the shop floor is scattered with tools and partially complete work, with copious explicit instructions and advice: anyone can pick up an unassigned programming task, read the documentation, and consult with other workers through e-mail, newsgroups, and chat. Work schedules are very weakly constrained, though there is no guarantee that a worker's contribution will ultimately be accepted: contributions to work within this "factory" come from all time zones and are accepted on the basis of a meritocratic process. Workers are free to leave with a copy of the product and to open up another manufacturing shop: programmers are always free to fork a development tree. Users are also "workers," as they may become producers of future versions of the code. Workers' inspection of each other's work, combined with effective management, ensures that the energies of an army of programmers, of whatever size, can effectively be focused on solving the problems of creating excellent code (Raymond 2001).

The corporatization of FOSS suggests a need, to the capitalist owner, for disciplining labor. But this disciplining is made difficult by the availability to workers of empowering technological advances, their education, and their independence as they choose schedules and work assignments. The corporate owner therefore must deploy a delicate mix of cooperation and co-optation. One form this co-optation takes is the introduction and promulgation of corporate ideals. As the FOSS community makes concessions — in the choice of licensing scheme,[21] in the mixing of proprietary and free software,[22] or in the diversion of labor to closed source projects[23] — these ideals are reinforced. The most seductive promises made by the corporate world remain those of venture capital funding, commercial success, and unlimited accumulation of wealth, all of which continue to require such concessions. As the FOSS community negotiates with the corporate world for acceptance, as open source projects turn into commercial enterprises (Pepperdine 2004), it becomes increasingly difficult for the community to maintain the purity of the original hacker ideals. The discussions this provokes in the FOSS community bring to the fore the rift between the free software and open source movements.

The exploitation of "free labor" is another potential locus of co-optation. This "intense collective labor of programmers, designers, and workers" has played an integral role in, and placed its stamp on, the development and enrichment of the Internet:

> Simultaneously voluntarily given and unwaged, enjoyed and exploited, free labor on the Net includes . . . building Web sites, modifying software packages, reading and participating in mailing lists . . . it is the spectacle of that labor changing its product that keeps the users coming back. The commodity . . . is only as good as the labor that goes into it. . . . The notion of users' labor maintains an ideological and material centrality. . . . [T]he best way to stay visible and thriving on the Web is to turn your site into a space that is . . . built by its users. Users keep a site alive through their labor. . . . Such a feature seems endemic to the Internet in ways that can be worked on by commercialization, but not substantially altered. (Terranova 2000)

This phenomenon clearly represents an "extraction of value" from continuous work, though Terranova's critique only points to the existence of labor uncompensated by traditional means such as money exchange: it trades on an old confusion by conflating "financially uncompensated" with "free." Compensations in the FOSS economy are diverse; a programmer who releases code freely may do so anticipating others will release code useful for him.

But the open source movement does provide evidence of the trend toward the co-optation of the digital economy by the corporate world.[24] This co-optation is inevitable, precisely because the cybereconomy reflects the economy in which it is embedded: "[I]t is . . . impossible to separate . . . the digital economy of the Net from the larger network economy of late capitalism. . . . [T]he Internet is always and simultaneously a gift economy and an advanced capitalist economy" (Terranova 2000). The co-optation is either implicit ("you must go open-source to get access to . . . the near-instantaneous bug-fixes, the distributed intellectual resources of the Net, the increasingly large open-source code base" [Leonard 1999]) or explicit ("what better way to shed staff than by . . . having code-dabbling hobbyists fix and further develop your product?" [Horvath 1998]), and signals a lack of reciprocity, especially of code-borrowing, prefiguring the eventual depletion of the FOSS sphere:

> [T]he open source question demonstrates the overreliance of the digital economy as such on free labor. . . . [It] is part of larger mechanisms of capitalist extraction of value which are fundamental to late capitalism. . . . Late capitalism . . . exhausts [free labor] by subtracting selectively but widely the means through which that labor can reproduce itself . . . [it] . . . nurtures, exploits, and exhausts its labor force. (Terranova 2000)

The corporate tendency to extract maximum value from any arrangement of labor and production exploits a tension in this sphere between the pragmatic techno-optimists (the open-source movement) and the quasi-altruistic communitarians (free software "zealots"). The question for the FOSS community is whether this extraction of value is to be resisted. If resistance is in order, what form might it take? As we will see, the array of FOSS licenses represents a variety of answers to these questions.

Co-optation, properly understood as the furtherance of another's goals under the mistaken impression of furthering one's own, could take several forms in the FOSS realm. One is the compromising of the goals of FOSS: for people to have agency over the software on their machines, and, subordinately, to write free software and encourage its widespread adoption. This compromise could be effected in a variety of ways: the number of FOSS programmers could decline, some lured away by enticing proprietary-software jobs, some unconvinced by the inadequate marketing of the technical and economic viability of FOSS, some thwarted by unforeseen shifts in the economy that render FOSS a financially unviable way to work. Furthermore, FOSS products could be driven out of the market by monopolistic pressures: Microsoft's Internet Explorer, which was originally based on the open-source Spyglass browser, essentially drove Netscape out of the browser market by being bundled with the Windows operating system. Thus, continued nonreciprocal borrowing of free software for use in proprietary products could increase the latter's market share without contributing to the software commons. Last, and most subtle, is the possibility of a weakening, after exposure to differing values, of the shared norms that bind the community.

The FOSS community does not have control over the first method (though sufficient exposure to FOSS norms could weaken the allure of enticing proprietary-software jobs). The second could be affected by executive decisions over the deployment of licensing schemes; keeping code free, and ensuring reciprocity in code sharing through licensing provisions such as those of the GPL ensures protection against co-optation. The third is controlled by discourse in the community. Here, significantly, the rhetorical thrust of the open-source community (Berry 2004), in sharp opposition to the language of the free software community, is an invitation to co-optation. The Open Source Initiative's pronouncements indicate that this language is deliberately employed in the cause of corporate acceptance. The constant refrain that there is "nothing special" about free software other than its development model — for example, "[Open source] is one tool among many that can . . . create business value. . . . [It] is just a way to put product in many users' hands inexpensively" (Olson 2006) — and the lack of attention paid to the cultural norms of the FOSS community is an indicator of this trend. The OSI's discourse is shot through with corporate jargon; the only time the corporate world pays attention to the GPL is when legal departments warn of potential violation of its terms in the mixing of free software with proprietary packages. The OSI thus enables a subtle exploitation of the programmer whose code may well be used to further corporate ends and undermine his own community.

FOSS reworks not only our understanding of labor relations but also that of the worker's relationship to the goods he produces. Traditional arrangements of commodity production locate the knowledge and decisions of technique outside of the worker. In FOSS, the conception of the open source user as empowered programmer[25] enables a reconfiguration of the relationship between worker and product that substantially addresses Marxian notions of worker alienation. The user of proprietary software is alienated from the product; he is unable to perceive its product's infrastructure or adapt it to meet his needs. The FOSS model, by making source code available, modulates this alienation by casting users as workers who might modify the product. This blurring of the programmer/user distinction thus acts to erase the consumer/producer distinction as well. Alienation from products is mitigated in the FOSS world because the worker can derive independent profit and surplus value from his work. The knowledge-based nature of software, revealed by its source code, resolves the problem of alienation because "the worker . . . achieves fulfillment through work [by finding] in her brain her own, unalienated means of production" (Terranova 2000).

The potential for such fulfillment is partially embodied in programmers' right to fork. While the technical rationale for the right to fork is protection against the incompetence of one set of code maintainers, it also preserves a spirit of entrepreneurship: a FOSS worker can seek independent commercial advantage from her copy of the code. A worker could leave the "factory" one day with a copy of the software and commence sales of the software, or a derivative of it, at any price he (and the market) sees fit. The success of this breakaway project is only limited by the worker's technical competence and ability to recruit codevelopers.

Furthermore, in FOSS, the extraction of surplus value from the product is under the control of the worker. To redress the absurdity of assigning a commodity value to software, a good whose marginal cost of production is zero, the market assigns it a phantom price, one that supposedly captures the cost of the labor and expertise of those who wrote it. As the sale-value of software is driven down by the marginal cost of reproduction, free software workers may leverage their freedom by selling, at market rates, services such as support and customization for products they know intimately.

Viewed through the lens of political economy, Bill Gates's intervention with the Homebrew Computer Club, based on the reasoning that users would pay a market-determined price for a commodity they were unable to develop on their own, showed a software entrepreneur's keen understanding of the true scarcity that lay ahead. In the software world, historically, the scarcity had not been one of material but of knowledge. Thus, while the problem faced by the personal-computing community in the 1980s, the lack of adequate software, was the same as those faced by consumers in the 1960s, one key difference between the two groups was that by the 1980s users had become excluded from participation in the development process. Ironically, commercial personal computing brought widespread access to computer software and hardware, but at the cost of a fundamental alienation of even the interested user from the product. The growth of the computer industry in the wake of the personal computer revolution has maintained this industrial image of the user separated from the code that runs his machines.

FOSS and Property

Like any digital good, software can be distributed, via the Internet, to facilitate a direct and "just-in-time" connection between producer and consumer. Unique to free software, however, is its close identification of its mode of production with its mode of distribution. Linux, as an archetypal example, was produced through a process of transnational accretion of repairs and improvements. This accretion was only possible because of the preexisting distribution mechanisms of the Internet; more important, consumers of Linux rely on the same distribution network as its producers. This leads to a unique situation:

> [I]n the world of zero-marginal cost, anarchist distribution — that is, distribution without exclusion from the act of distributing — produces inherently superior distribution . . . when the right to distribute goods with zero-marginal cost has to be bought and sold, there are inefficiencies introduced in the social network of distribution. When no such buying and selling, no such exclusion from the power of distribution exists, distribution occurs at the native speed of the social network itself. (Moglen 2003)

Adam Smith's original analysis of market economies relied on the context of particular kinds of goods, modes of production, and arrangements for exchange and compensation. But when the character of goods and production changes, the market in which these goods are exchanged must adapt on pain of gross inefficiency (Moglen 2003). The maintenance of these inefficiencies by the exercise of monopolistic power and regressive legal protections is not only anathema to a free market but also certain to fail. Thus, while the "invisible hand" pushes the market toward change, these interventions resist its benign influence.

In typical markets, producers provide property, in the form of goods, to consumers, a transaction underwritten by a particular monetary scheme through which exchange value is communicated and realized. When markets are structured around goods with a radically different nature, notions of monetary compensation and property change in turn. Most observers of the FOSS world agree that economic incentives and compensation are not exclusively monetary, supplemented by "reputationomics," gift cultures, network effects, barter economies, and the like. But perhaps the most significant feature of the FOSS economy is its explicit disdain for, and inversion of, traditional assumptions about the importance of private property.

David Hume famously suggested that property relations only make sense under conditions of scarcity (Hume 1978, 484–98). But in the software world, the scarcity is not of the good, but of an intangible commodity, the programmer's knowledge. That treating software as private property crucially affects its creation, use, and further development has long been recognized in the free software community: "If a program has an owner, this very much affects what it is, and what you can do with a copy if you buy one. The difference is not just a matter of money. The system of owners of software encourages software owners to produce something — but not what society really needs" (Stallman 1994). Control of the means of production of, and exclusion from, property through nondisclosure agreements, copyright, patent, and trade secret law is the fundamental scarcity-creation principle in proprietary software's property regime.

The rejection of software ownership by the free software community denies both these principles:

> The advance of digital society, whose involuntary promoter is the bourgeoisie, replaces the isolation of the creators, due to competition, by their revolutionary combination, due to association. Creators of knowledge, technology, and culture discover that they no longer require the structure of production based on ownership and the structure of distribution based on coercion of payment. Association, and its anarchist model of propertyless production, makes possible the creation of free software, through which creators gain control of the technology of further production. (Moglen 2003)

The FOSS world can therefore be considered as championing a great experiment in alternative property regimes:

> [W]e have made a social network committed to the proposition that the central executable elements of human technology can be produced by sharing — without exclusionary property relations. And that if the central executable elements of technology can be made by sharing, without exclusionary property relations, then the non-executable elements of culture — art, useful information, and so on — can be distributed without exclusionary property relations. (Moglen 2003)

That is, software can be successfully conceived as common property rather than private property, with implications for the development and dissemination not only of technology but also of culture. But the artificially asymmetric accumulation of intellectual resources created by the contemporary software industry's exclusionary property relations threatens any such progress.

Immanuel Kant's theory of private property highlights a constitutional incoherence in proprietary software. Kant assumes that the use of useful objects is a good and, further, that objects are not usable unless they are owned. Kant then argues for a connection between property and agency, as it would be an insult to agency and human personality if no system were devised for the use of useful objects: "It is a duty of right to act towards others so that what is external (usable) could also become someone's" (Kant 1991). He concludes that we are obliged to act in ways that make useful objects belong to someone. But as such an arrangement relies on a collectively agreed-upon property regime within which questions of ownership can be resolved, and because the appropriation of a resource as private property imposes new duties on a collective, a property regime cannot acquire legitimacy through unilateral action: it must be ratified by all involved in such a way that everyone's interests are protected equally. If a private property regime is to be established, the question of ownership cannot be begged but must be settled on a just basis. Such an agreement has not taken place in the software world: the free software community's resistance to the proprietary regime indicates it is not a universally accepted model. Both the technical and economic feasibility of the FOSS property model suggest an alternative is at hand. The proprietary-software property model, then, is incoherent: it is a system of ownership devised without a meaningful conception of property to underwrite it (Boyle 1996). The freedom to own proprietary software masks a property regime that rests on exclusion; it is a system that takes away liberties (Stallman 1992, 1994).

As a social construction, property is always subject to analysis in light of changed economic conditions or artifacts with novel characteristics. Thus property, both as a concept and as a mechanism for the distribution of resources, is always open to reform and revision (Gallie 1956). If all property systems are engaged in some distributive calculus of freedom, then no property system unequivocally contributes to liberty. Talk about property is inseparable from talk about justice: every ethical or economic justification for private property rests on the assumption that it will result in a more just distribution of resources. Locke, for instance, suggested a Pareto-optimal justification for private property: everyone will be better off in such a regime, or, at least, it will benefit some and leave others unharmed. Private property rights are grounded in a clear-cut utilitarianism: they are intended to bring about a greater social good than the alternatives. When this utilitarian calculus fails, other property regimes may become more attractive, as in the nationalization of certain tracts of parkland in the United States, or the Quebecois interest in nationalizing Canada's oil resources in the wake of increased fuel prices (*The Canadian Press* 2005).

The story of FOSS suggests an alternative calculus that may provide a more effective route to the production and distribution of high-quality software. Software, once freed, is not just nonrival, it is antirival: the more widely the software is distributed, the greater its value becomes as the result of collective debugging and improvement. The inhibitions on software distribution imposed by exclusionary property relations thus prevent the creation of maximal value in an economy based on nonrival and antirival goods. FOSS suggests a political economy of software based on nonexclusionary, equitable distribution of its resources. Stewardship and guardianship are viable alternatives to exclusion (Weber 2004, 228). Stewards of "private" property may be restricted in their use of it to the extent that each decision regarding its use requires collective consultation. To understand a programmer as the steward of his code would be to posit a different relationship of technology to society. Software becomes a carrier of socially constructed knowledge stewarded by the programmer.

The notion of property is still crucial to FOSS: software must have an owner/licensor who can license rights to the FOSS community. But this property is effectively common, not private: its usage is determined by rules that guarantee its access to all; its use is only restricted in order to protect this universal access. Any commons, though, is susceptible to the "tragedy of the commons," in which collective ownership depresses individual incentives for upkeep of the commons, resulting in its eventual degradation (Raymond 2000). But FOSS would only be vulnerable to this devolution if a licensing scheme were to allow it: thus, the choice of license is particularly important. Here again, the ideological differences between the free software movement and the Open Source Initiative are crucial, for the OSI's greater tolerance of noncopyleft licensing schemes, which allow nonreciprocal borrowing from the software commons, could lead to a depletion of the commons.

The unique perspectives on property characterizing the FOSS movement are most clearly articulated in software licenses; some differences among FOSS licenses are best understood as varying degrees of tolerance for the privatization of goods previously held as common property. FOSS licenses aim to create a common property system in which resource usage is regulated by rules whose raison d'être is to make those resources available for use by all members of society. Software licensed under the GNU General Public License (GPL) — the paradigmatic free software license — must remain under this license in perpetuity: if a programmer were to make changes to software licensed under the GPL, then distribute the changed code, it must also be licensed under the GPL. This ensures that the software, as common property, remains in common. The GPL influences the commercial potential of free software: if someone were selling a GPL-licensed product and a new version were released by an independent programmer, the "original owner" could integrate the new code into the old codebase and continue selling the product as before. Because the original owner in such a scenario commands market share, typically by virtue of so-called value-added services (such as support, documentation, and antecedent user community), the owner may be in a position to elbow out the new software product developed by the developer.

Alternatively, under the terms of licenses such as the Berkeley Standard Distribution (BSD) license, an independent programmer's code could be used by anyone else, who could make modifications and then release the code as proprietary. The original owner would not have access to the proprietary code, and thus would be unable to make changes or integrate it into older versions without recompense to the developer. The original unmodified code would still be open; the modifications would be the only part kept secret. Such secrets, however, are not trivial, and if juxtaposed with the superior marketing and market presence of a corporate heavyweight, could render the common version worthless in the face of a more heavily developed proprietary version.

The differences among free software licenses and their contrast with proprietary licenses hearken back to the original cleavage in the software world: Is software a commodity or a common good? The software market became viable by privatizing a class of property previously understood as held in common. It also created the possibility for programmers to be perceived as highly paid technocrats, a phenomenon that took on extreme proportions after the tremendous commercial potential of the Internet became apparent. Bill Gates's claims in the Homebrew letter still remain the core of any economic argument against free software. Indeed, it is not a stretch to say they are the only economic argument against FOSS.

The Future of FOSS

We only have hints about the shape the software economy would take in the absence of exclusionary property relations: without monopolies propped up by legal protections for owners a more fragmented market could result, accompanied by diminishing salaries and a shrinking demand for programmers. But perhaps the ubiquity of computing and the new availability of code would provoke a demand for customized code and the programmers to create it. Software could then revert to its original status as object of craft, with the relationship of craftsman to object, and customer to craftsman, worked out autonomously. This would create a decentralized cadre of freely operating workers who would have eliminated the potential for monopolistic or capitalist co-optation through their particular deployment of intellectual property regimes.

This vision of a return to software's roots is opposed by perspectives on the early era of computing that hold it was not conducive to the production of quality software, as it provided very little economic competition (Glass 2005). But this argument is reductive in the extreme: it suggests only one reason for the production of quality software, and disregards a constellation of individual and social motivations. Furthermore, this analysis fails to acknowledge the limited market that could not accommodate the production of a diverse range of software products; the first user-developed software was a response to the lack of software vendors in the fledgling market of the time.

The free software political economy is not cleanly separable from the larger political economy in which it is situated; neither is impervious to the influence of the other. The changes promised by the FOSS economy will remain only partially realized so long as software, a good that sits uncomfortably in any taxonomy of goods and products, is misconstrued as a commodity, and so long as the fundamental source of alienation, the failure to recognize a programmer's knowledge as the true source of value, remains in place.

If political economy is understood as the interplay between the political forces of the "outside" world and an "internal" economy, then the fracturing of the free software world by the creation of the Open Source Initiative was a crucial event, as external pressures forced a splintering of the free software political economy. The OSI intends to supply merely a software-engineering methodology — release code quickly, release often, involve users early in development — that can be transplanted into a corporate setting without much difficulty. IBM's adoption of open source has not caused any easing of their aggressive patenting regime; whatever the OSI's message about the openness of information, it has not permeated IBM's approach to its patent portfolio.

The open source movement is the apotheosis of hackerist pragmatism. The OSI claims, in a complete rejection of the social constructionist view of technology, that a development model's viability, desirability, and success depends only on the quality of the software it produces: the best technology "just bubbles up." This denies the role of contingency in technology and ascribes an autonomy to technological evolution that is philosophically implausible and historically ill-grounded. The OSI enables a subtle co-optation of the free software model; what makes its stance attractive to corporate interests is both the possibility of drawing upon the technical skills of a motivated worker force and the "freedom" to convert to closed source in the future.

The free software movement typifies technocratic idealism, yet it resists the technocratic impulse of the corporate world because it is willing to sacrifice technical and economic goods to preserve the intangible value of the freedom of software (Stallman 1992, 1994). Arguments for open source relying exclusively on engineering and economic factors, such as quality, reliability, cost, and choice (Raymond 2000) are a considerable distance from the altruistic notion of sharing that underwrites free software ideals.

The OSI, while portraying itself as an advocate for a revolutionary model for the software economy, remains hostage to its tolerance of proprietary software. The original motivation for the Open Source Definition (and the Open Source Initiative's attendant movement away from Free Software) was the concern that the word "free" was misleading and unattractive to potential corporate supporters. But as Richard Stallman's speech/beer refrain shows, there simply is no confusion when we say "free speech" — no one imagines we are giving away speech for free. Stallman's choice of terms reflects the commodification of software and makes clear the basis of the movement to (re)claim software as a general public good. The distance that open source advocates seek from the free software movement as they seduce corporate interests reflects the success of a long campaign waged by those very interests to privatize the historically public resource of software.

2

The Ethics of Free Software

"I would like to consider [the question of who gets to copy software] using a different criterion: the prosperity and freedom of the public in general. This answer cannot be decided by current law — the law should conform to ethics, not the other way around."

— Richard Stallman (Stallman 1992)

"Constitutions which aim at the common advantage are correct and just without qualification."

— Aristotle (Aristotle 1998, III.6.1279a17-21)

From an ethical perspective, one of the most pressing questions raised by free and open source software is the question of the rights granted to, and the restrictions placed on, users and collaborators by the creators of computer programs. What freedoms do software users and developers deserve, and how can those freedoms best be protected?

Free and open source software is generally classified according to the terms under which it is licensed. In 1996, Richard Stallman's Free Software Foundation[1] (FSF) provided the first formal definition of this class of software, the Free Software Definition (FSD) (The Free Software Foundation 2005). In the following year, Bruce Perens reframed this definition as the Debian Social Contract (Debian Project 2004), emphasizing the rights of, and programmers' responsibilities to, the community of users:

> Ean Schuessler came up with the idea for the Contract after a conversation . . . with Bob Young, the co-founder of a then-emergent commercial Linux distribution, Red Hat. Ean suggested that Red Hat might want to guarantee in writing that as they grew larger they would always provide GPLed software. Young replied that "that would be the kiss of death," implying that such a guarantee made to the users of free software could prove disastrous to his business. Ean (who was himself a business owner) was both amused and disturbed by Young's answer, and with other developers at the conference he decided that it would behoove Debian to provide such a guarantee in writing. (Coleman 2005, 357)

This document included the Debian Free Software Guidelines, which were then adapted by the Open Source Initiative[2] (OSI) to create the Open Source Definition (OSD) (Open Source Initiative 2006). These definitions — the FSD and the OSD — provide lists of conditions that software licenses must meet to be classified as "free" or "open source," respectively. Most software licenses meeting one definition meet the other as well; thus, the same freedoms are enabled by both free software and open source licenses.

The freedoms enumerated in the FSD and OSD embody an ethical stance that provides normative guidance to, and protects the rights of, the community of free software users and developers. Building on these definitions, free software licensing schemes grant a suite of rights and freedoms, to programmers and users alike, that are much broader than those granted by proprietary-software licensing schemes. At a finer granularity, the particular licenses take different approaches to protecting these rights and freedoms; hence, choosing a license is an important responsibility of the free software developer.

While the FSD and OSD fundamentally agree on the nature of software freedom, they enumerate these freedoms using radically different language; there is much moral and instrumental significance in this difference. FOSS licenses, by being based on these definitions, serve as constitutions for the communities of programmers and users; the choice of licensing scheme is crucial to maintaining the viability of the free software community. The implications of license choice for the community of free software programmers and users is illustrated by the conflicts engendered by the licensing of the X Window System, a ubiquitous graphical user interface for Unix workstations as well as GNU/Linux systems.

The X Consortium, developers of the X Window System, was historically opposed to the copyleft terms of the GPL. It expressed its opposition through a mixture of outright pressure — by refusing to include copylefted software in its X distribution — and quasi-ethical arguments that the restrictions of copyleft were too onerous (Stallman 1998). The Consortium asked free software developers, instead, to donate their software without copylefting it:

> "Join us in donating our work to proprietary software developers," they said, suggesting that this is a noble form of self-sacrifice. "Join us in achieving popularity," they said, suggesting that it was not even a sacrifice. But self-sacrifice is not the issue: tossing away the defense that copyleft provides, which protects the freedom of the whole community, is sacrificing more than yourself. Those who granted the X Consortium's request entrusted the community's future to the good will of the X Consortium. (Stallman 1998)

The X Consortium's policy was motivated by its desire to ensure corporate acceptance of the X Window system, effectively making corporations the arbiters of licensing decisions in this programming community.

In 1997, control of the X Window System codebase passed to The Open Group, who changed the licensing terms in 1998 with the release of the X11R6.4

version. The new license kept the source code open and continued to allow the creation of derivative work, but it required licensors who generated revenue from products that included X11R6.4 to pay a licensing fee. The imposition of this additional requirement, regarded as a betrayal by the free software community, made it difficult to develop software that incorporated or relied on the X Window System. Ironically, programmers, by agreeing not to use copyleft, had granted the X Consortium and The Open Group the power to add restrictions on the use of their code. In September 1998, several months after the restricted version of X11R6.4 was released, The Open Group rereleased it under the same noncopyleft free software license that was used for X11R6.3.

This story has an instructive moral: succumbing to the lure of commercial popularity can restrict the freedoms of software. Even had The Open Group not effectively closed the code for X, the licensing terms used for the release of the code had made it available for such a takeover; it was possible to take "nonreciprocal advantage" of the FOSS community's joint efforts — to receive unrestricted code from developers but then to impose restrictions on that code for private gain. For the free software community, it is vital that software be protected against the kind of opportunism practiced by the X Consortium and The Open Group.

The Software Freedoms

The fundamental difference between free and proprietary software lies in the nature of the actions that users of the software are permitted to take. Proprietary software, relying on trade secret, licensing, and copyright law, restricts user actions via End User License Agreements (EULAs); free software licenses eliminate, to varying degrees, restrictions on user actions. The difference between proprietary and free software, as established by software licenses, is not a question of price. A free software package may cost as much as a proprietary package; that it is "free" only affects what the user may do with it once she has procured it.

Free Software

The "free" in "free software" refers to a cluster of four specific freedoms identified by the Free Software Definition (The Free Software Foundation 2005):

> "Free software" is a matter of liberty, not price. To understand the concept, you should think of "free" as in "free speech," not as in "free beer." Free software is a matter of the users' freedom to run, copy, distribute, study, change and improve the software. More precisely, it refers to four kinds of freedom, for the users of the software:
>
> The freedom to run the program, for any purpose (freedom 0)
>
> The freedom to study how the program works, and adapt it to your needs (freedom 1). Access to the source code is a precondition for this.

The freedom to redistribute copies so you can help your neighbor (freedom 2)

The freedom to improve the program, and release your improvements to the public, so that the whole community benefits (freedom 3). Access to the source code is a precondition for this.

Taken together, these four freedoms describe a range of possibilities for user action; the commitment to uphold these choices provides a normative framework for the behavior of software developers. Each of these freedoms for the user can only be ensured through appropriate action on the part of software developers. Software users, particularly in the free software world, may become the developers of the next generation of software, in which case they, too, would become subject to these normative constraints. The sustenance of these freedoms over the course of time thus requires active dissemination and adoption of the values that undergird these freedoms.

In a rhetorically suggestive move, the first freedom is termed "Freedom 0." At one level, this is an example of playful hacker humor (in some programming languages, counting begins at 0), but it also signals a bedrock principle. Freedom 0 intends to protect the right of the user to deploy software in whatever fashion, towards whatever end, he or she sees fit. Correspondingly, the creator of the software must relinquish control over how his work will be used, granting full autonomy, and ancillary responsibility, to the user. In particular, this means that the software creator must give up the possibility of asserting rights, such as the *droit moral* granted to artists under European copyright law (Caslon Analytics 2006), over the disposition of her work. Freedom 0 is historically grounded in the hacker ethic, which values unfettered access to information. Hackers viewed themselves as free to uncover the inner workings of systems like telephone or computer networks; their investigations relied on putting the components of these systems to use in ways not envisioned by their designers. Restrictions on how phones, computers, or software could be used would limit the scope of such explorations. It is an aversion to such restriction, placed on the ability to tinker with technological systems, which appears to motivate Freedom 0.

At first glance, Freedom 1 appears to treat only freedoms important to programmers — the freedoms to examine and modify code. Yet all users, even those who are not trained programmers, should have the freedom to adapt software to their own needs, whether through their own efforts to learn how to program, or through contractors or friends who do the work for them; this freedom is a vital aspect of user autonomy. Distinctions between "developer" and "user" are erased by this freedom: the provision of source code creates the possibility for a user to become a developer. Freedom 1 enshrines the potential for transformation: both of the user, who may be transformed through study, and of code, which may be altered in form, content, and functionality. Both sorts of transformation rely on direct access to the source code; experimental study of high-level functionality, or even reverse engineering, that is, determining how the program was written by analyzing its binary code and output, is not sufficient.

The ethical content of Freedom 2 has little to do with the technical nature of its subject: it is a straightforward statement of communitarian principles. Yet the normative demand of this freedom — to be able to make copies freely — relies on software's nonrival character and ease of reproduction and distribution. The Open Group's imposition of licensing fees on X11R6.4 abridged Freedom 2; as the Free Software Definition clarifies: "[Y]ou should be free to redistribute copies, either with or without modifications, either gratis or charging a fee for distribution, to anyone anywhere. Being free to do these things means (among other things) that you do not have to ask or pay for permission." Any terms restricting redistribution, whether financial or logistical, violate Freedom 2.

Redistributing copies is not the only way to help one's neighbor by sharing software. A user could share her computer with a friend who stops by to write his community newsletter; he would be using the software but not making a copy for himself. Or, software could be provided as a Web service. The FSD's explicit protection of the freedom to make and distribute copies anticipates that users' freedom to share software would be most effectively restricted by blocking copying.

Freedom 3 is framed in terms of facilitating programmers' innovation and making the fruits of this innovation available to the community of programmers and users. This freedom is not only an extension of Freedom 1 but also an explicit statement of the importance of community. It is easily understood as the formal statement of an important component of Richard Stallman's initial announcement of the GNU project: "I consider that the golden rule requires that if I like a program I must share it with other people who like it" (Stallman 1983). Freedoms 2 and 3 most explicitly acknowledge the social context of code: it is written in response to a felt human need, and must be made available to all without restriction.

The benefits that accrue from these freedoms flow equally to users and developers. Each freedom is stated without reference to a particular political ideology; each valorizes a particular independence. Taken jointly, Freedoms 1, 2, and 3 work to ensure a "fair use" of software, and thus concomitantly make a statement against the inappropriate application of legal regimes in the domain of software: "protections" on software, whether enforced by copyright or trade secret law, should not restrict these freedoms.

Proprietary Software

In contrast to free software, proprietary software is licensed in terms antithetical to users' freedoms:

> When a consumer purchases a piece of software, say Microsoft Excel, she acquires along with the physical copy of the software and the manual . . . the right to use the software for its intended purpose — in this case, as a spreadsheet program. By

> opening the plastic wrap on the box, the consumer becomes bound by the so-called shrinkwrap license under which she is bound not to copy the work (beyond the single copy made for her own use), not to make derivative works based on the work, and not to authorize anyone else to do either of these two things. (St. Laurent 2004)

Thus, proprietary licenses most directly impact Freedoms 1, 2, and 3. Freedom 1, the freedom to study and modify the software, is only provided in the very limited sense that users can customize the handful of features the vendor makes available for their customization. This level of access precludes any meaningful study of the code. The restrictions on copying typically placed by EULAs directly affect Freedom 2; furthermore, without the provision of source code, Freedoms 1 and 3 are fatally compromised, as the code cannot be improved and redistributed. EULAs go on to restrict use of the software on more than one computer, reselling of purchased copies, and the use of the software for purposes other than those sanctioned by the original license, such as employing the software for commercial use if purchased under an educational license.[3] Thus, fundamentally, EULAs act to limit the "choices, options and actions" of users (Zymaris 2003).

The free software community's declaration of the four freedoms demonstrates the importance accorded to unmediated relationships between users and developers, relationships permitting broad autonomy for all. The terms of these relationships are negotiated between users and developers via intra-community discourse and concretized in software licenses. By contrast, proprietary software interposes a layer of bureaucracy, if not outright paternalism, by placing a third party, the vendor, in charge of the "welfare of the community." The financial viability of the vendor becomes a precondition for any sustained, if indirect, relationship between users and developers; the freedoms granted to users and developers alike are only those that support, or fail to threaten, this financial constraint.

Free and proprietary software licenses are two different responses to copyright law:

> In proprietary software, the license terms are designed to protect the copyright. They're a way of granting a few rights to users while reserving as much legal territory as possible for the owner (the copyright holder). The copyright holder is very important, and the license logic so restrictive that the exact technicalities of the license terms are usually unimportant. In open source software. . . . the copyright exists to protect the license. The only rights the copyright holder always keeps are to enforce the license. . . . [M]ost choices pass to the user. . . . [I]n open source software the copyright holder is almost irrelevant — but the license terms are very important. (Raymond 2002)

Thus, what free software licenses do or do not say is crucial to understanding which freedoms they facilitate. Because of software's modifiability and the possibility for future distribution, a license can affect the choices and freedoms of "downstream" users as well.

The effect of licensing terms on the relationships between users and software is most clearly demonstrated through example (Hannemyr 1999). Proprietary-software packages, such as Adobe PageMaker and Microsoft Word, which combine text editing and typesetting capabilities, have their free software counterpart in TeX,[4] a typesetting program easily integrated with any number of text editors, such as *emacs*.[5] Both TeX and *emacs* were explicitly designed to be freely customizable and extensible by their users, providing very fine control over both the user's interaction with the software and the final appearance of the typeset documents. Similar proprietary packages offer many powerful features, but are fundamentally inflexible in their relationships to the user. This inflexibility is evident in the way they allow or disallow, for example, user customizations of keystrokes. Different proprietary-software packages typically use different keystrokes to initiate particular actions: "Quit" might be represented by Alt-Q in one program and Ctrl-Z in another. Highly customizable programs (such as *emacs*) allow the user to "remap" the keystrokes corresponding to different actions, so that the interfaces of diverse programs can be synchronized, greatly simplifying the computing experience. But proprietary software rarely provides adequate mechanisms for achieving this kind of customization; customization of the core functionality of the software is even more rarely found in proprietary applications. Users confronted with proprietary software that lacks both desired functionality and sufficient customizability are then forced into choosing among several unappealing options: to make do with substandard performance, to compensate by spending many extra hours of work, or to revise their original expectations.

Proprietary applications such as those found in Microsoft's Office suite are often extensible in the sense that the user can add new functionality, but this is rarely the same as a capacity for arbitrary customization. Extensibility of proprietary software more often has to do with supporting the assimilation of other applications: proprietary software exploits extensibility to create dependencies that drive its continued adoption. So, for instance, a Microsoft Word user may extend its bibliographic capabilities by integrating another proprietary software package such as EndNote. The collaboration between the creators of Word and EndNote serves both: by providing tight integration with popular word processing software, EndNote increases its market share, and by providing programming facilities for such integration, Word's functionality is enhanced. Extensibility is provided not only for the user's convenience but for the sake of the vendors' market position. But the user is unable to make a customization and to share it with his friends or coworkers. They must rely upon the vendors' beneficence to provide these, a decision contingent on the vendors' analysis of the change's economic utility.

Freedom Zero

Freedom 0 of the Free Software Definition places no restrictions on the use of software. But software may be used to achieve ethically questionable ends. This highlights a tension in the provision of software freedoms: while the FSD explicitly forbids direct restrictions on users' freedoms, it does not address other means by which software may indirectly restrict freedoms. Suppose a developer creates software implementing an especially accurate method for dynamically calculating flight trajectories of powered aerial vehicles. This software has many applications, most of which have no potential to do harm. The developer, however, is opposed to the continued development of nuclear weapons, and does not want his software used in the guidance system of a nuclear missile.[6] This software could not be licensed as free software while simultaneously reflecting the developer's intended restriction on the military application of his software and its derivative works.

The discussion of the potential uses of software is no less complicated than a discussion of the application of scientific knowledge: particular restrictions run the risk of being vague, too inclusive, or perpetually subject to amendments in light of new developments. Perhaps placing restrictions on specific uses of software is a misdirected effort — our pacifist developer, rather than forbidding his software from being used in missile-guidance systems, should instead work toward global nuclear disarmament. Yet forbidding this particular application of this software may be a small step toward nuclear disarmament. These concerns are echoed in the history of science, as scientists raise concerns about the potential applications of the knowledge they create (The Pugwash Conferences 2002). Acting on these concerns, scientists have often employed political persuasion and appeals to conscience (Rees 2006), including voluntary abstention from work — all options available to programmers today. Thus, rather than seeking formally to proscribe a particular application of scientific discoveries, which might constrain other promising avenues of inquiry, concerned scientists seek to arrive at a consensus within the community regarding these decisions. These often-contentious discussions have historically highlighted political and ethical differences within the scientific community.

Notwithstanding the choices available to ethically sensitive developers, we can make a pragmatic argument supporting the provision of Freedom 0, relying neither on the premise that decisions about uses of software should be left to lawmakers nor on the premise that proprietary-software licenses do no better. There is an insuperable difficulty in circumscribing Freedom 0: restricting one use of software could easily lead to suggestions for more restrictions. If a particular license were to say, "You are not allowed to use this software to simulate nuclear explosions," then we could conceive of other licenses that forbid use of licensed software in stem cell research laboratories. The anticipation of problems like these motivates the "No Discrimination Against Fields of Endeavor" clause of the Open Source Definition, as these restrictions "tend to be moral or political . . . however well-intentioned such restrictions might be, they are antithetical to the notion of open source, and in practice are damaging to its objectives" (St. Laurent 2004, 10).

Placing such restrictions presents the unappealing prospect of a Balkanization of the free software corpus, with borders appearing along arbitrary ideological fault lines. Such a state of affairs would not serve the ends of a free society, as it grossly restricts the autonomy and choice of individual users. Such slippery-slope arguments are not hypothetical: they feature prominently in the debate surrounding the inclusion of restrictions on "Digital Rights Management" (DRM) and privacy-violating code in Version 3 of the GPL (GPLv3) (The Free Software Foundation 2006). While it is rare to find a defense or analysis of Freedom 0 in the FOSS community outside the text of the FSD and OSD, and while it is rare for proprietary-software licenses to impose restrictions on the use of software beyond those mentioned above, the inclusion of such restrictions in GPLv3 has sparked heated debate. Certainly, the language that appeared in the first discussion draft looked like an abridgment of Freedom 0:

> As a free software license, this License intrinsically disfavors technical attempts to restrict users' freedom to copy, modify, and share copyrighted works. Each of its provisions shall be interpreted in light of this specific declaration of the licensor's intent. Regardless of any other provision of this license, no permission is given to distribute covered works that illegally invade users' privacy, nor for modes of distribution that deny users that run covered works the full exercise of the legal rights granted by this License. (The Free Software Foundation 2006)

In response to comments from the free software community, this language was removed in the second draft.

Restrictions on the use of software seem destined to fail: software is an easily reproducible and disseminable artifact. In many jurisdictions, artists do have legally protected moral rights concerning the uses to which their works are put. Many of these rights are contingent on the tangibility and irreproducibility of the art in question — painters and sculptors may have a strong voice in where and how their pieces are exhibited. But it is difficult to imagine poets and musicians being able to restrict when and how their works are performed, particularly if these restrictions infringe the free speech rights of others.[7] Perhaps poets, musicians, and writers, as well as free software developers, realize the futility of trying to impose restrictions on the dissemination and use of easily reproducible artifacts. From the perspective of the enrichment of the cultural commons, placing restrictions on the use of works, whether fine art or software, seems particularly counterproductive — such restricted works would no longer be held in common. While we could conceive of an artist wanting to restrict use of his work during his lifetime, this work will ultimately fall into the public domain, at which time all restrictions on its use would lift.

Matt Butcher has suggested Rawls's "veil of ignorance" (Rawls 1971) supports an argument for Freedom 0. Consider free software projects to be communities focused on a common interest, and a free software license as a constitution agreed upon by the community. Suppose this community were assembled under a veil of ignorance: none of the group knows in advance which position in the community they will hold. Individuals would not know their social and political positions, or others' reasons for being interested in the project. Some will be users of the software; some will be core developers/maintainers, while others will write code and documentation. The group is then asked to determine what rights should be granted to whom. Most plausibly, the community would choose to grant Freedom 0 to everyone. If a particular subgroup in the community could decide for what purposes a program could be used, each member would be justified in fearing that such a subgroup could prevent his legitimate use of the software. The group could try to arrive at a set of restrictions by consensus, but such a process could be intractable if no one knows his or her eventual position in the community.

The question of whether Freedom 0 should be granted is orthogonal to a relative assessment of free- and proprietary-software licensing schemes. The fundamental distinction among contemporary software licenses is the issue of the availability of source code. If the most important question were, "How should software be used?" then the taxonomy of software licenses would have a much different form, one in which licenses were classified according to the usage restrictions they imposed. Conceivably, some who now find themselves in opposition regarding the availability of source code might find themselves in agreement over whether their software could be used to build nuclear missiles. Thus, we could decide what uses software could be put to without having decided whether source code should be available or not; we could decide whether source code should be available without having decided what uses software should have. Deciding what uses the original software could be put to — the only decision to which Freedom 0 applies — is distinct from the decision whether to make modifications to the supplied source, to distribute the modified product, and whether to distribute the modified source.

Our concern for the rest of this chapter will be with how the remaining freedoms can be best facilitated, with a focus on the software licensing schemes available to the free software community.

Toward an Ethical Analysis

The Free Software Foundation's licensing ideology is most clearly reflected by its use and advocacy of copyleft licenses, which require all distributed modifications of the licensed software to be released under the same licensing terms as the original. Copyleft is an alternative application of the provisions of copyright law: developers using copyleft licenses, rather than retaining all the rights granted by copyright law, license them to the user under the condition that all derivative works be licensed under the same terms. In the case of free software, copyleft licenses first grant the bundle of free software rights to the licensee, then further require all future distributed modifications of the software to be licensed under the same agreement and thus remain free. Non-copylefted software is not subject to this requirement; thus non-copylefted free software may become proprietary in future versions. (In what follows, we use the term "non-copylefted software" to refer to non-copylefted free software.)

Both the FSD and the OSD allow copyleft and non-copyleft licenses.[8] The GNU General Public License (GPL) is the archetypal example of a copyleft license that meets the FSD and OSD alike; the Berkeley Standard Distribution (BSD) licenses[9] are non-copyleft licenses that meet the FSD and OSD as well. So strong is the association of the GPL with free software that it is commonly assumed that "free software" is synonymous with "software released under the GPL." However, free software may be released under a non-copyleft license such as a BSD license.

Non-copyleft licenses such as the BSD licenses often enable the commercial success of the software they license (Rosen 2004); this success sometimes takes the form of inclusion in some proprietary application, as when source code from the Berkeley Standard Distribution of Unix was taken to Sun Microsystems by Bill Joy in 1982 (Weber 2004, 112). The use of these licenses is connected to the original motivation for writing the software — Berkeley Unix and the X Window System were both research projects intended to demonstrate the technical viability of a basic concept that would, if successful, be developed further by others (Rosen 2004, 30–32).

The distinction between copyleft and non-copyleft is roughly mirrored in the division between the free software and open source movements. While it is a gross oversimplification to identify the free software movement with copyleft licensing, they share tactical space in their approach toward the propagation of free software: both are grounded in an ideological commitment to the active protection and dissemination not only of code but also of free software ideals. Similarly, no facile identification can be made between the open source movement and non-copyleft licensing. But both subscribe to a perspective that values the autonomy of the developer and the meritocracy of code: open source software will achieve widespread adoption because of its technical superiority and the flexibility it offers its licensees, whether corporate or individual. Developers who identify with the free software camp may occasionally choose to license their code under a non-copyleft license. The Debian group is a stalwart component of the free software movement, yet the Debian GNU/Linux distribution incorporates software with a variety of licenses, and its developers are not compelled to use any particular licensing scheme. Open source developers similarly often use both the GPL and BSD licenses.

Thus, the communities of developers that make up the "free software movement" and the "open source movement" are diverse along many dimensions, and often overlap. Developers differ in their political beliefs, their commitment to the causes with which they are aligned, their preference for licensing schemes, even their choice of text editor. It is generally difficult, and undesirable, closely to identify a particular developer with a particular movement. Any discussion of a "movement" would do better to concentrate on texts or public pronouncements closely associated with it. Thus, we distinguish between developers at large in the open source community and the Open Source Initiative, which takes upon itself the role of leadership and advocacy for the "open source movement"; similarly, we will not assume the views of a "free software programmer" to be in perfect consonance with the public statements of the Free Software Foundation.

In what follows, we critique the position shared by the OSI and non-copyleft licensing; to that end we will freely move between discussion of the open source movement (particularly the OSD and OSI) and non-copyleft licensing. We will identify the FSD with copyleft licenses, as it explicitly argues the advantages of copyleft ("We believe there are important reasons why it is better to use copyleft"[10]). There are crucial distinctions between the spirits of the FSD and the OSD. The FSF makes clear its motivation in creating the FSD is the preservation of a social freedom rather than that of individual programmers. The preservation of the freedom of all software users, now and in the future, is a moral and social imperative. This concern for the freedom of future users is reflected by the use of copyleft in the GPL, which embodies an intolerance of proprietary software in any form. However, the OSI's drafting of the OSD, which emphasizes technical efficiency (acknowledging the technical strength of free software)[11] and neo-liberal business pragmatism (Berry 2004), is motivated by the desire for the widespread commercial adoption of the free software development model.[12] This motivation is demonstrated by its acceptance of the possibility that free software may be incorporated in proprietary packages.

The text of the FSD deploys an explicit language of freedom and community, while the terms of the OSD are presented in dialogue with explicitly business-oriented pragmatic "rationales" attached to each clause of the Definition. For example, Clause 6 of the OSD ("No Discrimination against Fields of Endeavor") reads:

> The license must not restrict anyone from making use of the program in a specific field of endeavor. For example, it may not restrict the program from being used in a business, or from being used for genetic research.

This statement is accompanied by the following rationale:

> The major intention of this clause is to prohibit license traps that prevent open source from being used commercially. We want commercial users to join our community, not feel excluded from it.

The FSD states the same requirements with this language:

> [Users must have the] freedom to run the program, for any purpose. . . . The freedom to use a program means the freedom for any kind of person or organization to use it on any kind of computer system, for any kind of . . . job, and without being required to communicate subsequently with the developer or any other specific entity.

Through its language and strong identification with copyleft licensing, the FSD appears to hold the collective interests of society paramount, while the OSD, with its concern for constraints on the individual (copyleft is perceived as one such constraint, although it is not explicitly identified as such in the OSD), seems to prioritize the interests of the individual licensee. A copyleft license need not use the ideological language of the FSD; it might simply state its requirements in pure legalese. That the GPL does borrow language and ideology from the FSD is a crucial decision by its drafters, indicating the adoption of a particular rhetorical strategy as part of its promulgation of free software. The difference between the two definitions delineates a classical opposition between community welfare and the protection of individual choice.

Non-copyleft licenses allow licensees the choice to restrict the freedom of others: while the source code is open to the licensee, he or she is free to make modifications and subsequently distribute the software without source code, thus curtailing the rights of future users to modify software. In this way, a licensee can create an ostensible commercial advantage for himself by drawing on the contributions of the free software community while keeping his modifications to the source code proprietary. A copyleft license such as the GPL restricts licensees' freedom by forbidding anyone to make the software, or any of its future derivatives, proprietary. In so doing, it preserves the freedom of future licensees of the source code. As the GPL's Preamble states, "To protect your rights, we need to make restrictions that forbid anyone to deny you these rights or to ask you to surrender the rights. These restrictions translate to certain responsibilities for you if you distribute copies of the software, or if you modify it." Thus, the authors of the GPL claim the enforcement of these restrictions ensures the freedom of software for all users, present and future. Towards this end, the GPL restricts one freedom of individual licensees.

Conversely, non-copyleft licenses rest on the principle that it is obligatory not to restrict anyone's freedom. The differences in the licenses are easily understood through the lens of the digital commons:

> The BSD license says: "Here is a commons. It is not defended by copyright against appropriation. Everything in the commons may be taken and put into proprietary, non-commons production as easily as it may be incorporated into commons production. We encourage people to put material into commons, and we are indifferent as to whether the appropriative use made of commons resources is proprietary, or commons-reinforcing." The GPL says: We construct a protected commons, in which . . . the phenomena of commons are adduced through the phenomena of copyright, restricted ownership is employed to create non-restricted, self-pro-

tected commons. The GPL. . . . says: "Take this software; do what you want with it — copy, modify, redistribute. But if you distribute, modified or unmodified, do not attempt to give anybody to whom you distribute fewer rights than you had in the material with which you began." It requires no acceptance, it requires no contractual obligation. It says, you are permitted to do [sic], just don't try to reduce anybody else's rights. The result is a commons that protects itself: Appropriation may be made in an unlimited way, providing that each modification of goods in commons are returned to commons. (Moglen 2003)

These differences are most succinctly expressed by a pair of haiku:[13]

GNU Haiku
You may use the source
Change at will, port, give away
But with the new source

BSD Haiku
You may use the source
Change at will, port, give away
With source if you want

The free software licensor is confronted with a choice of licenses and moral codes — a choice that seems to require prioritizing one group's freedoms over another's. This putative ethical dilemma can be resolved in favor of copyleft licenses such as the GPL because of their greater facilitation of freedoms, their conscious appeal to a broader community (that is, their responsiveness to the social context of code), and their commitment to "ethical foresight." The GPL ensures for itself, and facilitates on the part of the licensee, an ethical vision by using an explicit language of rights, responsibilities, moral injunctions, and freedoms. The restrictions it imposes ensure the liberties of each citizen; the only alternative it fails to provide — as a kind of freedom — is the possibility of restricting others. Thus, the fundamental difference among free software licenses is their differential valuation of the rights of the immediate and downstream licensees and the vitality of the software commons.

Though Hobbes famously defined freedom as the absence of restriction, political thought from Aristotle to Heidegger has been at pains to distinguish freedom from license. Lawrence Crocker (Crocker 1980), building on Isaiah Berlin's (Berlin 1969) distinction between positive and negative freedoms, characterizes positive freedom as the presence of alternatives (x may choose y' as an alternative to y) and negative freedom as the absence of restriction (x is not restricted by z).[14] Harbingers of these distinctions may be found in Maurice Cranston's analysis, which argues that in speaking of freedom we must ask "free *to do* what?" and "freedom *from* what?" (Cranston 1954)

Much philosophical debate has centered on whether freedom is properly analyzed in terms of positive freedoms alone, or only negative freedoms, or as a combination of the two. Crocker and Charles Taylor (Taylor 1979) both argue that positive freedom is the only kind of freedom — that talk of negative freedoms is redundant at best. Yet there are critiques aplenty of positive freedom, such as the contention that it overextends the notion of freedom to the point of meaningless-ness — if every social good can be described as the freedom from its opposite, then "freedom" loses its descriptive power (Benn and Peters 1959). This intense philosophical debate has political overtones. Modern liberal thought provides ide-ological space for the state to facilitate positive freedoms — to provide the means by which alternatives are made available to the polity. Libertarian and modern conservative thought would restrict the state to ensuring negative freedoms — to removing restrictions that inhibit the realization of citizens' individual potentials.

We contend, with Cranston (Cranston 1954) and Gerald MacCallum (Mac-Callum 1967), that the distinction between providing alternatives and removing restrictions is a vague one. We can plausibly view the removal of restrictions as the provision of alternatives; the presence of alternatives can be understood as the absence of restrictions. We treat freedom as inhering in both the provision of alternatives and the removal of restrictions. Our bedrock principle is that free-dom is a moral good. Social arrangements must ensure the greatest freedom for their constituents: "each person ought to grant to other persons an equal right to be free" (Pollock 1981, 13). The only justifiable violation of this principle is the restraint of a person whose actions interfere with the liberty of another. Such a conclusion is echoed in the claim that the primary purpose of a liberal political community is to create the public circumstances in which men and women are left alone to "do what they want, provided that their actions do not interfere with the liberty of others" (Ignatieff 1998).

Liberal theorists advocating the facilitation of positive freedoms are follow-ing a long tradition of political thought that suggests unfettered freedom can eas-ily become an absence of freedom. This notion is most famously expressed in Karl Popper's "paradox of economic freedom." Removing all restrictions on the actions of the rich would result in the total exploitation of the poor, and their sub-sequent loss of economic freedom:

> [T]he principle of non-intervention, of an unrestrained economic system, has to be given up; if we wish freedom to be safeguarded, then we must demand that the policy of unlimited economic freedom be replaced by the planned economic intervention of the state. We must demand that unrestrained *capitalism* give way to an *economic interventionism*. . . . State intervention should be limited to what is really necessary for the protection of freedom. (Popper 1966, 125)

More fundamentally, the paradox of freedom underwrites any argument for entering into social arrangements that involve the enactment and enforcement of laws, ostensible restrictions on freedoms. These derive their legitimacy from their enhancement of the freedoms all participants in these arrangements might have, only circumscribing those freedoms that constrain others' liberty. Free software licenses, as moral and legal documents, must be held to these standards.

The Licensing Schemes

The GPL is the archetypal copyleft license. Like its progenitor, the Free Software Definition, it employs an explicit language of responsibilities and freedoms, as in its Preamble:

> The licenses for most software are designed to take away your freedom to share and change it. By contrast, the GNU General Public License is intended to guarantee your freedom to share and change free software — to make sure the software is free for all its users. When we speak of free software, we are referring to freedom, not price. Our General Public Licenses are designed to make sure that you have the freedom to distribute copies of free software (and charge for this service if you wish), that you receive source code or can get it if you want it, that you can change the software or use pieces of it in new free programs; and that you know you can do these things.

The GPL states its larger objective immediately — to preserve the freedom of all software licensees — and makes prescriptions to implement this objective:

> To protect your rights, we need to make restrictions that forbid anyone to deny you these rights or to ask you to surrender the rights. These restrictions translate to certain responsibilities for you if you distribute copies of the software, or if you modify it . . . if you distribute copies of such a program, whether gratis or for a fee, you must give the recipients all the rights that you have. You must make sure that they, too, receive or can get the source code. And you must show them these terms so they know their rights.

The moral imperative for the GPL is that every member of society should be free to inspect, use, and modify software. Furthermore, no one should have the right to take nonreciprocal advantage of another's code. To ensure this, the license enjoins any action that closes code. As a corollary, it is clear that one user's right to free software may not infringe another's right to the same.

Both the FSD and the OSD view software freedom as residing in the four software freedoms. The language with which these freedoms are expressed, however, differs significantly. For example, where the FSD discusses "[t]he freedom to improve the program, and release your improvements to the public, so that the whole community benefits," the OSD requires compliant licenses to "allow modifications and derived works, and must allow them to be distributed under the same terms as the license of the original software." A non-copyleft license could comply with either definition by allowing modifications and derived works, without requiring the modified source to be kept open. Such licenses, then, implicitly grant licensees rights that have the potential to impinge on the rights of others, specifically the rights of later licensees to have the same freedoms. Non-copyleft licenses can demand very little from licensees while complying with both the FSD and the OSD. The latest version of the BSD license only requires derived works carry the original copyright notice:

> Redistributions of source code must retain the . . . copyright notice, this list of conditions and the following disclaimer. Redistributions in binary form must reproduce the . . . copyright notice, this list of conditions and the following disclaimer in the documentation and/or other materials provided with the distribution.

Similarly, the MIT license only requires the original author's name be kept on the credit list of all derived works. Prima facie, these licenses read like models of permissiveness with respect to the requirements of the GPL. But works derived from BSD- or MIT-licensed code need not be distributed with the modified source code. A non-copyleft licensor then, is committed to releasing the source code for a program, but need not commit to keeping future versions of that program free.

Non-copyleft licenses do not significantly constrain their licensees, avoiding any mention of "freedom" or restrictions on future usage in their text; the GPL, while making explicit mention of "freedoms," places more restrictions on its licensees. But any proprietary software license acts to restrict the freedoms of its users; it is this kind of restriction that copyleft licensing resists. Copyleft licensees cannot distribute modified works without providing source code — they must pass along all the freedoms they themselves enjoy, with the net effect of increasing the global availability of free software. In contrast, non-copyleft licenses, by allowing licensees nearly unrestricted use of the licensed code, do not actively resist the diminishment of users' freedoms.

What, then, is the moral course of action — to copyleft or not? Is it morally justifiable to restrict the freedom of another in order to prevent the compromise of the overall freedom of the community of users and developers? Is it morally justifiable to restrict developers' freedoms to protect the software commons? To answer this question, we first must clarify the nature of the "restriction," the contours of the "community," the concept of "overall freedom" and the extent of its "compromise."

The Copyleft Bargain

Toward this clarification, we begin by examining which freedoms (positive and negative) are facilitated by the two licensing schemes — that is, which alternatives are provided and which restrictions are made by each scheme. The copyleft restriction constrains the actions of its licensees via precise conditions on redistribution and future use of the software. The GPL requires of the licensee that all future versions of the program be released under the terms of the GPL: "You must cause any work that you distribute or publish, that in whole or in part contains or is derived from the Program or any part thereof, to be licensed as a whole at no charge to all third parties under the terms of this License."

Importantly, these restrictions are contingent. *If* the licensee decides at some point in the future to make modifications *and* to distribute the modified program, *then* certain terms must be obeyed. This circumscribes a very narrow set of future actions of the licensee. Furthermore, because the programmer is aware of the restrictions placed by the GPL as he first makes use of the code, he is not blindsided by any of its provisions. The GPL's restriction is not paternalistic: it does not restrain an individual for his own good but simply restricts his ability to restrain others. If the programmer wants to modify the program for personal use, for internal use in a corporation, or even as part of a Web-based proprietary service, such as Google's search engine, then he is not obliged to make the source code public. Copyleft does not restrict the ability of its licensees to earn a living — indeed, the question of having access to source code is orthogonal to programmers' subsistence. A programmer using code licensed under the GPL can, for example, contract to provide services or further modifications to the code; a programmer working on proprietary code may struggle financially because of unfavorable markets. Neither proprietary nor free software is necessary or sufficient to earn a living, but access to the code is necessary to enable the positive freedoms identified in both the OSD and the FSD.

Furthermore, there is no coercion inherent in the GPL. A programmer is free to study copylefted code carefully, to note its workings, to replicate its functionality by writing new code and to distribute it under any conditions he desires, including making this new code proprietary. These freedoms are never usurped. He is not free, however, to distribute the copylefted code in a manner the original licensor did not want:

> [I]nstalling, using or even modifying GPL-licensed software implicates no term of that license. Any user is completely free to undertake any of these actions. There are no limitations on the number of installations of the software that a user may undertake and no requirement that the user pay royalties in exchange for use . . . only if the user intends to distribute the original code or modified versions does the GPL come into effect. (St. Laurent 2004, 151)

The licensor's decision to release code under a copyleft license indicates a desire to maintain the freedom of source: she has either written the code from scratch and copylefted it, or she has modified copylefted code. In both cases, she has accepted copyleft and its accompanying restrictions. It is this acceptance the GPL expects the licensee to respect.

In contrast to the GPL, the non-copyleft BSD license has permissive redistribution terms:

> Redistribution and use in source and binary forms, with or without modification, are permitted provided that the following conditions are met: Redistributions of source code must retain the above copyright notice, this list of conditions and the

following disclaimer. Redistributions in binary form must reproduce the above copyright notice.

Therefore, if the licensee decides to distribute modifications, and further decides to distribute the source code for these modifications, then the only requirement placed by the BSD license is that the original copyrights and permissions be included along with the source distribution. This means that future modifications are not required to include source code distribution. After one round of modifications the freedom of the software may no longer be protected. The proprietary licensor is thus able to draw upon the work of the free software community, and yet not give back to it. While he is not obligated to do so under the letter of the license, this act of non-reciprocity diverges from the spirit of the free software community. Using free software in a proprietary package thereby entails the furtherance of proprietary software while yielding no advantage to the free software community:

> The GPL is about giving free software an immune system so that Forker du jour can't hire all your developers away to work on a closed fork of the codebase the way Netscape gutted Mosaic, BSDI shredded the Berkeley CSRG [Computer Science Research Group], and the two Lisp companies drained the original MIT AI lab.[15]

Thus the argument that the BSD licenses' terms are benign because "the original source remains open, even if it is used in a proprietary package" fails: if the free software community considers closed source harmful, whether on moral or technical grounds, then licenses that permit free software to propagate closed source must be harmful as well. Non-copyleft licenses only provide alternatives for the immediate licensee, as she is free to do what she pleases with the code; their concern does not extend to future licensees, whose alternatives may be reduced as a consequence.

The most controversial restriction placed by the GPL has to do with the commingling of free and proprietary software. In particular, if GPL'd software is linked with another piece of software, the entire product must be GPL'd:

> This General Public License does not permit incorporating your program into proprietary programs. . . . [I]f [independent] sections [of a work] are distributed as part of a whole which is a work based on the Program, the distribution of the whole must be on the terms of this License, whose permissions for other licensees extend to the entire whole, and thus to each and every part regardless of who wrote it.

Thus the linked code must be free as well. Critics of the GPL view this clause as a burdensome restriction because dependencies between GPL'd and non-GPL'd code require the non-GPL'd code to be freed (Weeks 2005; Albert 2004). Suppose Richard writes a program and releases it under the GPL. Bill, who would like to use this program because it provides much-needed functionality for his proprietary software product, combines the first program with his to make a new one.[16] This program will have to be released under the GPL. If, however, the "independent sections" are released separately, they do not need to be licensed under the GPL. These situations are commonplace in software development:

> [I]t is not uncommon for a particular program to be capable of both integration with other software to form a unified whole, such as into a calculator program that performs a variety of functions, and also functioning with minimal or no modifications as a separate entity, such as a program that only calculates square roots. This provision of the GPL allows the author of such software to license the software under another license (typically a proprietary one) when distributed by itself and under the GPL when the license is distributed as part of a larger work, including GPL-licensed programs. (St. Laurent 2004, 40)

Depending on perspective, the new program has either been "freed by" or "infected with" the GPL:

> [T]he "viral" characteristics of the GPL make it impossible to combine that work with other code without "infecting" that code with the GPL license provisions. If you have a proprietary business model, this does "prevent" you from using that software. (O'Reilly 2001)

In a burst of hyperbole, Microsoft CEO Steven Ballmer, while speaking of Linux, described the GPL as a "cancer" (Greene 2001). Richard Stallman, however, terms this the "spider plant clause," a considerably more benign characterization (Stallman 2005).

But simply distributing a software package on the same media (such as a CD) as a GPL'd program does not require all software on that media to be GPL'd. The GPL does not intend to "claim rights or contest your rights to work written entirely by you; rather, the intent is to exercise the right to control the distribution of derivative or collective works based on the Program." For copyleft provisions to apply to a software package, it must be "integral to and/or derivative of a program that is GPL-licensed" (St. Laurent 2004). Both the intention and the effect of the GPL's restrictions, then, are to provide more alternatives to the users and potential developers or extenders of the hybrid product: copyleft is designed not only to protect freedoms but also to propagate them.

Free software licensing schemes require varying compromises from their licensees. A strong copyleft license like the GPL might compromise technical efficiency with its requirement that every modification, including those incorporating proprietary software components, be released under the GPL. This could result in a slower rate of development, as programmers re-implement code that previously existed as only free or only proprietary. Proprietary developers may provide their own implementations of code licensed under the GPL so as to avoid placing their code under the GPL, or free software developers may provide free implementations of previously proprietary code. But copyleft advocates are not blind to the possibility of compromising for technical efficiency:

When you work on the core of X . . . there is a practical reason not to use copyleft. The XFree86 group does an important job for the community in maintaining these programs, and the benefit of copylefting our changes would be less than the harm done by a fork in development. So it is better to work with the XFree86 group and not copyleft our changes on these programs. Likewise for utilities . . . which are close to the core of X. . . . [T]he XFree86 group has a firm commitment to developing these programs as free software. The issue is different for programs outside the core of X. . . . There is no reason not to copyleft them, and we should copyleft them. (Stallman 1998)

Free software remains in a public-domain-like space because copyright law protects it; copyleft extends these protections. The act of distributing code under copyleft ensures that there can be no nonreciprocal borrowings from the software commons. Such borrowings, in the economic context of software, can quickly deplete the commons. This paradox of freedom needs, for its resolution, the intervention of the GPL: "The GPL is the embodiment of the principle that certain types of freedom require rules in order to be preserved" (Laurent 2004). Non-copyleft licenses remain vulnerable to the non-reciprocity the GPL guards against.

Thus, one distinction between copyleft and non-copyleft licenses is that copyleft licenses display more sensitivity to the range of actions future licensees may wish to take. Reflecting the FSF's approach to the propagation of free software ideals, copyleft licenses are imbued with ethical foresight.

Ethical Foresight

Moral agents are capable of deliberative agency, of thinking through the effects of their actions, directly and indirectly, in the context of some moral principle. Even if not the calculating agent of utilitarian analysis, a moral agent is capable of understanding the effects of its actions, of realizing the import of a moral obligation or imperative. Refusing to think through the effects of actions, denying one's autonomy or agency, or disregarding moral considerations are failures to be avoided by a moral agent. To possess ethical foresight, then, is to be able to deliberate upon the moral stance implicit in one's actions and pronouncements and to act with an awareness of the consequences of one's actions.

The FSF, through its writings, keeps its ethical principles in clear view at all times:[17] "above all, society needs to encourage the spirit of voluntary cooperation in its citizens" (Stallman 1994). This perspective permeates the language of the GPL. The OSI and the OSD, however, carefully avoid any explicit ethical statements. While both the free software and open source movements agree that moral behavior includes free distribution of source code, the language used by the OSI and in non-copyleft licenses fails to look beyond the immediate freedoms granted to developers.

The OSI makes clear that its central ideological commitment is the widespread commercial adoption of free software, based on the technical superiority of its development model:

> When programmers can read, redistribute, and modify the source code . . . the software evolves. . . . [T]his can happen at a speed that, if one is used to the slow pace of conventional software development, seems astonishing. . . . [T]his rapid evolutionary process produces better software than the traditional closed model. . . . [The] Open Source Initiative exists to make this case to the commercial world.[18]

The origins of this "case," as described in the OSI's retelling of its own history, lies in a deliberate distancing from the free software movement: "We realized it was time to dump the confrontational attitude that has been associated with 'free software' in the past and sell the idea strictly on . . . pragmatic, business-case grounds" (The Open Source Initiative 2006). The free software movement's explicit statement and promulgation of ethical principles is thus interpreted as a "confrontational attitude." Even portions of the OSD prima facie couched in ethical language, such as its antidiscrimination provisions (licenses must not discriminate against any person or group of persons) are rationalized with language about "the process" and its "benefit": "In order to get the maximum benefit from the process, the maximum diversity of persons and groups should be equally eligible to contribute to open sources. Therefore we forbid any open source license from locking anybody out of the process." Besides a nod to the openness of source code, there is no talk of freedom in the OSD: the word "free" is deliberately excluded because of the claim that potential corporate licensors would find it confusing.[19] Similarly, the sparse language of non-copyleft licenses precludes the explicit statement, and thereby the future protection, of community-wide goals or aspirations. The only social context the OSD acknowledges is the business community the OSI is courting.

By contrast, copyleft was devised to protect particular freedoms for a broader community, an intention made explicit in the Preamble to the GPL: "The GNU General Public License is intended to guarantee your freedom to share and change free software — to make sure the software is free for all its users." The strong copyleft provisions and particular language of the GPL reflect a desire not only to protect and propagate freedom, but also to do so self-consciously. As Clause 7 makes clear, the demands of the license trump all other distribution-related obligations the licensee faces:

> If you cannot distribute so as to satisfy simultaneously your obligations under this License and any other pertinent obligations, then . . . you may not distribute the Program at all. . . . [I]f a patent license would not permit royalty-free redistribution of the Program . . . then the only way you could satisfy both it and this License would be to refrain entirely from distribution of the Program.

The language of the OSD is much more tolerant of the permissiveness of non-copyleft licenses: "The license must allow modifications and derived works, and must allow them to be distributed under the same terms as the license of the original software." Crucially, this clause does not require modifications to be distributed under the same terms — it "allows" them. The OSD does not mention the possibility of protection for future versions of the code and offers no argument for any particular compliant licensing scheme. With this weaker language, the OSI looks away from the potential consequences of its permissiveness: the growth of closed code and the shrinking of the software commons.

The FSF is unabashed about its political and moral roots — "The Free Software Movement was founded in 1984, but its inspiration comes from the ideals of 1776: freedom, community, and voluntary cooperation" (Stallman 2001) — a self-consciousness that finds expression in the explicit language of rights, responsibilities and freedoms of the GPL. The GPL's careful legalese, which anticipates and closes off various paths through which it might be defeated, is testament to the care it takes to preserve its moral spirit: "We wish to avoid the danger that redistributors of a free program will individually obtain patent licenses, in effect making the program proprietary. To prevent this, we have made it clear that any patent must be licensed for everyone's free use or not licensed at all." The GPL is uncompromising on the demands it makes on users. Any use of the licensed program automatically indicates acceptance of the license; if the use is not in conformance with the license, it is illegal. Furthermore, Clause 6 automatically licenses recipients of redistributed code with the same license.

The GPL seeks to make its licensees moral agents by inculcating ethical foresight in them. To this end, it reminds the licensees of its original goals:

All of the FSF's decisions . . . are guided by the two goals of preserving the free status of all derivatives of our free software and of promoting the sharing and reuse of software generally.

and urges them to propagate the freedom of software using a copyleft license:

If you develop a new program, and you want it to be of the greatest possible use to the public, the best way to achieve this is to make it free software. . . . [I]f you distribute copies of such a program, . . . you must give the recipients all the rights that you have.

The FSF facilitates the freedoms of users and developers not only by providing free software but also by highlighting the ethical issues at stake:

Any software license gets its main effect from being applied to certain code. But the code alone would not spread the philosophy of free software. To do that, we must talk about the philosophy. If I had only written free software, and not explained about the freedom it gives you, the code might have contributed to the advance of technology but it would not have contributed much to the advance of human freedom.[20]

The goal of the OSI is widespread acceptance; in the name of meeting this goal, it disclaims moral responsibility:

> We think the economic self-interest arguments for open source are strong enough that nobody needs to go on any moral crusades about it. (The Open Source Initiative 2006)

The disavowal of the language of the FSD by the framers of the OSD thus indicates a discomfort with explicit ethical statements, as if the realm of technical enterprise would be compromised by such traffic.

Traditional moral philosophy holds that the only justifiable restriction on freedom is one that prevents harm to others (Pollock 1981; Mill 1975). It is the limitation of alternatives and undermining of the free-software community, whose resources the proprietary community would like to utilize, that the restrictions placed by the GPL prevent. Whether or not the GPL's provisions are truly a constraint on freedom is contingent on how we ascribe moral responsibility for such constraints, "and this in turn depends on which theory of moral obligation one holds. Debates about social freedom cannot be separated from wider debates about social obligation" (Miller 2006). The GPL licensor, if morally obligated to prevent the harms of closed code, is then not imposing any restrictions: "The GPL prohibits trampling the freedom of others. Those who wish to make non-free software, those who would not respect the freedom of others, often cry bloody murder about this 'restriction.'"[21] Indeed, any explicit statement of rights implicitly proscribes actions that infringe those rights: "Technically speaking, the bill of rights is a list of restrictions. Can't shut people up, can't take the guns away, can't impose a religion on people."[22] Thus, criticisms of copyleft licensing as being overly restrictive — such as those below — are misplaced:

> [T]he GPL forces people to do things just the same as a traditional license forces people to do things. You speak of freedom yet you took that freedom away with the GPL. If you really believed in freedom then the GPL would just be the same as the public domain. *That's* freedom. The BSD license is far closer to a truly free license, the GPL isn't even remotely close to a free license. . . . [T]he GPL . . . [is] a fine license if your goal is to have things done out in the open with no hoarding. . . . The GPL absolutely positively does not grant me all the rights I want, it took substantial portions of my freedom away. I am not free to use GPL source in any way I wish and neither is anyone else.[23]

The statement merely expresses a non-obligation to future licensees, failing to recognize the hypocrisy of those that wish to use GPL'd code in proprietary packages: "But even as they complain that they cannot put our code into their non-free products, they are refusing to let us put their code into our free software packages."[24] Copyleft licensing is grounded in a particular theory of moral obligations; it is this moral perspective that should be the target of analysis and criticism. We would view critiques of the GPL's "restrictions" differently if we understood them as critiques of its specific request for reciprocity. Non-copyleft licensors ostensibly share much of this moral commitment, but act differently — not more or less restrictively — to uphold it.

The Licenses and Classical Ethical Analysis

Our evaluation of the manifestos and licensing schemes of the free software community has proceeded from ethical concepts, such as freedom and community, invoked by those texts themselves. But if our concern is as universal as these concepts suggest, it behooves us to continue this examination using the evaluative frameworks of moral philosophy, which provide normative guidance for decision making in moral and ethical matters. Utilitarianism relies on the use of an explicit calculus, while deontological frameworks such as Kantian ethics bid us look for categorical imperatives. As ethical dilemmas such as the trolley problem (Shall I kill one to save five?) (Thomson 1976) or Benjamin Constant's example of truth-telling to a murderer[25] demonstrate, these frameworks often compete for the attention of our moral intuitions in ways that leave us unsatisfactorily short of a decision. The utilitarian resolution of the trolley thought experiment clashes with our moral revulsion at taking a life, while the deontological injunction that we always tell the truth does not seem to outweigh the utilitarian value of a white lie.

As the singular application of an ethical framework invariably forces an impoverished dichotomy upon us, truly interesting ethical scenarios require multiple theoretical frameworks for satisfactory assessment. Thus, it would be a mistake to use a purely utilitarian or deontological framework in our evaluation of these licensing schemes. Still, when we are engaged in moral decision-making, these frameworks usefully clarify the ethical standing of an action or statement, and often adduce evidence in favor of a candidate decision.

Prima facie, the language of copyleft — specifically, the GPL — is strongly deontological, while non-copyleft licenses suggest a utilitarian grounding (Zittrain 2004). An individual developer who chooses to release non-copyleft software might reason that the utility of the license — its attractiveness to those who would use her code in proprietary products, for instance — trumps the deontological undergirding of a copyleft license. But matters are not so straightforward. Both kinds of licensing schemes enjoin obligations on the part of licensees and, concomitantly, both the FSD and OSD can be viewed as evangelical documents, promising the greatest good for all. While the OSD might appear grounded in a facile utilitarianism, it also has the flavor of a deontological scheme: the Rationale for Clause 9 states that, "Distributors of open source software have the right to make their own choices about their own software"; licensors therefore have an obligation to uphold this right. Indeed, the GPL may be more strongly utilitarian in its argument that compromises of individual freedom — constraints on downstream developers' choice of license — are necessary for the greatest benefit of the greatest number. Richard Stallman states this explicitly: "we should perform a cost-benefit analysis on behalf of society as a whole, taking account of individual freedom as well as production of material goods" (Stallman 1992).

The software definitions and licensing schemes in question, however, differ on the social goods they aim to provide: high-quality software by the OSD, freedom in the use of all software by the FSD. Thus, we can make no judgment favoring one over the other until we decide which of the goods has a higher utility. A utilitarian conclusion in favor of the FSD and copyleft licensing would require us to assign a higher utility to the provision of freedom and less to the technical values of efficiency and software quality. The justification for assigning higher relative utility to freedom than to technical efficiency must be made on other, extra-utilitarian, grounds, perhaps by taking refuge in the clarity of the deontological assertion that we have a duty to preserve freedom. Deontological and utilitarian strands run through both these licenses; choosing one license over another requires a decision informed by both intuitions.

When we evaluate the licensing policies using a Kantian framework, which bids us to act on the basis of universalizable maxims,[26] we find copyleft and non-copyleft licenses are equivalent. Both the non-copyleft and copyleft licensor can rationally will all software be licensed under their chosen licensing scheme. This equivalence for the immediate licensee shows the consideration of secondary effects, such as the potential for the closing of free code by a future licensor, to be especially important. If the BSD licensor can rationally will all software be licensed under her chosen licensing scheme, that is, that all software be free, then why would she not use a copyleft license? The desire to release code under the BSD license, rejecting the copyleft option, acknowledges the possibility that the code might become closed by future licensees, whom the BSD licensor does not want to turn away. If that is the case, the BSD licensor's stance is not fully universalizable, thus introducing a hint of incoherence in the original licensing decision.

Licenses as Constitutions

FOSS software licenses may be understood as providing social structure and a set of values that regulate their respective communities, functioning thus as "de facto constitutions" (Weber 2004). For instance, one way to think of the BSD license is that, "it serves to credit the researchers, protect them and the university from liability, and then let people do what they want, as they see fit, with the product" (Weber 2004, 181). As constitutions, these licenses are fundamental documents, written and changed with care, not to be taken lightly. More important, as constitutions, they act as blueprint and vision for a community. A good constitution represents, but does not impose, the shared values of its constituents. The drafters of a constitution aim to create a document that encodes their values and anticipates future challenges to it: writing constitutions especially requires its drafters to possess ethical foresight. For example, the GPL draws on the hacker ethos that privileges sharing, demonstrating both mutuality and inclusiveness, because of the expectation that users will interact with the license as both licensor and licensee. Underlying the BSD is a laissez-faire attitude that does not discriminate against developers of proprietary software. Free software licenses also reflect the hacker value on the meritocracy of code, which they implement by allowing structures for power sharing in the community, most importantly through the right to fork.

A comparison of the language used by the FSF and the OSI is useful in developing an understanding of the kinds of communities they intend to sustain. As the FSF states in the Free Software Definition, it explicitly intends to uphold the right of all citizens to use, inspect, and modify software: "Free software is a matter of the users' freedom to run, copy, distribute, study, change and improve the software." The OSI concerns itself with programmers, specifically with the rights of software businesses: "The Open Source Initiative exists to make th[e] case [for the technical advantages of the open source development model] to the commercial world." Thus, it is concerned with making itself attractive to those who might want to keep code closed in the future, that is, precisely those that feel little resonance with the original technical and moral imperatives of free software. Free software licenses that do not include copyleft terms are similarly attractive to this group because of their apparent permissiveness in allowing business imperatives to trump moral ones.

Historically, the evaluation of constitutions is accompanied by debate of their provisions among those that would be affected (The European Convention 2003; Bailyn 1993); ongoing discussion about the merits of these licensing schemes is part of such an evaluation. The intense discussion of Version 3 of the GNU Public License — the first new version of the license in fifteen years — bears witness to the importance to the community of public critical discussion of its provisions. For example, the first proposed draft of the new version of the license contained the clause, "no permission is given to distribute covered works that illegally invade users' privacy." After six months of public debate, the second discussion draft no longer contained this clause, a change rationalized as follows:

> The clause referring to illegal invasions of users' privacy was intended to provide developers a weapon, based in copyright, to combat spyware and malware, in order to supplement enforcement efforts of public authorities. The considerable public reaction to this provision, however, was overwhelmingly negative, and we therefore have decided to remove it. (The Free Software Foundation 2006)

These discussions are strongly normative in character; at stake is a shared vision of the values of the programming community and how those values might best be sustained by the license.

The ethical position enshrined in a free software license is an important determinant of the conduct that license users feel is expected of them. By accepting the terms of, or releasing code under, a license, a user or developer implicitly adopts its values, much as taking up citizenship of a nation makes an explicit statement of adherence to its constitutional values. Whether a nation's constitution has a significant effect on the behavior of its citizens is not clear, but it is an important standard of permissible behavior. The U.S. Constitution, for example, is the ultimate standard for the laws of the land; any citizen may challenge the constitutionality of any law.

Typically, constitutions set out to do the following: define — in their preambles — the goals of the polity, bestow rights such as voting or free speech, and define and limit powers of government officials or other authorities. The GPL does all of these. It defines the goals of its community, bestows rights upon its users, and limits the powers of those who exert authority over code. The unifying principle that underwrites both the copyleft restriction and the absence of restrictions on specific uses per Freedom 0 is the value placed on community autonomy and self-determination. A non-copyleft license distributes rights among its users differently, transferring the right to control the distribution of future versions of the code from the licensor to the licensee.

Constitutions define an ethical code of conduct for a community. In determining the coherence of such a code, we can assess whether the constitution adequately protects against the propagation of values it opposes. A state committed to democracy will not tolerate features in its constitution that could lead to a co-optation of democratic principles; the U.S. Constitution has been amended on several occasions to provide more effective protection of democratic principles. The central mystery of the permissiveness of the OSI and non-copyleft licensing then confronts us: If closed software is inimical to their core values, why do they tolerate the possibility for free code to be closed? Why do they condone proprietary nonreciprocal borrowing from the open source community? What is the core value of the Open Source Initiative: software freedom, or economic and technical efficiency?

Toward the Creation of a Virtuous Space

Copyleft and non-copyleft licensing schemes are each predicated on, and committed to furthering, a particular vision of a society underwritten by technology. The moral content of these visions may be examined via virtue ethics, which employs the Aristotelian notion of a virtue as the mean of two extremes (Aristotle 350 BC/1962): for example, the virtue of character is elevated by self-discipline and corrupted by self-indulgence. Virtues are acquired through practice: a compassionate person is one who repeatedly acts compassionately. The determination of what is virtuous is inflected by the moral agent's community, which, rather than giving rules for ethical behavior, provides guidance about what sort of people we should be. The ideal response to this guidance is to develop one's virtues in consonance with the community's ethical values. Thus, virtue ethics creates a benign conflation of the virtuous person and the ethical person. The goal of community-determined standards of "virtue" is to build a virtuous community, so we may interrogate rival codes of conduct to determine the contours of their intended communities. Reading free software licenses in this fashion, they become guidelines to answering the questions, "What kind of person would I become if I abide by the terms of the license?" and "What sort of community would this license create?" These questions prompt the further question, "Would I like to belong to such a community?"

The Open Source Initiative is directed toward the establishment of a programming community constituted for one purpose: to write high-quality code. To this end, the language of the OSD privileges the technocratic virtue of producing good code. The Free Software Foundation assigns less value to this virtue: sharing is its primary concern, even at the expense of technical efficiency. Specifically, the GPL enjoins us to practice the virtues of generosity, by sharing the source code, and reciprocity, by giving improved code back to the free software community. The free software movement's vision of a community based on these virtues entails clear expectations of its members. The OSI and the OSD, by not adequately articulating the virtue of reciprocity, fail to inculcate it within their community. Thus, viewed through the lens of virtue ethics, the FSF and the GPL provide clearer enunciation of the values of its community and explicit guidance to its adherents.

Ensuring the Rights of Constituents

In evaluating a constitution, we consider not only the "goods" it provides but also the mechanisms it puts in place to ensure their provision:

> A legal system begins with a constitution, takes its strength from it, and conforms with it. . . . If a constitution is useless and if its breaching is inconsequential to governing, then it should be no surprise that the general public has no use for it. . . . Evaluating the Constitution's machinery. . . . is a matter . . . of foreseeing how given mechanisms will work in the future. . . . [It] must focus on the operational aspect, that is, whether the constitutional mechanisms were constructed in a manner that will facilitate their rational application (Letowska 1997).

A constitution framed so its injunctions are unenforceable is ethically irresponsible; thus, a judgment of the ethical content of free software licenses must include an evaluation of their legal enforceability, a subject of much debate (Blakeslee and Ferguson 2006; Wacha 2004; Gatto 2006). Some doubt, for example, that acceptance of the GPL constitutes contract formation between the licensor and future downstream licensees (Wallace 2004), a claim disputed by those that suggest the GPL should be understood as a license rather than a contract (Jones 2003). Due to the tremendous variation in legal jurisdictions in which the GPL is deployed, an evaluation of these claims must rest on a similar breadth of analytical perspectives. Licenses, however, because they incorporate all legal machinery necessary for their enforcement, may be applied regardless of jurisdiction. In particular, in

2004, a German court, in deciding *Welte v. Sitecom Deutschland GmbH*, found that the GPL was a "valid and enforceable copyright license" (Carver 2005).

The GPL includes specific requirements on code modification and redistribution, following these with explicit language to ensure enforceability through successive generations of code: "Each time you redistribute the Program (or any work based on the Program), the recipient automatically receives a license from the original licensor to copy, distribute or modify the Program subject to these terms and conditions." This language creates contractual privity, the legal state in which two or more parties are bound by contractual obligation, between the licensor of the original work and all present and future licensees of that work. Further, even if it is interpreted not to create contractual privity between the original licensor and downstream licensees, "This provision, by creating a direct relationship between the licensor and each future licensee, reserves the licensor's right of legal remedy against future licensees notwithstanding the presence of intermediate distributors who may have no interest in upholding the license" (St. Laurent 2004, 43).

Although free software is rarely distributed in a manner that affords licensees an explicit opportunity to accept its licensing terms (such as clicking an "I Accept" button as the software is installed), the framing of the GPL provides legal protection against a licensee's noncompliance. The ingenuity of the GPL becomes apparent in its use of copyright law to regulate the distribution of modified code. According to copyright law, users have no rights to use, modify, or redistribute copyrighted code unless they possess a license to do so. Thus, if a licensee were to claim that he is not bound by the GPL because he did not enter into a contract, then he would simultaneously be surrendering his rights to the code.

But the most important enforcement mechanism for the GPL, even in jurisdictions with weak copyright protection, is the self-regulation of the free software community: the act of redistributing GPL'd code without acknowledging it as such is reckoned a moral wrong, an awareness of which is in itself an effective enforcement mechanism. The inculcation of this principle proceeds through the explicit language of rights, freedoms, and social goods that undergirds the GPL and the FSD. As *Welte v. Sitecom Deutschland GmbH* showed, plaintiffs keen to enforce the GPL did not care much for financial damages but wished to prevent non-reciprocal advantage being gained:

> Welte did not win damages, but rather an injunction and GPL compliance. . . . What motivates those, like Welte, that seek to enforce the GPL? The answer can be found in the philosophy driving the GPL itself. The netfilter team members . . . chose the GPL for the work that it does as a license. . . . Software developers spend a great deal of time creating such software, and when they are not being paid directly . . . they may seek other forms of compensation . . . such as the assurance that others will always be able to study, modify, improve, and share the work that they have begun. Welte is one of many free software developers who has made a conscious choice to

use the GPL because it prevents others from making proprietary derivatives of his work. When asked why he pursued this legal action, Welte said, "Because I write code under the GPL and not the BSD license." (Carver 2005)

Linus Torvalds expressed similar thoughts on his choice of the GPL:

> I really want a license to do just two things: make the code available to others, and make sure that improvements stay that way. That's really it. Nothing more, nothing less. Everything else is fluff. It may sound like a very simple concept, but even most open-source licenses fail my criteria very fundamentally. They tend to fail in allowing somebody to limit the availability of improvements some way. (Shankland 2004)

The OSI's emphasis on popularizing a software development model in the business world is unlikely to have this profound effect. Rhetorical choices in framing manifestos are not merely linguistic ones; they have long-term implications for the communities they define.

Protecting Software Freedoms Through Copyleft Licensing

Free software makes available the knowledge and innovation inscribed in its source code. This dissemination breeds independence in, and facilitates the agency of, the community of software users and developers. Both the OSI and FSF demonstrate a commitment to the idea of free software. The OSI's deliberate choice of different language in its public pronouncements, however, brings into question the depth of their commitment. Similarly, non-copyleft licenses, through their permissive terms, reflect a willingness to tolerate the non-reciprocity that is a potential consequence of their use.

The Rawlsian argument in support of Freedom 0 may be adapted and used against non-copyleft licensing. A community of free software developers assembled under the "veil of ignorance" plausibly would deny a user the freedom to make a proprietary version of free software, recognizing that such a freedom is potentially harmful to the community; each member of the community would rightfully be concerned that if this freedom were granted, he or she would be adversely affected. The history of the X Window System illustrates the pitfalls of such permissiveness; similarly, the story of the Linux kernel and BitKeeper illustrates the fundamental incompatibility of the ethical principles of the proprietary and free software domains.

BitKeeper

In 2002, Linux kernel developers decided to begin using a proprietary software tool called BitKeeper to manage the millions of lines of Linux kernel source code. BitKeeper's author, Larry McVoy, licensed it in two versions, for commercial and noncommercial use respectively. He did not provide source code for either version.

Moreover, both licenses forbade users from "reverse engineering" the program — that is, trying to determine how the program was written by analyzing its binary code representation and the data it produces. The switch to BitKeeper was bitterly contested by several veteran programmers, including Richard Stallman and Alan Cox, who were concerned about both the use of proprietary tools to facilitate the development of a free software project and the restrictiveness of BitKeeper's license terms. While McVoy added features to facilitate partial interoperability between Linux's BitKeeper servers and developers using software version-control systems such as CVS and Subversion, the decision remained a divisive one, as bitter disagreements continued to arise on the project's mailing lists.[27]

In 2005, Andrew "Tridge" Tridgell, a programmer highly respected in the FOSS community for his work in creating Samba, a free version of a once-proprietary Microsoft file-sharing protocol called SMB, turned his attention to BitKeeper. Guided by the desire to have all information relevant to the development process freely available, he began examining data produced by BitKeeper, particularly data about source-code revision history that was not made directly available to developers. The result of his work would have been a free version of BitKeeper that, like most other source-management applications, would make this useful "meta-data" visible to its users. When McVoy became aware of Tridgell's work, he withdrew the noncommercial version of BitKeeper, thereby temporarily halting progress on not just the Linux kernel but many other free software projects as well.

While this dispute was reported by the media as an internecine "flame war" within the FOSS community, as Torvalds expressed displeasure over Tridgell's actions (Orlowski 2005), and Bruce Perens vehemently disagreed (Orlowski 2005), the issue — as the participants in the discussions were keenly aware — was one of norms of behavior in the free and open source communities. The kernel developers' original motivation for using BitKeeper, though it was not free software, was its functionality. But as this history demonstrates, it would have been better to have used a free tool all along. While the argument for using BitKeeper was that it would speed up the development of free software, its withdrawal dramatically slowed the rate of development on the same project. This phenomenon arises repeatedly in the contemporary history of FOSS, as the community has experimented with the coexistence of free and proprietary software. The stories of the Mozilla Public License, the Netscape Public License, and the Sun Common Source License indicate that the intermingling of proprietary and free software interests is rarely effective (Weber 2004). The simplicity of the GPL and its unyielding requirements may well be virtues, not weaknesses.

In the event, BitKeeper was replaced by *git* for Linux version control in June 2005, a happier outcome for the FOSS community. The Bitkeeper fiasco had one salutary effect: it had illustrated the dangers of confusing the "free" of free speech with the "free" of free beer (Stallman 2005). McVoy had made his software available for "free" but it clearly was not "free" in a way compatible with the free software community's interests. Short-term decisions made on grounds of technical expediency can render entire communities vulnerable.

Forbearance and Forced Generosity?

Before we leave our discussion of the relative merits of the licensing schemes, we consider two possible ethical objections to copyleft. First, it might ask for too much forbearance on the part of its licensees and hence commit the error of making unrealistic claims[28] on moral agents (Sidgwick 1981). Second, copyleft might coerce the virtue of generosity, thereby reducing its moral import (Machan 1998).

The forbearance that copyleft licenses demand is the sacrifice of some kinds of commercial advantage, along with some technical and logistical efficiency. But some copyleft licenses, such as the Lesser GPL, facilitate an important technical requirement, the ability to link free and proprietary-software libraries. Furthermore, the ability of a developer to earn a living is not precluded by copyleft licenses: programmers have ample opportunity to derive income from free software (Raymond 2000). The text of the GPL itself includes two examples of how commercial value may be created on top of copylefted software: "You may charge a fee for the physical act of transferring a copy, and you may at your option offer warranty protection in exchange for a fee."

Furthermore, because the GPL's restrictions on distribution do not apply to software made available as a networked service, Web-based application providers such as Google, whose gigantic server farms run Linux, have built multibillion-dollar corporations using copylefted code while keeping their kernel customizations private. Thus, copyleft licenses embody the spirit of generosity in a golden-mean fashion: they avoid both the foolish generosity of the patsy and the stinginess of the miser.

> But is the generosity demanded by the GPL coerced and hence not morally praiseworthy?
>
> The virtue of generosity is a spontaneous . . . rationally cultivated, disposition of persons to extend their help to others. . . . [G]enerosity presupposes that persons can make free choices. . . . Its full flourishing . . . requires . . . that the rights to liberty of action are fully respected and protected. . . . Coerced "generosity" is not virtuous. . . . Only if men and women are left free . . . can they be expected to act as they should, including generously, when that is appropriate. (Machan 1998)

The "coerced" generosity that copyleft licenses appear to demand only applies to those programmers who choose to release their modifications of previously released software. The original choice to work with copylefted software was not coerced, as the programmer could have begun an independent implementation. Whatever coercion is present is secondary to the programmer's free embrace of copyleft and his desire to use the distributed software.

"Political Agnosticism"

The disdaining of explicit moral or political language by the OSI and non-copyleft licensing can be charitably characterized as "political agnosticism." Coleman's anthropological study of hacker communities shows the agnosticism reflected in the sparse language of non-copyleft licenses is also expressed in intracommunity discourse within, and governance of, parts of the free software community (Coleman 2005). The Open Source Initiative's "depoliticized" efforts to popularize free software development may thus be construed as the "stealth propagation" of free software ideals in the commercial world: the apparent altruistic nature of the process could encourage similar behavior in commercial settings. This may be the intent, but, as the BitKeeper and X Windows stories show, this kind of agnosticism imposes a serious vulnerability on the free software community. Those who are averse to "the political" may prefer ideological neutrality, a choice we contest for its real and undesirable effects. The GPL's strategy of explicitly propagating free software and its ideals may be most effective in sustaining the free software community.

Political agnosticism finds its polar opposite in the uncompromising rhetoric of, and ideology espoused by, Richard Stallman, the founder of the Free Software Foundation. His language and tactics are viewed by many as unnecessarily combative and inflexible to the point of naïveté (Williams 2002; Zawinski 2000; Drepper 2001; Raymond 2001). But it is equally plausible to suggest that it is the purity of his vision, the ascetic ideal he represents, that helps the FSF and the GPL mark out an ideal position to which others may aspire. Stallman's repeated articulation of the free software ideals is as important to the sustenance of the free software community as the terms of the GPL.

While criticisms are often made of Stallman's use of the word "free" because of the potential confusion between price and liberty that this terminology engenders, his deliberate choice of this language, holding the discussion to a moral and political plane, is a strategic masterstroke. Rather than mounting simplistic anticorporate tirades, which would likely not gain much traction in these times, Stallman's appeal to ideals of freedom enables him to build a broad alliance across many ideological divides. The term "free" demands a vigorous political and philosophical defense: picking a morally inflected language is crucial in being able to awaken a moral conscience. This is where the language of the Open Source Initiative, and the Open Source Definition, fail.

Is the availability of source code only a tiny freedom, only of interest to a tiny community, of little use without a context of much broader freedoms? If software is viewed in an exclusively technical light, then perhaps so. But not if code is properly viewed as an enabler of technical and social imperatives. To this end, FOSS licenses impose a particular ethical vision and provide a normative critique of legal frameworks that impact software, a genuine alternative that relies heavily on a liberal vision (Coleman 2005). The copyleft provision, which enriches the digital commons by granting to licensees all rights reserved under copyright law, does not work in isolation but rather as a protective clause of specifically enumerated freedoms. It is these freedoms that are preserved: a defense of copyleft licensing is a defense of the four freedoms enumerated in the Free Software Definition.

The Open Source Initiative represents a schism in the free software movement: it seeks greater acceptance among corporate developers for the free software development model, but not for its attendant political and ethical message. In disdaining the explicit ideology of the FSF, the OSI is forced to make facile claims that writing software is just engineering, that free software is not a moral or social imperative. But these claims ring hollow in a world where software is deeply implicated in the creation and maintenance of contemporary social and political structures, from electronic voting to public education to an ever-increasing suite of economic transactions. The OSI's position reflects a naïveté about technology's place as a singular socioeconomic force. Its deliberate narrowing of the free software ideal represents the injection of a problematic moral agnosticism into a domain created and sustained by idealism.

3

Free Software and the Aesthetics of Code

"Because the objects of art are expressive, they communicate. I do not say that communication to others is the intent of an artist. But it is a consequence of his work."
— John Dewey (Dewey 1934, 104)

"When I speak about computer programming as an art, I am thinking primarily of it as an art *form*, in an aesthetic sense. The chief goal of my work as educator and author is to help people learn how to write *beautiful programs*. . . . My feeling is that when we prepare a program, the experience can be just like composing poetry or music."
— Donald Knuth (Knuth 1992, 7)

Eric Raymond, self-proclaimed anthropologist of the open source software movement, once observed, "Given enough eyeballs, all bugs are shallow." On first reading, this seems simply to be a pithy inversion of "Too many cooks spoil the broth," but this statement is in fact a critical claim about the unique aesthetic qualities of free software.

All programmers have participated in conversations about "beautiful" code: beauty is a strangely comfortable topic for computer scientists. If we interpret aesthetics in the modern sense, as the science of the judgment of artifacts, then the programmer's activity is essentially aesthetic: the programmer brings informed judgments to bear on the process of creating and refining software artifacts. But while computer scientists have a well-developed suite of techniques for approaching questions such as "Is this code efficient?" or "Is this code correct?" it is less clear how to work with questions such as "Is this code beautiful?" Such questions are difficult because of the spectrum of forms in which software artifacts may simultaneously exist, ranging from directly executable machine code subject primarily to analysis of its functionality and behavior, to highly expressive source code further subject to inspection, criticism, and transformation.

If it makes sense to talk about the beauty of code, then it must be that aesthetic theories have something to tell us about software artifacts and their creation. These theories engage as soon as we begin to consider what makes a particular piece of code "beautiful," based on factors ranging from the pragmatic, such as computational efficiency, to the intangible, such as "code that instantiates a beautiful algorithm." These factors may be unique to computer science as a discipline, but they are nonetheless grounded in age-old aesthetic concepts such as judgment, taste, and the act of interpretation.

But aesthetics is also concerned with creativity and the creative process: we must consider the relationship of the artist to her work. It is in this light that the uniqueness of free software becomes readily apparent. Contemporary descriptions of FOSS development that emphasize its "spontaneous" (Raymond 2001, 52), "unorganized" (Shankland 2000), or even "chaotic" (House 1998) qualities resonate with traditions in art criticism that valorize spontaneity and overlook or ignore the structures that facilitate and sustain the production of art. Examining the FOSS environment, a carefully structured workspace with distinctive architectural features that facilitate group collaboration and creativity, reveals instructive truths not only about the aesthetic qualities of FOSS works in particular, but also about software development in general.

In free software, the anticipated gaze of users and collaborators redounds to the artistic act of design and production. Just as any creative endeavor is inseparable from critique, free software programmers benefit from a worldwide audience of critics and collaborators. Developers of a software system whose source code will be released for the scrutiny of other talented programmers anticipate a critical response as they work and hone their skills, perhaps guarding against ridicule from peers or bidding for a higher reputation in their community. This environment and its emergent coding practices make the greatest contribution to the quality of free software: free software design and development creates better programmers, not just better programs. Free software's mode of unrestricted collaboration imposes strong aesthetic constraints, supporting a unique relationship between artist and artifact: it is an aesthetic that modifies both artist and artifact, thereby making bugs inherently shallow.

Code as Artifact

The study of aesthetics is concerned not only with determining what "art" is but also, more generally, with exploring what "beauty" is. Our oldest associations with beauty — those of harmony and order — are central preoccupations of most considerations of code. The notion of "beautiful code" enters many discussions of programming.[1] Clearly, code evokes emotional responses associated with beauty. The code for FreeBSD's *ping* utility, excerpted below, has been described as "beautiful" on the Slashdot.org webforum;[2] our concern for the remainder of the chapter will be to discover the basis of such an evaluation.

```
        if (source) {
                bzero((char *)&sock_in, sizeof(sock_in));
                sock_in.sin_family = AF_INET;
                if (inet_aton(source, &sock_in.sin_addr) != 0) {
                        shostname = source;
                } else {
                        hp = gethostbyname2(source, AF_INET);
                        if (!hp)
                                errx(EX_NOHOST, "cannot resolve %s: %s",
                                    source, hstrerror(h_errno));
                        sock_in.sin_len = sizeof sock_in;
                        if ((unsigned)hp->h_length > sizeof(sock_in.sin_addr) ||
                        hp->h_length < 0)
                                errx(1, "gethostbyname2: illegal address");
                        memcpy(&sock_in.sin_addr, hp->h_addr_list[0],
                        sizeof(sock_in.sin_addr));
                        (void)strncpy(snamebuf, hp->h_name,
                        sizeof(snamebuf) - 1);
                        snamebuf[sizeof(snamebuf) - 1] = '\0';
                        shostname = snamebuf;
                }
                if (bind(s, (struct sockaddr *)&sock_in, sizeof sock_in) == -1)
                        err(1, "bind");
        }
```

Attempting to treat software as a form of artistic expression is fraught with challenges. Software is the original digital artifact: intangible, infinitely reproducible, with copies indistinguishable from the original. Indeed, the notion of an "original" copy of a piece of code is illusory, as operating systems autonomously copy and recopy data files between and throughout permanent and temporary storage. Walter Benjamin eloquently anticipated theoretical questions about the difficulties created by such reproducibility for our understanding of art:

> Mechanical reproduction of a work of art . . . represents something new. . . . In the case of the art object, a most sensitive nucleus — namely, its authenticity — is interfered with . . . The authenticity of a thing . . . is transmissible from its beginning. . . . from its substantive duration to its testimony to the history which it has experienced. Since the historical testimony rests on the authenticity, the former is jeopardized by reproduction when substantive duration ceases to matter . . . what is really jeopardized when the historical testimony is affected is the authority of the object. One might subsume the eliminated element in the term "aura" . . . that which withers in the age of mechanical reproduction is the aura of the work of art. (Benjamin 1969)

Benjamin, who did not live in a digitized era, perhaps would have struggled to make sense of the standing of code.

Contemporary theorists see this loss of aura as the starting point for a new theory of the virtual; specifically, the virtuality of digital artifacts represents a new sort of aura. Code might not have the aura Benjamin speaks of, but its perfect reproducibility enables a preservation and transmission of aura that Benjamin did not consider. With access to a program's source code, we can examine an exact replica of the programmer's work. This replica is different from a mechanical reproduction, for it is perfectly indistinguishable from the "original." If we examine the source code, we examine the programmer's work directly. Code's aura is both destroyed and preserved by its perfect reproducibility.

Software's status as art is suspect not only because of its digital ineffability but also because of the multiple forms of expression that it subsumes. It may occupy many points on the continuum established by the extremes of text-like source code and digital machine code (Tyre 2001). It is understood sometimes as literature, sometimes as mathematics, yet most of its users view software as purely instrumental. Attempting to place software in aesthetic categories simultaneously reveals the ease with which software can be fitted into these categories and the unease that accompanies such a classification (Cox, McLean, and Ward 2004; Fishwick et al. 2005).

A traditional aesthetic analysis of source code might begin with the question, "Is this software pleasing to the senses?" At minimum, it may be pleasing to the eye: the elegance of code's design is often reflected in a visually structured presentation on the screen or printed page. But programmers mean more when they speak of beautiful code: as when scientists speak of beautiful theories or mathematicians of beautiful proofs, it is often an appreciation of an ingenious solution to a problem. Theories, proofs, and code all have expressive content specific to their discipline that is subject to aesthetic analysis.

Code and Theories of Aesthetics

Theories of aesthetics aim to provide conceptual analysis of aesthetic concepts; they aim to define the extension of aesthetic predicates such as "beautiful" and "sublime." The domain of such an inquiry is certainly not restricted to human artifacts, as centuries of argument about the meaning of beauty in nature demonstrate. The notions of art and beauty are related yet separable: ugly artifacts can be reckoned as art while beautiful objects may not be art. Our study of software aesthetics proceeds, then, in two directions: we ask whether software meets the conditions specified in some definition of "art," and we try to determine whether it possesses the qualities required to be called "beautiful."

Theories of art often contain prescriptive elements, but the necessary conditions they set out for works of art are rarely met by software. Code does not fit into a neoclassical or realist sensibility, as do the nineteenth-century novel or the output of the 1950s Italian school of neorealist cinema. Code is not useful in its encouragement of patriotism, piety, or social change as is the drama of Henrik Ibsen. Nor is code "progressive" in the sense that Marx prescribed — it does not especially support the cause of the working classes. Code is similarly rejected by avant-garde notions of art that disdain functionality. For Tolstoy, art was the evocation of emotion: the artist expresses some felt emotion in the artwork that is thereby induced in the viewer (Tolstoy 1960); software rarely meets this requirement.

John Dewey (Dewey 1934) and Richard Collingwood (Collingwood 1938) both thought of art as a communicative language, one of equal stature with verbal or linguistic communication. Dewey expressed this most strongly in his claim, "objects of art are expressive, they are a language . . . art is the most universal form of language . . . it is the most universal and freest form of communication" (Dewey 1934, 270). Code is a symbolic form of communication, conveying ideas and information to both humans and machines; machines are imbued with informational content only when code is running on them. Yet, as we will see, code can also trigger a spectrum of emotional responses. Code as a language possesses the unique quality of being simultaneously executable on a machine and readable by human and machine alike (Galloway 2004; Thacker 2004). Code is also a form of expression, a means of communication among those fluent in the language of programming (Tyre 2001); it is precisely in its expressive potential that its aesthetic qualities lie. Source code is prose much as a mathematical proof is prose, but the blending of the theoretical, the abstract, and the pragmatic makes writing code an act of simultaneously composing text, providing a proof, and doing an experiment. Some of this multiplicity is captured in programmers' description of their work as "programming," "writing code," or, simply yet powerfully, as just "coding." The first speaks to an act of engineering — of imbuing a machine with a capacity to solve a problem — but it also sounds the most prosaic, reminiscent of facile tasks like getting a VCR to work. The second captures the literary character of creating source code. The third speaks to the transformation of an algorithm into code. Programmers view themselves as artisans. Very few describe their craft as "producing" software; rather, they "make" it.

Programming is often regarded as the craft of representing abstract algorithms in concrete forms executable by a computer: in bringing an algorithm to fruition, the programmer is engaging in the artist's task of partly completing "what nature cannot bring to a finish" (Aristotle 1984, 340). Thus, we might view code as an attempt to capture the beauty of an abstract object, the algorithm. Much as an artist extracts form from objects of experience, such as the human body, and imposes that form on matter, such as canvas, the programmer imposes the form of an abstract algorithm in, and on, a particular programming language. The programmer uses the medium of a programming language to render the algorithm in the material substrate of digital circuitry.

Important distinctions can be made between the aesthetic appreciation of works of art that are primarily experienced visually, such as painting and photography, and those mediated by text, such as poetry and prose. An appreciation of code grounded only in a sensory modality such as vision fails to acknowledge its polymorphous character: we apprehend code visually, but treating code as textual expression, applying aesthetic notions derived from literature, turns its appreciation into a literary act. This point is taken to its logical conclusion in the argument that programming is the process of creating works of literature (Knuth 1992), a perspective that captures both the creative effort required to write code and the kind of aesthetic pleasure that reading a program can induce. Great works of literature resonate primarily with our emotional and psychological sensibilities, as they may evoke memories, inspire trains of thought, and enable introspection. It is the author's technical mastery of the textual medium and keen appreciation of the reader's sensibilities that makes a novel a work of art. A similar appreciation of programmers' abilities informs our aesthetic assessments of code.

While assessing the beauty of code by visual standards alone restricts us to a superficial appreciation, nonetheless a connection exists between the code's visual qualities and its technical clarity. Programmers' visual styles are distinctive; visual elegance is generally regarded as a precondition for "beautiful code," code that is a pleasure to read — and easy to understand. This comprehension, as in prose, is facilitated by good writing style; books on programming style, regarded as indispensable by experienced programmers, include advice familiar to writers in other genres:

> Write clearly — don't be too clever.
> Say what you mean, simply and directly.
> Write clearly — don't sacrifice clarity for "efficiency."
> Parenthesize to avoid ambiguity.
> Don't stop with your first draft.
> Use the good features of a language; avoid the bad ones (Kernighan and Plauger 1978)

Unsurprisingly, programmers' writing styles distinguish the work of a veteran from a novice.

The aesthetics in code also manifests at the intersection of ingenuity and whimsy. Oliver Schade maintains an archive[3] of 980 (and counting) programs, written in several hundred different languages, each of which prints the complete lyrics to the song "99 Bottles of Beer on the Wall." The example below, written in Perl, is one of the top-rated (and most-discussed) examples on the site:[4]
This program, when executed, produces the following output:

> 99 bottles of beer on the wall, 99 bottles of beer!
> Take one down, pass it around,
> 98 bottles of beer on the wall!
> 98 bottles of beer on the wall, 98 bottles of beer!

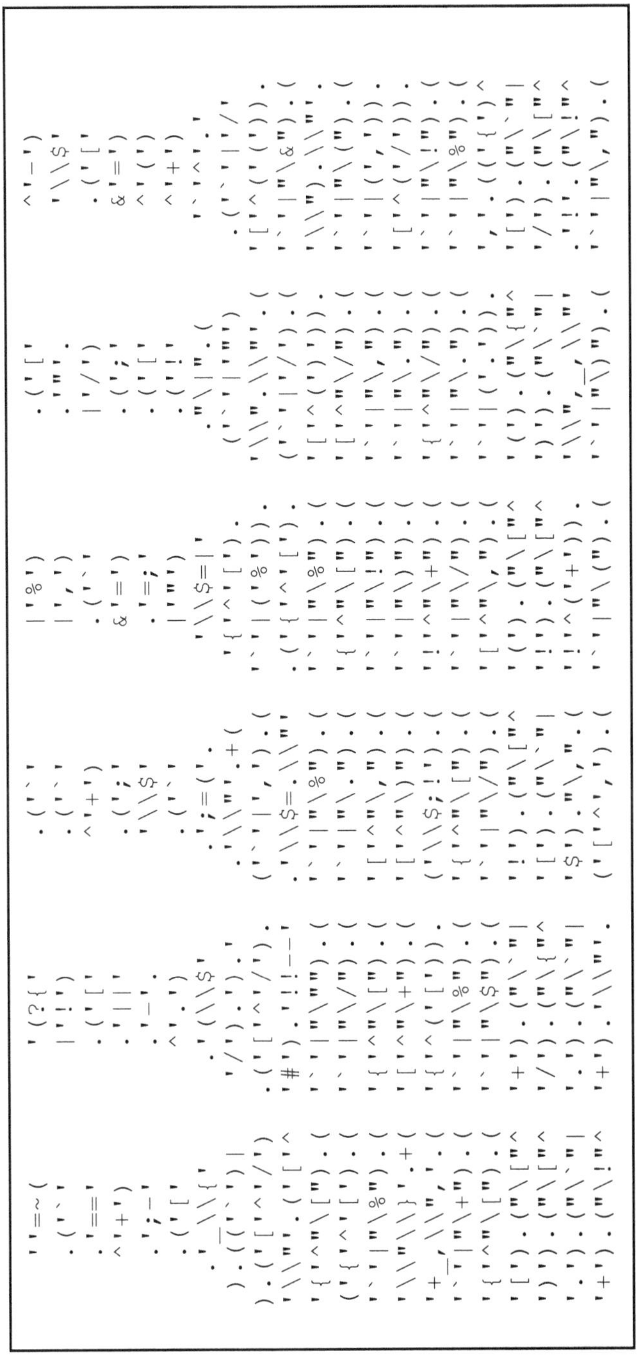

Figure 3.1

Take one down, pass it around,
97 bottles of beer on the wall!
. . .
1 bottle of beer on the wall, 1 bottle of beer!
Take one down, pass it around,
No bottles of beer on the wall!

Despite the appearance of the text of the program as formatted punctuation marks, it nonetheless produces coherent, if unsophisticated, text output. The appreciation of this code by other programmers lies in their recognition that the writer has submerged the semantics of the code in a visual pun.

Sometimes the aesthetics of code derives from a broader political and social context, as in the online DeCSS gallery, which displays samples of code that enable the decryption of copy-protected DVDs and are therefore illegal under the terms of the U.S. Digital Millennium Copyright Act.[5] While little of the code on display has overt aesthetic value, each piece, and the exhibit as a whole, is a political protest against the criminalization of the act of writing code.

"Good" code could not be visually ugly unless the programmer intentionally makes it so by obfuscation.[6] It is no coincidence that Donald Knuth, a computer scientist famously obsessed with beauty in programming, is also the creator of TeX, a typesetting program renowned for its beautiful renderings not only of mathematical symbols and formulae but also documents as a whole. In the domain of source code, one finds a close relationship between visual "clarity" and "clarity" as a cognitive concept: to "see" something refers both to a visual act and to an act of understanding. It is easy to confound a reader's understanding of a piece of code by manipulating its visual appearance with respect to its syntactic structure. These two code fragments, in the programming language C, have precisely the same meaning to the machine, but, as beginning programmers quickly discover, the difference in indentation significantly affects initial perceptions of the code's functionality:

```
if (edition == HARDCOVER)              if (edition == HARDCOVER)
    if (sales > 1000)                      if (sales > 1000)
        printPaperback();                      printPaperback();
else                                   else
    remainderBin();                        remainderBin();
```

The indentation of the "else" gives a strong visual hint about the logical structure of the code, but compilers for most languages ignore such cues. As in the Perl example above, the visual formatting of code is almost exclusively a matter of communicating with human readers.

George Simonyi, the lead programmer of Microsoft Word,[7] explains his understanding of the different modalities of code aesthetics:

I think the [program] listing gives the same sort of pleasure that you get from a clean home. You can just tell with a glance if things are messy — if garbage and unwashed dishes are lying about — or if things are really clean. It may not mean much. Just because a house is clean, it might be a den of iniquity! But it is an important first impression and it does say something about the program. I'll bet you that from 10 feet away I can tell if a program is bad. I might not guarantee that it is good, but if it looks bad from 10 feet, I can guarantee you that it wasn't written with care. And if it wasn't written with care, it's probably not beautiful in the logical sense.

But suppose it looks good. You then pick deeper. To understand the structure of a program is much, much harder. Some people have different opinions about what makes the structure beautiful. There are purists who think only structured programming with certain very simple constructions, used in a very strict mathematical fashion, is beautiful. That was a very reasonable reaction to the situation before the sixties when programmers were unaware of the notion of structuring.

But to me, programs can be beautiful even if they do not follow these concepts, if they have other redeeming features. It's like comparing modern poetry with classical poetry. I think classical poetry is great and you can appreciate it. But you can't limit your appreciation to just classical poetry. It also doesn't mean that if you put random words on paper and call it poetry, there will be beauty. But if a code has some redeeming qualities, I don't think it needs to be structured in a mathematical sense to be beautiful. (Lammers 1989, 12–13)

Software is understood as an art form not by making it conform to the necessary and sufficient conditions of some conceptual analysis but by viewing it through the Wittgensteinian lens of the "family resemblance" shared by related art objects. This approach enables us to study the relational properties of art and the historical and social contexts within which it is produced. Furthermore, a contemporary understanding of software as art is emerging on two fronts. On an institutional level, the art world has recognized works of software as works of art: in September 1999, in a "Duchampian" maneuver (Berry 2002), the jury of the ".net" category of the Ars Electronica festival awarded its top prize, the Golden Nica, to Linux. In its statement, the jury specifically noted the collaborative aesthetic of the Linux kernel:

[We] sought out pieces that are community building, self organizing, distributed, impossible without the Net, and have grown beyond the original design of the artist. [Linux] has birthed an aesthetic showing how something can be built on the Net through an intentional, but not necessarily direct, description. [It] relies on the contributions of thousands of volunteer programmers who collaborate online in a group effort. . . . [T]he community that has assembled around this anarchic effort demonstrates how strong an aesthetic can be in bringing a community, assets, ideas and attention together. (McCullagh 1999)

On a theoretical level, critics have begun reading manifestos of art movements into the software world, particularly noting parallels between collaboration in software and collaboration in the production of art:

> [T]he comparison between avant-garde art and free software does more than point out the collective nature of cultural production; it also points to the revolutionary effects this realization may have when the consumer and the producer become indistinguishable. This same dream of indistinctness also underpins the avant-garde wish to dissolve art into life or, better, to realize art as a practice of life. . . . A radical realization of art, then, would be the deposition of the sovereign producer and a return of the shared wealth of creativity to its true owners: the multitude. (Berry 2002)

Aesthetics in Science and Mathematics

Our inquiry into notions of beauty in programming has many historical antecedents in the sciences. While the classification of scientific works as art appears to face many of the difficulties we see in classifying software, scientists have little trouble in using the predicate "beautiful" in judgment of scientific works (Kragh and Hovis 1993; Heisenberg 1974). Indeed, scientists often place as much value on the aesthetic component of theories and experiments as on their technical merits: scientific discourse is shot through with discussions of "art" and "beauty" (Farmelo 2002) to the extent that Nobel Prize–winning physicist Subhramanyam Chandrashekhar dedicated an entire series of lectures to aesthetic motivations in science (Chandrashekhar 1990).

Art and beauty take on specific meanings in the scientific context. When we describe Newton's masterwork, the *Principia Mathematica*, as beautiful, we speak not of its turgid prose but rather of its revolutionary content. While Maxwell's equations superficially appear as forbidding arrays of mathematical symbols, they convey to physicists a proportion, elegance, order, and simplicity that is beautiful.[8]

$$\oint_{\substack{closed \\ surface}} \vec{E} \cdot d\vec{A} = \frac{Qenc}{\varepsilon_0}$$

$$\oint_{\substack{closed \\ surface}} \vec{B} \cdot d\vec{A} = 0$$

$$\oint \vec{E} \cdot d\vec{s} = -\frac{d\varphi_B}{dt}$$

$$\oint \vec{B} \cdot d\vec{s} = \mu_{0\varepsilon 0}\frac{d\varphi_E}{dt} + \mu_0 i_{enc}$$

Assessments of these equations as beautiful are not based on their visual aspect, but on a deeper aesthetic quality, one shared by Euler's famous identity, $e^{i\pi} + 1 = 0$, itself described as "uncanny and sublime" and "filled with cosmic beauty" (Crease 2004). Scientists' responses to scientific theories and works clearly have an aesthetically inflected emotional component.

Programmers and practitioners self-consciously note that much of their aesthetic concern is inherited from other sciences. In his discussion of elegance in programming, software engineer Harlan Mills draws parallels with mathematics, noting that much evaluation of mathematical beauty rests on notions of powerful simplicity:

> A mathematics theorem is elegant, not because it is complicated or hard to understand, but because it says more with less wasted motion. . . . [M]athematics can be a source of great power in organizing ideas and describing processes. . . . [I]t is easy to mix up the simplicity that comes from a deep analysis with a simple-minded analysis, which leads to hopeless complexities. (Mills 1983, 8)

This concern for simplicity also underlies the poetics of the fundamental equations of physics: "They are short and are organized according to some principle, and the most beautiful of them convey the hidden symmetries of nature," (Kaku 1994, 130) or "[Y]ou can recognize truth by its beauty and simplicity. When you get it right, it is obvious that it is right. . . . The truth always turns out to be simpler than you thought" (Feynman 1965, 165). This simplicity is often difficult to characterize. Sometimes it is descriptive simplicity, a measure of the complexity of the theory's description of reality, sometimes ontological simplicity, as when a theory makes particularly perspicuous use of Ockham's Razor.

The history of scientific practice provides ample support for valorizing simplicity. The success of the special theory of relativity may be partially attributed to its simplicity of statement, which did away with much ontological clutter.[9] Or, perhaps this principle is a pragmatic one: "the simpler hypothesis, the one with fewer parameters, is initially the more probable simply because a wider range of possible subsequent findings is classified as favorable to it" (Quine 2005). Similarly, mathematicians struggle to devise simple definitions in their effort to derive the most powerful theorems; complicated definitions produce theorems of restricted scope. Scientists strive for simple theories under the historically justified assumption that this effort brings them closer to a successful solution.

Quine's pragmatism finds resonance in Buckminster Fuller's oft-quoted assertion about the connection between beauty and functionality: "When I'm working on a problem, I never think about beauty. I think only how to solve the problem. But when I have finished, if the solution is not beautiful, I know it is wrong." The computer scientist Edsger Dijkstra similarly described the relationship between aesthetics and function: "In the design of sophisticated digital systems, elegance is not a dispensable luxury, but a matter of life and death, being a major factor that decides between success and failure" (Dijkstra 1999). That is, beauty is not incidental to the investigative enterprise of programming. The beauty of a solution is part of its technical assessment.

Contemporary programmers echo this concern with beauty, functionality, and simplicity:

> I'm thinking about things like simplicity — how easy is it going to be for someone to look at it later? How well is it fulfilling the overall design that I have in mind? How well does it fit into the architecture? If I were writing a very long poem with many parts, I would be thinking, "Okay, how does this piece fit in with the other pieces? How is it part of the bigger picture?" When coding, I'm doing similar things. (Heiss 2002)

Programmers also link beauty and simplicity when they describe the mental states required to produce good code: clarity of thought accompanied by trance-like states of concentration. Code created by an uncluttered mind manifests the simplicity of origins; messy code, because it is a symptom of a messy brain, is likely to be incorrect code as well.

Aesthetic Judgment and the Creative Process

Art is predicated on creativity. In order for a work to be judged as art, it must have been brought about through a creative process: one of the prominent evaluative terms attached to artworks is "creative." Artworks are made objects first and foremost: art is the paradigmatic form of human creative making, in contrast to mechanical or biological reproduction and routinized mass production. Thus, part of the investigative territory of aesthetics is the relationship between art and creativity. If we say something about how an artwork came to be, the processes that led to its making, to the creative style embodied in it, we are not simply providing annotation but are adding to our aesthetic understanding of the work. Any account of creation requires an account of production: our perception of drawings, for example, is informed by an understanding of them as effects of actions that were guided by certain purposes toward particular ends (Maynard 2003). This kind of perception differs from our perception of natural objects: looking at artworks is properly informed by an awareness of them as created objects.

Historically, the creative process has been susceptible to mystification and romanticization, from the Platonic notion of inspiration to Kant's insistence on the indeterminacy of the rules for producing beautiful things (Kant 1790/1987), to the Romantic view of poetic inspiration as mystery verging on madness, to Freudian theories that take creativity to be grounded in the unknowable unconscious (Freud 1994). Similarly, some contemporary views on creativity either treat aesthetic properties as not amenable to explanation in terms of their generative processes, or argue that creativity is unpredictable and unrepeatable (Hausman 1981). Some contemporary developmental psychologists, however, see creativity as a cognitive process susceptible to systematic empirical investigation (Campbell

1960; Simonton 1988). In our investigation of what makes code beautiful, we will treat creativity in programming as a phenomenon particularly facilitated by a combination of contingent social, technical, and organizational factors.

Our focus on the creative process is in theoretical opposition to formalism, which concentrates solely on properties of the art object (Beardsley 1965), and institutionalism, which stresses relational properties of artworks (Dickie 1974). These theories stress that the appropriate focus of aesthetic analysis should be the finished work's "inherent, artistically relevant features" (Gaut and Livingston 2003, 3): inquiries into the work's provenance are simply irrelevant. Our approach is akin to intentionalist views that relate the correct interpretations of works with the intentions of their makers, with the process through which a work comes into being (Wollheim 1980).

The creativity inherent in writing software has not always been obvious. Some early popular perceptions of computer programming viewed it as the rote application of syntactic rules: by keeping these rules in mind, writing correct code would be effortless. In more recent times, it has been suggested that the increasing power and expressiveness of programming languages would relax even this demand on programmers, as in this marketing pitch:

> The integrated WINDEV language, W-Language, is powerful, simple and intuitive.
> . . . [I]ts commands are highly sophisticated, and replace dozens or hundreds of
> 4GL commands, simplifying programming. No more unnecessary complexity . . .
> no more useless programming! . . . [C]oding is intuitive. (PC SOFT 2006)

This persistent misunderstanding appears to be grounded in a belief that programming is an activity that takes place in tightly structured environments, using formal languages and standardized techniques, apparently leaving no room for creativity.

Working within the constraints of a particular programming language (a "medium"), and relying on established algorithms (a set of "techniques") may be understood as an adherence to a kind of tradition. If creativity is in opposition to tradition, then programmers' work does not appear to be particularly creative. But this distinction is not a perspicuous one: artists belong to traditions, so creativity and adherence to tradition are clearly not in opposition. Some degree of tradition is necessary for creativity to transpire, to allow the artist to discern his options and to serve as a background against which creativity becomes recognizable (Carroll 2003). Moreover, "rules, concepts, and conventions . . . provide, together with the cultural environment . . . the conditions for the making of a literary work. . . . [This framework] creates the condition for creativity" (Olsen 2003, 206).

Unsurprisingly, the belief that programming is a genuinely creative act is espoused most commonly by programmers themselves, with their intimate understanding of the demands of their craft:

> Two programmers may solve the same problem with very different programs; that
> is, the results are highly variable. . . . Thus as long as programming is primarily the

job of writing everything down in some order, it is in fact highly variable. But that in itself is not creative. It is possible to be creative in programming, and that deals with far more ill-defined questions, such as minimizing the amount of intermediate data required, or the amount of program storage, or the amount of execution time, and so on. Finding the deep simplicities in a complicated collection of things to be done is the creativity in programming. (Mills 1983)

Software engineer Richard Gabriel observed similarities between writing code and writing poetry:

So, because you can program well or poorly, and because most of it is creative . . . my view is that we should train developers the way we train creative people like poets and artists. . . . Writing code certainly feels very similar to writing poetry. When I'm writing poetry, it feels like the center of my thinking is in a particular place, and when I'm writing code the center of my thinking feels in the same kind of place. It's the same kind of concentration. . . . [I]f you look at the source code of extremely talented programmers, there's beauty in it. (Heiss 2002)

As they reflect on the beauty of code and the creativity inherent in coding, programmers teach us much about how beauty is defined in computer science, informing us both about how good code is best produced and about where creativity resides in the programming process.

Most early practitioners of computer science brought with them an aesthetic apparatus grounded in mathematical notions and placed the same demands on good code that they would on a good proof. Early work on software engineering — the study of design and management techniques for the production of complex software systems — from which emerged the principles of structured programming, was explicitly grounded in logic and mathematical recursion theory (Mills 1983). But even then it was recognized that the programmer was engaged in a unique enterprise, one calling on notions of beauty in a fashion unique to the act of coding.

Programmers regularly deploy aesthetic language as they discuss the merits of code. Even before they refer to the beauty of code by using specialized terminology, they use a simple lexicon of subjective judgment: code evokes pleasure or displeasure. Programmers will respond to badly written code with language which is remarkably emotive: "ugly" (Seiwald 2005; Atwood 2006), "horrible" (Evans 2006), "irritating" (Kalnichevski 2005), "kludgy" (*Kludge* 2006) (i.e., remarkably inelegant), or "inscrutable" (Hylton 2002). The language used to describe good code is similarly emotive: "beautiful" (Sutton 2004), "clean" (Fells 2004), "amazing" (Ammerman 2006). Like any aesthetic judgment, programmers' opinions of code are subjective and open for contestation:

Programmer#1: Hey, Lisp's paren[these]s are a big part of the reason Lisp is beautiful!

Programmer #2: They're also a big part of why it's ugly — and I speak as a person who's long ago gotten over the parenthesis-phobia. (Tanksley and Krishnaswami 1999)

These terms are often embedded in discussions that employ a highly technical vocabulary, but the fact that appreciating software requires such technical mediation does not disqualify it from being beautiful. As Chandrasekhar observed, "[works of art] are accessible to each one of us *provided we are attuned* to the perception of strangeness in the proportion and the conformity of the parts to one another and to the whole" (Chandrashekhar 1990, 73, emphasis added). Appreciation of art is contingent on a particular kind of literacy, claims about accessibility to the masses notwithstanding. Music appreciation classes induce concept revision and ontology refinement; casual wine drinkers can become oenophiles through structured wine-tasting experiences. In programming, this attunement is brought about by competence in the craft: a person who has never written code cannot appreciate code. Programmers may not always be able to articulate explicit standards of beauty in code, or to provide necessary and sufficient conditions for a piece of code to be beautiful, but they can draw upon a shared vocabulary and its antecedent usage, confident their assessments of beauty will be understood by their peers.

The need for competence in the craft of programming as a precondition for its aesthetic appreciation marks an important difference from other genres of aesthetic work: to appreciate *Crime and Punishment*, one need not be a writer; to enjoy Rembrandt's *The Night Watch*, one need not be an artist. But, much as it is difficult fully to grasp the beauty of *Eugene Onegin* without understanding Russian — translators struggle to convey the aesthetic qualities of the original, knowing they must inevitably present a substantially different work — it is hard to understand the beauty of code without "speaking" it. To regard code as "just instructions to a machine" is as impoverished a perspective as regarding Shakespeare as "just ink on paper."

Just as artistic or cultural literacy is the ability to abstract away from the words on the page or the notes in the score to bring the work into dialogue with cultural, aesthetic, and historical contexts, literacy in code is the ability to abstract away from syntactic minutiae toward a perception of the programmer's mastery of his craft. The contention that "perception is thought and sensation fused" (James 1950) is more aptly applied to the appreciation of code than to the visual and auditory arts, where the illusion of unmediated contact is more successfully sustained. The appreciation of software cannot call upon as broad a sensibility as the appreciation of painting: the audience of software appreciators is thereby circumscribed. Programming is an esoteric art, in which exposure to relevant aesthetic concepts is necessary before a work can be appreciated. This interpenetration of fact and value turns the apprehension of the aesthetic qualities of software into "an exercise of our conceptual powers — not merely of our sense organs" (Putnam 1995).

To understand the aesthetic appreciation that its practitioners have for code is to understand a "form of life" (Wittgenstein 1953/1999); speaking about code and its qualities is an archetypal language-game:

> [Wittgenstein] speaks of just how much would be required to appreciate African art as a native appreciates it, and how different such appreciation, e.g., the ability to point out relevant features, is from the appreciation of the same art by even an informed connoisseur. (Putnam 1995)

Programming is a synthetic form of life in which code appreciation is a native skill. No one is born into this form of life, however; its participants all undergo the same literacy training, overcoming similar cognitive obstacles. Learning how to program affects appreciation of code: most programming students will point to their appreciation of programming as starting from the point that they were able to read and write code. A student exposed to the austere formalism of the Turing machine, the first mathematical model of computation, may be overwhelmed by the mathematics. Turing machine programs do not look pretty; they are nearly impossible to read. Their beauty emerges as the reader understands that Turing's machine and its formal description solves the puzzle of representing arbitrary computational activity using a physical apparatus. The abstraction at the heart of the Turing machine is the key both to understanding the machine and to appreciating its beauty. The beauty of code, then, is apprehended by the aesthetic sensibility of programmers conversant with its constraints and particular demands.

The Struggle with Complexity

Edsger Dijkstra once said, "When we recognize the battle against chaos, mess, and unmastered complexity as one of computing science's major callings, we must admit that 'Beauty Is Our Business'" (Dijkstra 1980). Beauty, then, is an integral part of the practice of computer science; the disciplines of software engineering and complexity theory are both chartered to uncover techniques for mitigating the complexities of the development and execution of programs. One of the fundamental missions of computer science is to comprehend the relationship between the physical limits of machines and the abstract notion of computation that drives them. Aesthetic appreciation in computer science is rooted in the profoundly humbling knowledge of the difficulties of marrying computation and materiality. In its attempts to master the physical substrate, computer science deploys architectures, operating systems, and programming languages. As man-made systems, programs, and machines impose order, programmers perceive an emergent beauty and harmony.

This struggle with the complexity of computing grounds the discipline's understanding of elegance. The programming world has matured slowly toward a set of shared standards for assessment of code—aversion to baroque structures and techniques, and appreciation of simplicity, breadth of application, and efficient use of resources. These standards are sometimes reflected in the programming standards documents used by large programming projects. Such standards specify — often in excruciating detail — the style and form of the code, seeking to make it, "clean, consistent, and easy to install. . . . portable, robust and reliable. . . . [and] more maintainable by others."[10] They do not mandate conformism, however: their restrictions are not quantitative but qualitative. Standardization does not act as a damper on creativity but rather imposes constraints, the successful handling of which requires creativity: "it is not standards that inhibit such creativity in the programming process; it is simply the lack of creativity in the programmers themselves" (Mills 1983, 108).

While the aesthetics of code can be meaningfully judged on grounds similar to those used in science and mathematics — a Perl script may be appreciated for its simplicity of concept or cleverness of expression — judging the technical quality of code remains a challenging area of inquiry for engineers, one to which several institutes,[11] as well as many credit-hours of university instruction,[12] are dedicated. While quantitative techniques for assessing technical quality are continually debated, programmers agree that high levels of abstraction are a desirable ideal. Indeed, the history of computing is marked by a steady increase in abstraction in programming practice. Dijkstra's foundational contribution to software design, "structured programming" (Dijkstra 1970), introduced greater abstraction through the relegation of separate functional concerns into distinct sections of code. The development of programming techniques such as data encapsulation was motivated by the need for abstraction; the ascendance of the object-oriented and aspect-oriented paradigms evinces a need for even greater degrees of abstraction. Similarly, the uncluttered ontology of Unix contributes to its perception as an elegantly designed operating system. Legions of programmers have commented on how its radical simplicity — "everything in Unix is a file" — aids their use and understanding of the system and contributes to their ability to assess the design shortcomings of other operating systems. Similarly, the rapid adoption of XML as a nearly universal data-presentation format for the Internet was driven by the need to separate data formatting and definition from its content, thereby introducing another layer of abstraction (W3C 2003).

We have a glimmer of the aesthetic imperative of good code: beautiful code is an elegantly designed implementation — one using the "right" data structures and the "right" programming language — of an efficient algorithm. We are closer to a connection between the qualities of harmony and order, which have obsessed those struggling to define beauty through the ages, and the provenance of a technical artifact.

Aesthetics and Ingenuity

The physical substrate confers on software one of its primary meanings: the actions taken by that software as it manipulates and interacts with its physical environment during its execution. Software that is known to perform incorrectly rarely elicits a positive aesthetic evaluation. Aesthetic judgments of code quality rest jointly on the function of the code and the manner in which it is achieved. Beyond the binary assessment of whether a program works lies the subtler aesthetic concern with how the behavior of the program was wrought by the programmer: part of the aesthetic assessment of software depends on how the code demonstrates its creators' ingenuity.

Understanding how a particularly ingenious piece of code confronts and subsequently masters constraints is crucial to understanding creativity and beauty in programming. Programmers have a deep sense of how their work is made more creative by the presence of the physical constraints of computing devices. Programmers who worked in the early era of computing struggled, in particular, to write code that would work in the tiny memory banks of the time — the onboard mission computer for the Apollo 11 project had a memory of 72 kilobytes, less than that found in today's least-sophisticated cell phone. This struggle was reflected in the nature of the appreciation programmers accorded each other's work. Steven Levy's ethnography of the early programming culture, *Hackers,* describes the obsession with "bumming" instructions from code:

> A certain esthetic of programming style had emerged. Because of the limited memory space of the TX-0 (a handicap that extended to all computers of that era), hackers came to deeply appreciate innovative techniques which allowed programs to do complicated tasks with very few instructions. . . . [S]ometimes when you didn't need speed or space much, and you weren't thinking about art and beauty, you'd hack together an ugly program, attacking the problem with "brute force" methods. . . . [O]ne could recognize elegant shortcuts to shave off an instruction or two, or, better yet, rethink the whole problem and devise a new algorithm which would save a whole block of instructions. . . . [B]y approaching the problem from an off-beat angle that no one had thought of before but that in retrospect, made total sense. There was definitely an artistic impulse residing in those who could use this genius-from-Mars technique (Levy 1994).

These programmers experienced the relaxation of the constraint of system memory, brought on by advances in manufacturing techniques, as a loss of aesthetic pleasure.

The relative abundance of storage and processing power has resulted in a new aesthetic category. One of the most damning aesthetic characterizations of software is "bloated," that is, using many more instructions, and, hence, storage space, than necessary; laments about modern software often take the shape of complaints about its excessive memory consumption (Wirth 1995; Salkever 2003). Huge executables are disparaged as "bloatware," not least because of the diminished ingenuity they reflect (Levy 1994). Judgments of elegant code reflect this concern with conciseness: "I worked with some great Forth hackers at the time, and it was truly amazing what could be accomplished with what today would be a laughingly tiny memory footprint" (Warsaw 1999).

The peculiar marriage of constraints, functionality, and aesthetic sensibility in source code highlights a parallel between programming and architecture. An awareness of gravity's constraints is crucial in our aesthetic assessment of a building, as we assess its ability to master the weight of materials, to make different materials cohere. While striving to make the work visually pleasing, the architect is subject to the constraints of the requirements of the structure's inhabitants, much as the programmer is subject to the constraints of design specifications, user requirements, and computing power.

Artists in other genres struggle similarly: creative artistic action is often a matter of finding local maxima of aesthetic value, subject to certain constraints (Gaut and Livingston 2003). These constraints may be imposed on the artist, as in censorship laws; they may be voluntarily assumed, as when a composer decides to write a piece in sonata form; or they may be invented by the artists themselves, as in Picasso and Braque's invention of Cubism. Whatever the origin of the constraints, "creative action is governed by them," and "artistically relevant goals," such as the facilitation of communication between artists and the public, are advanced by them (Elster 2000, 212). The connection between creativity and coping with constraints is explicit in programming: "It is possible to be creative in programming, and that deals with far more ill-defined questions, such as minimizing the amount of intermediate data required, or the amount of program storage, or the amount of execution time, and so on" (Mills 1983).

While pioneering computer scientists applied their aesthetic considerations to implementation details, contemporary concerns with beauty in code extend to the usability of systems, which imposes its own constraints on programming. For example, the field of interface design is charged with the investigation of techniques to ease human-computer interaction. The assessment of the Xerox PARC's work on graphical user interfaces as particularly creative rests in part on their ingenious deployment of metaphors such as "the desktop," "buttons," and "windows" which impose a layer of abstraction between the user and the services provided by the machine.

Thus, the act of programming, in its most creative moments, endeavors to meet constraints imposed by nature through the physicality of computation, by the users of the program and their desires for functionality and usability, and by the programming community through the development of shared standards.

Free Software, Beautiful Code, and Collaboration

Different fields of creative endeavor have their own aesthetic imperatives: we expect software and its creators to have one that reflects the unique nature of its artifacts. The relationship between the programmer and his source code is grounded in a classical conception of aesthetics, in an ancient connection between objects and art. Classical Greek aesthetics understood art as the knowledge of how to make an object; good art was by definition produced by an artisan proficient in that art. By analogy, good code is that written by a good programmer. A study of the art of software must, therefore, seek to understand how someone becomes a good software artisan. As we will see, the free software aesthetic confirms the converse of the relationship between art and artisan: good coders are produced by good code.

In science and mathematics, aesthetic quality is often related to advances in the discipline. A beautiful theory typically carries more explanatory weight; a beautiful proof may introduce new notation or new analytic tools. Beautiful code, however, may not bring anything new to the discipline of computing; beauty is not related to advances in our collective understanding. Instead, code can be beautiful when viewed as a work in progress: it may fire the imagination of its readers with ideas of how to modify and improve it, or how to incorporate it into other projects.

Programming is no more or less collaborative than any other technical discipline. Scientific results must be reproducible. Many experiments depend on hundreds of scientists for their successful execution. But programming is collaborative at a much finer granularity. Programs are modified, extended, improved, recombined. Modern programming languages and techniques, such as the object-oriented paradigm, are explicitly intended to facilitate this sort of collaboration. In this sense, code is beautiful to the extent it provides an affordance for collaboration, or shows off its recombinatory potential, by virtue of clean design, readability, and ingenious expression.

Reflecting on the significance of collaboration, the dichotomy between free and proprietary software is a difference in the scope of possible collaborators. Bill Gates, arguably the world's foremost defender of closed code, is an ardent advocate of peer review:

> [T]he best way to prepare [to be a programmer] is to write programs, and to study great programs that other people have written. . . . You've got to be willing to read other people's code, then write your own, then have other people review your code. You've got to want to be in this incredible feedback loop where you get the world-class people to tell you what you are doing wrong . . . If you ever talk to a great programmer you will find he knows his tools like an artist knows his paintbrushes. It's amazing to see how much great programmers have in common in they way they developed. . . . When you get those people to look at a certain piece of code, you get a very, very common reaction. (Lammers 1989, 83)

Gates describes the anticipation of peer review as guiding him while writing code; he invokes the memory of an old acquaintance, "Norton," who provides critiques of his code and catches bugs (Lammers 1989, 76). To facilitate this sort of feedback loop, free software relies on the broadest possible population of collaborators; copyleft licensing's requirement of openness in perpetuity particularly protects this possibility.

The free software approach to collaboration is a remarkable mode of creative production. Here, creators begin work on a piece, but rather than working in relative seclusion, they periodically release perfect copies of their works to their audience. The audience's response is not limited to mere criticism: audience members may go in different creative directions with their copies of the work, or they may make modifications (possibly improvements) and send these back to the creative originators, who may or may not incorporate these changes as they proceed. In this model, documenting the rationale behind creative decisions is an integral part of the process; it is critical for creators to share their work with others to receive critique, corrections, and modifications embodying a community-wide logic of taste.

While there are certainly examples of works in the fine arts[13] that experiment with radical collaboration along the lines of free software, in general it is neither artistically nor logistically sustainable.[14] Where artists request critique from peers and consumers, they do not permit modification of their work. Writers do not permit readers to send in opening paragraphs or snappy segues, they do not worry that readers will take commercial copies of their books and work on them to produce a better ending; sculptors do not let viewers bang away with chisels on their stone works. For example, Remix Reading, an artistic project based in Reading, in the United Kingdom, aims to bring together artists working across several genres to share their work, be mutually inspired, and create "remixes."[15] While artists have exhibited works at these meetings, they are unhappy with audience members modifying the originals (Chance 2006). This kind of participation is sometimes sought in the film world when films are prescreened before a variety of audiences to test the reception of different endings. The almost universal contempt reserved for this marketing technique among serious cinephiles — the sense that the director is not doing his work as an auteur if he needs to consult the audience — shows this kind of participation cannot easily be implemented in other realms. But the digital realm facilitates a different sort of "collaboration," the kind found in "fan edits" of popular films, most famously *The Phantom Edit* of *Star Wars Episode I*, regarded by many critics as a stronger film than the original.[16] In free software, such participatory "viewing" is determinative of the genre.

This cultural significance of this mode of collaborative work was heralded in Walter Benjamin's 1934 speech "The Author as Producer":

> [A] writer's production must have the character of a model: it must be able to instruct other writers in their production and, secondly, it must be able to place an improved apparatus [of production] at their disposal. The apparatus will be the better the more consumers it brings in contact with the production process — in short, the more readers or spectators it turns into collaborators. (Benjamin 1992)

When the source code for a work is not open, and therefore closes off collaboration, "the model character of the work must be understood as functioning otherwise or not at all" (Berry 2002).

Benjamin's claims can be fruitfully illustrated through analogy. Consider a schoolteacher who asks students for a problem. He solves the problem without explaining his solution; none of his steps can be questioned. This is proprietary code. If he leaves his work behind on the blackboard, the students can attempt to reproduce the solution or to improve on it. Or, he could explain each step, providing justification and allowing for criticism. The students can copy these to their notebooks and, while the teacher continues work on the solution, attempt it for themselves. This is free software. It embodies a pedagogical aesthetic in requiring its practitioners to teach others how their code works. The availability of the source code of other programmers is a design feature of the free software environment, much like the "view source" option was a design feature of the World Wide Web. This feature enabled webpage makers to collaborate as their designs were made available for others to appropriate, modify, and improve.

In a profound aesthetic move, the free software "apparatus of production" blurs, nearly to the point of invisibility, the conceptual lines between artist and critic, between programmer and user, between owner and licensee. Programmers deprecate any special authorial relationship to their code, effectively saying, "In order to innovate, to create, I do not block you from making it your own." The pressure to allow others to fix your code (or to be able to tolerate this kind of intrusion) leads to a redefinition of ownership and a humility that will not permit the "test-pilot syndrome":[17] though it is the artist's work, his authorship does not grant him exclusive creative control. Exclusive authorial control may be lost, either voluntarily, when the programmer moves on to another project, or involuntarily, through forking.

Forking

The clearest indicator of the fundamentally different nature of free-software authorship is the potential for any programmer to begin a new line of development based on a copy of an existing free software project — even, perhaps especially, if so doing is contrary to the wishes of the recognized "owner" of the code. Such an occurrence is a "fork" in the development process. While many scientists look askance at work that seems to tread on the toes of an established researcher, the free software community views the right to fork as one of its foundational characteristics. There is little debate about the ethics of forking, except in a very narrow technical sense of whether it represents a good solution; so loose has the concept of ownership become that the notion of exclusive control is not taken seriously.

While forking may in some cases be an action agreed upon by parties in both "branches" of the fork, the decision is more often a destructive, resource-consuming one:

> [T]here are fewer effective core developers working on the project — their efforts are divided with each fork; the project is a less attractive platform to application

software developers because they have to build and test for each fork; it is also less attractive to deployers because they run the risk of running a fork that falls out of favour and ceases to be supported; users lose confidence because they are presented with the difficult choice of choosing which fork to run; service and support offerings have to try to target variant versions. (Smyth 2004)

When a criticism is leveled against some free software project, the developers are not the only ones entitled to a constructive response. Their critics may attempt to demonstrate the correctness of their critique by starting a new branch — a fork — of the development tree. The possibility of forking places unique creative pressures on the software craftsman. As long as the software meets the functional and aesthetic approval of the community, the location of creative control is unquestioned. If community support wanes, forking is a drastic solution. Avoiding forking — and there is considerable community pressure to do so — may require a significant compromise of the original vision of the work.

In the case of Samba, a tool for allowing computers, even those running different operating systems, to share files and printers, the fork that occurred in 2000 was an amiable split: some developers wanted to work on a "next-generation" version of the software that would likely be incompatible with the established product. Andrew Tridgell, founder and lead programmer of the original Samba project, wrote at the time:

> Despite some hilarious reports this is actually a good thing. . . . I am delighted that this split has occurred. Many of the design decisions in Samba are showing their age, but as Samba is so widely used it can be difficult to try radical new approaches while keeping the code as stable as users have come to expect. . . . There has been only one viable SMB server solution for the free software community for far too long, and a world with only one choice is a boring place indeed. (Tridgell 2000)

The fork of *gcc* (the GNU Compiler Collection) was a more complicated story:

> Sometimes a fork becomes so successful that, even though it was regarded even by its own instigators as a fork at the outset, it becomes the version everybody prefers, and eventually supplants the original by popular demand. (Fogel 2005)

As a result of technical disagreements, some of *gcc*'s most active developers chose to begin work on their own compiler collection, dubbed the Enhanced GNU Compiler System (*egcs*). Their goal was to create the best, if not necessarily the most stable, compiler; they incorporated modifications more rapidly than the official *gcc* project, with the result that *egcs* came to be much more popular among developers than *gcc*. Realizing this, the developer community agreed to merge the two codebases, resulting in a new and much improved *gcc*. The fork disappeared, and a better software product emerged.

Forking constitutes an important judgment: the artist's work has been deemed unacceptable, and an individual or group has decided to launch a competitive work. Thus, the critic is no longer limited to commentary but can intervene to impose his own artistic vision. Given the nature of creative production, the critic must enlist collaborators. Then two competing visions strive to convince the community of peers that their code meets the community's shared standards of taste and judgment better than the others'. Sociological perspectives on theory choice in the sciences suggest that while such appeals to standards are made in the context of supposedly objective arguments for a candidate theory, they are more accurately understood as persuasive efforts to build consensus (Kuhn 1962).

Audience-Artist Interaction

Reaching a complete understanding of the creative process depends on analysis not only of the performers but also of the relationships between performer and audience (Sawyer 2003). In the case of free software, the audience, the source of critical feedback, is the community of the programmers' peers, composed of committed users and competent programmers. Free software is constantly workshopped, just as a new stage production or short story might be. This places a different responsibility on the programmer: she now must justify technical and aesthetic decisions not only to herself but also to her audience. When the focus of programming moves from merely getting the code to work to being able to explain what it does to other intelligent programmers, the pressure of creativity changes. (The claim "I can file a tax return without errors," takes on a very different meaning when defended in front of an accounting class.) When preaching to the converted or the heathen, there is little or no creative pressure, given the difficulty of the task in the latter case and the ease in the former. When the community of critics and peers lies in the middle of this spectrum, the artist's drive to convince them is at its strongest: when preaching to those we might potentially convert, we work the hardest. Free software requires that the artisan work in this spotlight at all times: exposing the code to the critique of peers raises the standards that a programmer must meet. This is a hypertrophic form of scientific peer review, which, at its best, constitutes an intense public examination of the scientist's work.

   In free software, the community of critics — those who can provide meaningful feedback to the artisan — is much smaller than the community of users. To recall Chandrasekhar's remark about the relationship between aesthetics and accessibility, it takes much experience to become technically and aesthetically attuned to a work of software. Nearly any experienced programmer is capable of being a critic: free software offers the full realization of that capability. Users are not only encouraged to offer criticisms, in the form of bug reports or feature requests, but also are taken more seriously if they attempt to remedy the root of their dissatisfaction themselves.

   Programming does not allow for an aesthetic akin to the pure mathematician's credo that some things ought to be done for their own sake. Thus, programs are initially created in a very different way from other written works. Novels can be written without any felt need for them, but programs are always written in response to an existent problem: many programs start as an effort to "scratch an itch" (Raymond 2000). An attempt to solve a programming problem assumes it will be used by at least one person, even if only the programmer herself. A free software programmer's anticipation of the usability of his work includes an expectation others will read it to see how he has solved some problem — the critic is always present. Free software expands our notion of what it is for software to be useful. Source code and executable must not be separated; software is not whole without both; software must be read as well as run.

Robert Frankston, the creator of the original spreadsheet program VisiCalc, has observed, "A good programmer needs an aesthetic sense, combined with a guilt complex and a keen awareness of when to violate that aesthetic sense. The guilt complex forces him to work harder to improve the program and to bring it more in line with the aesthetic sense" (Lammers 1989, 157). The free software community acts as an external, communally imparted conscience for the programmer: when the programmer implements an inelegant solution, his awareness of it is enhanced by the community's response to it.

Free software development resonates with literary-theoretic claims that the author needs the reader to experience the text, that both author and reader are creators (Eco 1984). The artist's anticipation of the reader's response, whether technical or aesthetic, is crucial. Artworks are "infinite" in this sense; while they may arise from an individual artist, they are infinitely reinterpreted by the audience (Eco 1989). All writers struggle to "get it just right"; the free software programmer struggles similarly, knowing that the appreciation or criticism of a community of peers is within his grasp.

The act of revealing the code is a bold step, placing trust in, and responsibility on, other programmers and users, a fact about software development recognized in the early 1960s. While the software itself may work, it may be revealed to do so badly:

> A software system can pass its performance and capability acceptance tests and still be an internal nightmare of ad hoc designs put together as a *tour de force* in the short term memories of a team of programmers that is disbanded and scattered as soon as the tests are completed. (Mills 1983, 186–7)

In such a situation, pressures to rewrite the code or to dismiss the program altogether will follow almost inevitably. Public scrutiny of the code mitigates against such nightmares:

> As a consequence of its infancy and adolescence, software development has been practiced as a black art — not maliciously, but because it never seemed possible or necessary to make a public practice out of it. But software development technology

is coming of age and moving from private art to public practice. (Mills 1983, 186–7)

Programmers who inadequately anticipate this public gaze risk irrelevance. As computing power has increased, easing some of the physical constraints that fuel creativity and prompting accusations of "code bloat" and "brute force" programming, the expectation of other programmers' criticism is an important generative force in the creation of better code. Closed-code communities attempt to match this intensity of gaze through the deployment of code-review teams and rigorous testing schedules. But the possibility of forking is, to most programmers, a more compelling concern than the possibility of lost market share. The programmer's community of peers re-creates the environmentally imposed constraints that programmers contended with in an earlier era. This is free software's contribution to the set of constraints a programmer must face: his code must pass muster with his peers.

Over thirty years ago, Mills identified correctness, efficiency, robustness against errors, documentation, maintainability, modifiability, and reusability as desiderata for good code. The latter four are directly motivated by the collaborative nature of software production. The mode of collaboration under the free software regime is, in many ways, the apotheosis of Mills's vision for software production: programming is carried out by self-organized communities of interest rather than by transient cells organized by management (Mills 1983).

In FOSS we find not only a unique form of collaboration but also a debunking of many common myths about the creative process: that inspiration always precedes execution, that artists never edit their work, that everything made is released to the world. Programmers' ongoing iterative refinement of their code is closely related to painters' "relentless" drive to improve and perfect their work: in both cases, the creation of new work rests on the destruction of the old (Graham 2000). In free software, this iteration is broadened and accelerated.

Artists often reflect on the transformative impact their work has on themselves. But these transformations are mostly emotional; they do not directly correspond to changes in the artists' abilities. Free software enables transformation of both creative talent and the artifact by the artists' peers: critical feedback becomes a form of community participation in the act of creation, affecting the quality not only of the artifact but also of the artisan. External transformative pressure comes in the form of critical/audience response, and internal pressure is generated by the anticipation of the audience's gaze. Dewey characterized this anticipation: "even when the artist works in solitude. . . . the artist has to become vicariously the receiving audience" (Dewey 1934, 106). The programmer's fear of the loss of reputation in his community acts as a damper on hastily written bad code and as a pressure to innovate.

Programmers may intentionally join a free software project as a way of measuring and increasing their programming stature, as an act of self-edification.

While we have spoken of the transformation of the creator of a piece of code, programmers who have access to the innovation and knowledge of the creator are able to engage in a similar act of self-edification; thus, the free software aesthetic changes both for the better.

The Aesthetics of Group Collaboration

Our assertion of the particular creative and aesthetic potential of FOSS contests the romanticization of the individual creator expressed not only by the exaltation of the mythical solitary poet but also by contemporary application of patent and copyright law. The centrality of collaboration to creativity and artistic work reveals a dynamic interdependence between individual and group:

> The contemporary western emphasis on an individual artistic identity connected to a distinctive individual style arose in the Renaissance . . . but the execution of the work was still accomplished in groups: the best known example, Michelangelo's Sistine Chapel, required the joint labor of thirteen workers. . . . [T]here are several forms of co-construction in the visual arts: . . . the shared activity of many artists engaged in large works, such as churches, frescoes, and . . . large-scale murals. (John-Steiner 2000, 73)

Contemporary art criticism recognizes this trajectory from individual to collective as well:

> Modernist aesthetics is certainly predicated upon the concept of an individualized vision or oeuvre, but it also subsumes . . . modes of collective production. . . . [T]his individualized concept has been under attack from many quarters. With the. . . . increasing use of new technology, group practices and collaborations have increased dramatically. . . . [I]n certain practices the process of collaboration has been paramount, the growth or enabling of individuals or groups being the goal. . . . [I]n situations where there are ideas to be communicated more widely, aesthetic power becomes especially important — it is central to the work's ability to speak beyond the confines of any single group. The "beauty" of such images derives from the imaginative interpretation of meanings embodied in the ideas. . . . This . . . results from a transformation through critique, collaboration, and communication. . . . [T]he work forms a lens that creates a focal point in the energies of transformation. Desire focused is passion, and what is socialized passion but aesthetics? (Dunn and Leeson 1997)

Modern theories of collaboration and cognition reject the primacy of the individual as the locus of cognitive development: "cognition is people jointly constructing knowledge under particular conditions of social purpose and interaction" (Resnick, Levine, and Teasley 1991, 2); "joint mediated activity is the proper unit of psychological analysis and hence, is inherently socially shared" (Cole 1991).

In *Collaborative Aesthetics* (John-Steiner 2000), Vera John-Steiner brings a developmental psychologist's perspective to bear on well-known artistic collaborations. Her study notes the psychological valuation of the social dimensions of cognition (Vygotsky 1978; Vygotsky 1962), recast through a developmental psychology that emphasizes social context and codetermining relationships with other thinkers: "the forms and functions of cognition are shared among individuals, social institutions, and historically accumulated artifacts" (Cole 1991). This theoretical framework focuses on the cognitive characteristics of famous collaborations in the arts and sciences such as Picasso and Braque, Stravinsky and Balanchine, the Curies, and Miller and Nin (John-Steiner 2000) and of large-group collaboration, including the brilliant Xerox PARC group (Bennis and Biederman 1998).

These reports on collaborative creativity map very closely to the operation of collaboration within FOSS development. While the FOSS world has its own mythology of the lone programmer, and continues to recognize the originator of a package as the "author,"[18] the openness of the code inherently transforms software development into a social activity, one in which individual accomplishments are subordinate to the work of the community of developers. FOSS collaboration, indeed, "thrives on diversity of perspectives and on constructive dialogues between individuals negotiating their differences while creating their shared voice and vision" (John-Steiner 2000, 6). Just as the apotheosis of "transformative partnership" is the discarding of individual identity and attachments (John-Steiner 2000, 8), the FOSS development process slowly obliterates individual authorship on a line-by-line basis: change logs may record who made which changes when, but in the code, identity vanishes, as many contributions are woven into the finished whole. This phenomenon emerges in part from the willingness to "look at the written material as text rather than claiming 'that this is his or my idea'" (John-Steiner 2000, 50). Conversely, FOSS enables one of the most important psychological dynamics of collaboration, mutual appropriation, or the process of taking something from another and making it one's own.

Mathematician Philip Davis quotes James Thurber to describe his approach to collaboration: "Don't get it right, get it written" (John-Steiner 2000, 50), a sensibility that uncannily echoes Raymond's characterization of the FOSS approach to development as "Release early, release often" (Raymond 2000). Davis self-consciously uses his collaborators to "get it right," just as FOSS developers intentionally rely on their co-developers to find and resolve flaws. The FOSS developer who helps realize an incomplete development project is providing a rare sort of collaboration: "'I know a lot of people who are good critics. If I want to know what is wrong with my idea, they will tell me. But not very many — it is much more special — to have someone who is going to try to take your idea and help to develop it'" (John-Steiner 2000, 51). The "trust and mutual regard" that is necessary for this kind of relationship is the hallmark of a successful FOSS project.

A vibrant FOSS project is sustained by ongoing conversation, ranging from outright hostility to deep appreciation, in the form of vigorous debate and discussion facilitated by project listservs and chat channels (Weber 2004; Coleman 2005). This form of collaborative "virtual" conversation, utilizing physical networks that concretize information transfer and preservation, is a more tangible form of the "shadow networks," such as the intense conversations leading up to the founding of the Impressionist movement, that have for centuries held together large collaborations (John-Steiner 2000, 72). These shadow networks, by their nature relying upon informal, private communication, have perpetuated the myth of the individual creator, a myth that FOSS development, depending on a public, global network, renders unsustainable. The network, then, is a crucial part of the creative framework: "Techniques of distribution do not just disseminate what has been created elsewhere but have themselves a creative or productive potential" (Strathern 2005). This communication further broadens the mutual inspection of developers' individual approaches to problem solving, a method that has its antecedents in the study of art: "The Impressionists studied Delacroix and Japanese painters. The young artist copies masterworks. Atelier students working with the same model watch, criticize, and appropriate each others' visual understanding" (John-Steiner 2000, 74). The FOSS developer who writes code in anticipation of critical feedback from the community of co-developers and testers is taking advantage of "oppositional complementarity" (John-Steiner 2000, 52), in which collaboration takes the form of criticism toward the end of clarifying and refining the work.

"Integrative collaboration," the power of collaboration to transform not only the work but also the artistic community, is exemplified by the Picasso-Braque collaboration, which gave birth to Cubism (John-Steiner 2000, 203). Such collaboration is vital to the maturation of the individual artist. A FOSS community with its mailing lists and discussion boards therefore provides zones of "proximal development" (Vygotsky 1978) for the developer community, an environment in which a novice programmer may mature into a master craftsperson.

The collaborative environment of FOSS produces works that display a distinctive diversity in unity:

> One of the most prominent characteristics of an aesthetics of collaboration is the weaving of diverse images into a unified whole. The goal is not the subordination of the individual, but the harmonizing of alternative visions. The source of authenticity of collaborative work does not come about by paring it down to a single essential image; it is created through the accumulation of varied points of view. Thus, communally designed work extends the promise of the modernist convention of multiple points of view, from representing the fracturing of individual consciousness to the reuniting and reweaving of social, collective consciousness. (Gude 1989)

This "weaving" grounds attempts to understand FOSS itself as an aesthetic statement, perhaps as a form of artistic production heavily reliant on reuse, sampling, and bricolage (Century 2001). The use of these techniques can be read as FOSS's postauthorial manifesto, or as the starting point for investigations into the nature of authorship in domains where individual and collective creativity combine. FOSS projects reconcile diverse styles in a unique mingling of abstract and concrete: one author's contribution of a crucial abstraction, such as an algorithmic technique, may be realized in code by another. The simultaneous merging of the individual into the collective work and the precise detailing of the provenance of every line of code constitute a bivalent claim about authorship.

The Facilitation of Creativity

The creative nature of software programming is well understood by programmers, who experience it as an important aspect of the aesthetic component of software:

> I think [software] developers already know but are a little afraid to admit that writing software is a creative activity that requires a lot of interaction with the people who are going to use it. Writing software is a highly iterative, dynamic process requiring user feedback. . . . [I]t's like writing poetry in that you write some of it, and then you respond to it, which triggers more creativity, and you keep going. (Heiss 2002)

In software development, even if many details of the final functionality are known ahead of time, the particular techniques used to achieve it are not. The appreciation of code relies on the knowledge of how it is enabled. If the emergence of creativity depends on particular social arrangements (Novitz 2003), then the claim that free software communities produce better code can be understood as the claim that their organizational structures significantly enhance programmers' creativity.

Whatever our understanding of creativity in FOSS, it cannot be one that privileges a facile notion of novelty, one that disqualifies derivative works. Claims of originality take two forms: either they are aesthetically vacuous assertions having to do with temporality and superficial novelty, or they are assertions of newness with respect to aesthetic properties. In the more meaningful latter understanding, the aesthetic significance of the originality of the work rests in its aesthetic qualities and has little to do with its newness: in a series of paintings by a master, the newness of the last makes it no more valuable than the first (Vermazen 1991).

Creativity may be simply a measure of the possibility of recombination of ideas in ways that are both useful and surprising to experts in the field (Novitz 2003). Indeed, some creative work is best explained in terms of the "retrieval and application of previously acquired knowledge" (Gaut and Livingston 2003, 19). For instance, Picasso's *Guernica* has often been understood as an "extension, application, and refinement of his works of the 1930s" (Gaut and Livingston 2003; Weisberg 2006). The notion of "original creativity," then, may be only as meaningful as that of the "individual author."

Psychological studies of creativity suggest the creative process proceeds in four stages: preparation, incubation, illumination, and verification (Wallas 1926). The preparation and incubation phases must include the generation of many variants from which the best may eventually be selected. Poincaré, James, and Einstein, writing on their creative moments, confirmed that the times in which they felt most creative were the ones in which they generated and rejected many ideas (Campbell 1960; Simonton 1988). This form of creative destruction is seen in the "bazaar" model of software development, as incremental releases of source code test possible development paths to identify the most promising:

> The group as a whole can see the results of a proposed change in short cycles. Version control allows the group to reverse decisions and to test both forks of a branching decision. . . . These advantages allow a software developer to experience the future, or at least the short-term future, rather than merely trying to predict it. This ability in turn allows them to build a culture made on modeling multiple futures and selecting among them, rather than arguing over some theoretical "best" version. (Shirky 2005, 485)

Rejected alternatives are not lost but survive in the "change logs" of the project, which allow the recreation of earlier versions of software projects. Thus, the history of a FOSS project is even more directly accessible, to researchers and coders alike, than *pentimenti*, the visibility of layers of revision in oil paintings (Livingston 2003; Bourbakis 1998).

FOSS environments allow students and novice coders to study the work of more experienced programmers, a method of learning critical to the development of creative faculties. Kant believed that the study of the works of geniuses facilitated the creativity of their followers by helping them infer the genius' aesthetic principles (Kant 1790/1987, 47 AK 309–10). The importance of this phenomenon in the free software setting is well documented: "As with all creative arts, the most effective way to become a master is to imitate the mind-set of masters, not just intellectually but emotionally as well. Or . . . to follow the path: look to the master, follow the master, walk with the master, see through the master, become the master" (Raymond 2001). Software engineer Richard Gabriel offers a similar observation in his critique of software developers' training:

> But what do people do when they're being trained, for example, to get a Master of Fine Arts in poetry? They study great works of poetry. Do we do that in our software engineering disciplines? No. You don't look at the source code for great pieces of software. Or look at the architecture of great pieces of software. You don't look at their design. You don't study the lives of great software designers. So, you don't study the literature of the thing you're trying to build. . . .
>
> MFA programs create a context in which you're creating while reflecting on it. For example, you write poetry while reading and critiquing other poetry, and while working with mentors who are looking at what you're doing, helping you think about what you're doing and working with you on your revisions. Then you go into writers' workshops and continue the whole process, and write many, many poems under supervision in a critical context, and with mentorship. We don't do that with software (Heiss 2002).

The failures that Gabriel bemoans are inevitable when source code is not available for study. It would be unthinkable for a student of poetry not to have access to the work of his peers and predecessors. More generally, artistic creativity is vitally dependent on a rich public domain. Thus FOSS production, which both draws upon and enriches the public domain, facilitates creativity in the most fundamental sense.

Group Creativity

In *Group Creativity*, Keith Sawyer investigates the phenomenology of creativity in group settings, particularly improvisational jazz and theater (Sawyer 2003). He asserts that the improvisational character of the settings studied enhances the key characteristics of group creativity: process, unpredictability, intersubjectivity, complex communication, emergence, and reliance on "readymades" and convention. Sawyer's study is but a logical extension of the art world's long-standing acknowledgment of the importance of collaboration to artistic innovation. While the creative setting of FOSS is far less synchronous and spatially compact, its structure is such that it can nonetheless be understood as an ensemble traversing an improvisatory path toward a finished product.

Sawyer, applying the slogan "the process is the product" to improvisational performance, takes these groups to be engaged in the production, not of a particular work, but of their improvisation itself. FOSS projects provide a particular interpretation of this slogan by treating software as work-in-progress that is subject to a more flexible understanding of its form, functionality, and responsiveness to user requirements. Improvisation, imbued with unpredictability and contingency, is built into the FOSS governance model, in which forking ensures that there are at least as many possible futures for a project as there are developers. From a finer-grained perspective, every line of code, as it becomes simultaneously visible to the developers' community, is an invitation to recombination. Every proposed modification to the code will be accepted or rejected — and always recorded — by the community: the project's path through its developmental trajectory is one pushed and prodded at every moment by the complex and diverse decision-making processes of the developers.

To maintain the coherence of this process, FOSS participants evolve a measure of "interactional synchrony." In improvisational settings, this is an acute sensitivity to coperformers' physicality; and in FOSS a harmonization of individual idiosyncrasies as a governance technique (Weber 2004, 158–66). The meaning of each participant's contribution is determined in part by contemporaneous and subsequent contributions: whether new code fixes a bug or introduces new ones depends on its interaction not only with existing code but also with other new code. Just as in the performances Sawyer studies, FOSS projects must be constantly negotiated and constructed from moment to moment. Because of this unpredictability, each programmer may have a different understanding of the project and its evolution; to maintain intersubjective agreement, developers negotiate, from both technical and aesthetic grounds, among their distinct representations.

This negotiation is facilitated by complex communication, in which developers, while making their contributions, are able to offer criticism of other contributions as well as reflexive commentary on their own work. This criticism and commentary arises on two levels: conversation with other programmers about the others' work, generally transacted on mailing lists, discussion forums, or IRC channels (Weber 2004; Coleman 2005), and comments in code, typically in the programmers' own contribution.

As in Sawyer's collaborative subjects, the eventual form and content of a FOSS project is an emergent property: simply recounting the contributions of each developer is not sufficient to characterize fully each developer's role in the project. Any simple tally — of line counts, bugs fixed, files modified — will fail to capture the subtle yet significant effects one contributor's code may have on other developers. A developer's bad code might even serve as a bad example or illustrate an algorithmic technique that then becomes prevalent among her peers.

In the FOSS community, improvisation relies on broad cultural knowledge, such as that of programming languages and operating systems, functional components held in easily available libraries, and a wide array of programming idioms and patterns acquired through experience. In the settings that Sawyer studies, improvisation depends on a solid grasp of both culturally acquired conventions and so-called "readymades," small stock ideas that can be deployed in the process of improvising a larger whole. To a greater extent than any proprietary software, a FOSS project itself may contribute to the public stock of readymades, which are explicitly maintained by repositories such as freshmeat.net and sourceforge.net.

These perspectives on group improvisation are theoretically grounded in Dewey's emphasis on improvisation and Collingwood's view of collaboration as fundamental to art. Dewey implicitly argues that improvisation is an essential element of any artistic endeavor: "A rigid predetermination of an end-product. . . . leads to the turning out of a mechanical or academic product" (Dewey 1934, 138). FOSS projects may be easily characterized in terms of their functionality, but the structure of the solution that grants this functionality is rarely known in advance. Nor does achieving that functionality signify the end of creative work, as the openness of the code provides for unlimited revision and extension. Collingwood describes the artist's relationship with her audience, whether fellow artists, critics, or appreciators, as necessarily collaborative:

> [T]here must be an audience whose function is not . . . a merely receptive one but collaborative too . . . the artist thus stands in collaborative relations with an entire community. . . . [A]ll artists have modeled their style upon that of others, used subjects that others have used, and treated them as others have treated them already. A work of art so constructed is a work of collaboration. (Collingwood 1938, 318)

This assessment of the importance of collaboration led Collingwood, writing in the 1930s, to propose relaxations of copyright law to ameliorate the constraints it placed on creative collaboration (Collingwood 1938, 325). FOSS projects display the best features of collaborative group efforts by maintaining a space in which individual contributors can flourish even as they contribute to a codetermined whole.

"Does FOSS Produce Better Code?"

The most commonly cited evidence for the claim that the FOSS development model produces better software is the success of some of its most famous products: Sendmail, BIND, Apache, Mozilla Firefox, *emacs*. Other arguments rest on a variety of technical factors such as "reliability, performance, scalability, [and] security" (Wheeler 2005). Objections to these claims about the superior quality of free and open source software fall into several camps. Some of these are refinements or contestations of the "Raymond Principles" (Raymond 2000). For example, attracting collaborators requires the work explicitly display a minimal affordance for collaborative work — clear specifications, a minimal level of functionality, or well-defined open problems (Kesteloot 1998). Indeed, the artist that shows a radically incomplete piece to an audience of critics and potential collaboration risks getting feedback that is misdirected, irrelevant, or potentially destructive. Furthermore, overly large communities of free software developers may produce suboptimal code: perhaps an "effective bazaar size" is sufficient for free-software-like development (Cavalier 1998). Or debugging communities may diminish in size over time, with the result that the effectiveness of the FOSS model diminishes as well (Cavalier 1998). Nonetheless, the FOSS model of development permits a more rigorous selection, from a large pool, of developers for these small groups. Indeed, Firefox's highly modular design, enabling small groups to work on tightly focused modules, reflects such a selection (DiBona, Cooper, and Stone 2006, xxviii).

The free software model may not be especially unique, as communities demonstrating characteristics of free software may be found within groups manufacturing proprietary software. Producers of closed code, such as Microsoft, use the free software development model internally because "it very usefully advocates modularity, refinement, and aggressive peer review" (Eunice 1998). The tenor of this argument is that free software development is not so different from proprietary approaches, that corporate in-house development is just a scaled-back version of true free software development, capturing all its essential structural features with a smaller workforce. This claim, however, overlooks the role the free software development model has in fostering creativity and innovation: a FOSS project is always open to the entry of a new talented programmer and his contributions, but there is a far more complicated recruitment mechanism in a corporate setting. The proprietary approach may be just as effective at fixing bugs internally, but it falls short in its potential to take code in new directions. Furthermore, a proprietary software group may not have the time or inclination to work on problems found by its users, a weakness addressed by the openness of a FOSS community:

> If a bug report makes it back to a closed source developer group, and they don't have time, don't see the need (they may have a different notion of the program's purpose), lose the report, can't find the solution, or for any reason fail to fix the bug, the user is at a loss. But with open source, anyone in the community can (and therefore at least sometimes will) step up to the plate and fix the bug themselves. (Boring 1998)

Others directly disdain the quality of code found in free software projects. Glass aims to debunk some FOSS "myths," beginning with the claim that FOSS programmers are, as a group, the best programmers (Glass 2005). Glass points out that the so-called Programmer Aptitude Tests have been shown not to correlate well with qualitative measures of programming ability; therefore, we cannot identify the best programmers, whether or not they are working on free software projects. If we were to ask programmers to rank themselves, we would run afoul of the common behavioral bias in which subjects overrate the abilities of both themselves and their community members: a FOSS programmer is more likely to identify the best programmers as fellow FOSS programmers. In the absence of objective measures for programmer quality, we must rely on assessment of the quality of the code they produce. Thus, claims about FOSS programmers' quality are essentially claims about the quality of FOSS code, for which there is ample empirical evidence.

Glass suggests that the voluntary nature of the FOSS model, particular with respect to code review, is vulnerable to problems of selective interest. If developers only read code that is of interest to them, then large swaths of code will go unreviewed for long periods of time, and there is no way to document the frequency and thoroughness of these reviews. But the Mozilla group's exacting code-review system, for example, suggests that a successful FOSS project can and does solve the problems of selective attention (Baker 2005). We note, too, Clay Shirky's observation that an effective design aesthetic "changes the speed at which things happen by letting designers develop different parts of the system at independent rates" (Shirky 1998). Glass further disputes the utility of having code available to be read, as this is only of use to a small number of technically qualified programmers, and asserts that forking is not an effective guarantor of quality because it is technically and socially impractical. We suggest, however, that the former claim misses the point, while the long history of successful forks in the FOSS community is the only debunking required of the latter claim.

Perhaps FOSS projects suffer from the net-negative producer (NNP) phenomenon, in which programmers introduce more problems than they solve: the very openness of the project is an invitation to bad programmers as well as to good (Fitzgerald 2005). This, however, is an axis along which comparison to closed code simply cannot be made; it is likely this phenomenon is more closely correlated with code complexity than with openness.

The most compelling attacks on FOSS development are those grounded in actual inspection of FOSS code. Unix designer Ken Thompson, after his inspection of the Linux code base, asserted that it was no better or worse than other software he has read, though perhaps with more variance in quality (Thompson 1999). More specifically, a systematic study of one module of Linux's networking code reported numerous failings of design and implementation, ranging from poor or absent documentation to inadequate specification of internal interfaces and separation of functionality:

> We found nothing that we could identify as a precise specification of the module and nothing that we consider to be good design documentation. This is a serious fault. . . . Functions from the ARP module call functions from other modules. . . . [O]ften those functions call some other functions in some other module. There are many indirect invocations resulting in many potential cycles. Some of those functions return values, most of which are not explained. We are not told what the returned values represent, and cannot even find some reasonable comment about them. We can only guess what they represent. (Rusovan, Lawford, and Parnas 2005, 116–18)

This module comes off poorly when compared to code with the same functionality produced in more controlled environments, perhaps serving as evidence for the claim that too many cooks spoil the broth (Brooks 1995). It is unlikely, however, that only FOSS suffers from poorly written modules; proprietary software may include similarly weak code, code whose adequate functionality obscures its failures of design. This study beautifully exemplifies the strengths of free software: the authors were able to inspect the code and to publish their results openly, to the benefit of students, programmers, and researchers. Their criticism is now part of the FOSS development model, and may result in the reimplementation of the flawed code. Microsoft, tacitly acknowledging the power of this model, opened the source of its troubled Vista operating system to "blue hat hackers," inviting selected non-Microsoft programmers to probe systematically for security weaknesses (Lohr and Flynn 2006).

Open source is neither necessary nor sufficient to produce good code; neither is there a nomic positive correlation between "degree of openness" and the quality of the code. Whatever relationship exists between quality of code and its freedom is one afforded by the potential for the freedom of the code to facilitate a collaboration that can produce beautiful code. Free software addresses Donald Knuth's claim that the best software is written when programmers face challenges. For a programmer, the most intense challenges are likely to come from a community of like-minded programmers. While Raymond's characterization of FOSS development as a bazaar stresses the rapidity of change, that is not a central concern; that a broad community of programmers have access to a developer's code is more crucial than the speed at which corrections are made.

Programmers speak of their pleasure in unraveling a program's design by reading its source. Thus the act of decoding the code is made easier by the transparency of the code; the free software programmer is required to make his code decodable. The technical quality of free software is a logical outcome of its employment of a model of artistic collaboration that has been proven to work well across both history and genre. Its novelty resides less in its mode of organization than in the technical realm in which it finds application.

4

Free Software and the Scientific Practice of Computer Science

"This vessel, the accumulated canon of copyright and patent law, was developed to convey forms and methods of expression entirely different from the vaporous cargo it is now being asked to carry. It is leaking as much from within as without. Legal efforts to keep the old boat floating are taking three forms: a frenzy of deck chair rearrangement, stern warnings to the passengers that if she goes down, they will face harsh criminal penalties, and serene, glassy-eyed denial."

— James Boyle (Boyle 1997)

Computer science has a history more deeply steeped in the industrial sector than those of most of its sister disciplines. Perhaps due to its relative youth and predominantly technological character, the history of computer science parallels the increasingly industrial basis of modern scientific practice. This interweaving of the academic and industrial spheres of computing, with their divergent imperatives, can challenge the scientific vitality of the discipline. Computer science is a science whose relationship with technology is fundamental, prompting debate within the discipline about its scientific character, a question with implications for the objectivity of its disciplinary practices.

The history of free software, at the border of science and industry, suggests that it has normative implications for the practice of computer science qua science, the relationship between academy and industry, the peculiar application of proprietary ideas in computer science, the pedagogy of computer science, the funding and dissemination of academic and industrial research, and modern scientific inquiry broadly conceived. While computing has always been more than the academically inflected practice of computer science, its historically scientific character is at the heart of its ever-renewing potential for innovation. Free software and its constitutional principles have played, and will continue to play, a vital role in the scientific vigor and innovative capacities of both computer science and computationally demanding scientific inquiry.

Computer Science as a Science

Before we can begin to evaluate the scientific practice of computer science, we must establish that computer science is indeed a science. For our immediate purposes, it would suffice to make the nearly self-evident argument that computer science has a significant scientific component, but a brief exploration of this issue points toward the centrality of free software in the science of computing.

Though we can think of hackers and hobbyists as practicing a "naturalist" computer science in its early days, it did not acquire all the trappings of a scientific discipline until the establishment of university computer science departments some twenty years after ENIAC. Through the 1960s, computer science had to struggle to be recognized as a discipline within the academy as it competed with older applied sciences such as electrical engineering and applied mathematics. In particular, it had to combat the perception that computers were just clerical tools to be used for mundane administrative chores. Aiding in the recognition of computer science as an academic discipline, George Forsythe, a mathematician at Stanford University, created a Division of Computer Science within the Mathematics Department in 1961, which split off in 1967 to become the first computer science department (Ceruzzi 2003, 102). At that time Forsythe defined the "computer sciences" as "the theory of programming, numerical analysis, data processing, and the design of computer systems" (Knuth 1972).

Other stalwarts in the field had already made a formal definition of computer science. Herbert Simon, Alan Perlis, and Allan Newell wrote a letter to *Science* in 1967, defining computer science as the "study of computers" (Newell, Perlis, and Simon 1967). Their letter defended their definition and argued for the legitimacy of computer science as a science in response to a varied set of objections, including one claiming that computers as man-made artifacts were not a legitimate object of study for a "natural science." The trio argued, "[Computers] belong to both [engineering and science], like electricity (physics and electrical engineering) or plants (botany and agriculture). Time will tell what professional specialization is desirable . . . between the pure study of computers and their application." Newell and Simon went on to remark, in their 1975 Turing Award acceptance lecture:

> Computer science is an empirical discipline. We would have called it an experimental science, but like astronomy, economics, and geology, some of its unique forms of observation and experience do not fit a narrow stereotype of the experimental method. None the less [sic], they are experiments. Each new machine that is built is

an experiment. Actually constructing the machine poses a question to nature; and we listen for the answer by observing the machine in operation and analyzing it by all analytical and measurement means available. Each new program that is built is an experiment. It poses a question to nature, and its behavior offers clues to an answer.

But as basic scientists we build machines and programs as a way of discovering new phenomena and analyzing phenomena we already know about. Society often becomes confused about this, believing that computers and programs are to be constructed only for the economic use that can be made of them. . . . It needs to understand that the phenomena surrounding computers are deep and obscure, requiring much experimentation to assess their nature. (Newell and Simon 1976)

In 1996, a later era in which the economic use of computing had only grown in importance, Frederick Brooks argued that computer science was grievously misnamed, that its practitioners are not scientists but rather engineers (specifically, "toolsmiths") (Brooks 1996). As he described the distinction, "the scientist *builds in order to study*; the engineer *studies in order to build*" (emphasis in original). Or, "sciences legitimately take the discovery of facts and laws as a proper end in itself. A new fact, a new law is an accomplishment, worthy of publication. . . . But in design, in contrast with science, novelty in itself has no merit."[1] Brooks might be construed as asserting that computer science does not employ the traditional scientific method and should therefore be thought of as an engineering discipline. But computer scientists do frame hypotheses — say, a conjecture about the resource consumption of a distributed implementation of a new pattern-matching algorithm; then design experiments, perhaps implementing the algorithm and its experimental scaffolding; observe phenomena by gathering data from executing this implementation; support or reject hypotheses, for example, when the software performs unexpectedly poorly on large data sets; and formulate explanations, such as, "Network latencies had an unexpectedly severe impact on load-balancing." These hypotheses and experimental designs may be refined and repeated.

Brooks's distinction between scientists and engineers is a fair one, but he significantly undercounts situations in which computer scientists "build to study." In addition to obvious practical applications, computer scientists study computation by building models of computation, whether physical computers, software simulations, or design elements of programming languages. Brooks himself agrees that there is a significant distinction between computer science and the engineering disciplines: "Unlike other engineering disciplines, much of our product is intangible: algorithms, programs, software systems." These products eventually take tangible form as the internal states of a running computer change during the course of executing a program. George Forsythe frequently stressed the value of experimental as well as theoretical computer science: "To a modern mathematician, design seems to be a second-rate intellectual activity. But in the most mathematical of the sciences, physics, the role of design is highly appreciated. . . .

If experimental work can win half the laurels in physics, then good experimental work in computer science must be rated very high indeed" (Forsythe 1967).

The practices of computer science have a close kinship, both historically and currently, with those described by Giambattista Vico in *La Nueva Scienzia*: scientists understand the phenomena they study by making and constructing models that validate their theories (*Verum et factum convertuntur* — the true and the made are convertible) (Miner 1998). Artificial intelligence, which grew out of Norbert Wiener's cybernetics program, a direct inheritor of Vico's principle (Dupuy 2000), is a model-making discipline par excellence; many of its practitioners improve our understanding of feats of cognition such as vision and hearing by striving to create machines that replicate them (Brooks 1991). More broadly, computer science is plausibly viewed as the use of computers and programs as models to study the properties of information rather than of energy and matter, the traditional objects of study for the natural sciences. This use of models is constitutional of computer science: the study of computational complexity, for example, would be impoverished were it limited to theoretical analysis without access to the practice of writing and running programs.

It is both difficult and unnecessary to dispute that many aspects of computer science are concerned with matters of design as Brooks articulates them, and that many research publications essentially report solutions to engineering problems — the design of a new programming language, a new chip, or a new grid computing architecture. But it is equally difficult to ignore the many subfields predominantly concerned with uncovering new facts and laws and the practitioners of the discipline who comport themselves as scientists. For example, informatics is broadly and succinctly characterized as "the science of information. . . . the representation, processing, and communication of information in natural and artificial systems. . . . [I]nformatics has computational, cognitive and social aspects" (Fourman 2002). Similarly, algorithmics has enormous applications in computer programming, but also sports vibrant experimental and theoretical branches.

While Brooks attempts to make the case that computing is not science, he simultaneously chastises the discipline for "honor[ing] . . . the 'scientific' parts of our subject more," and thereby "misdirect[ing] young and brilliant minds." This polemic appears to be directed toward theoretical computer science, which by its very nature is rarely concerned with real-life design problems. But this field has uncovered "facts and laws" about the limits and applicability of computation that are not only meritorious in their own right but also critically inform nearly every design problem that Brooks locates at the center of the discipline. Alan Turing's discovery of uncomputable problems was both a scientific triumph and an early voice in an ongoing dialogue, in both theoretical and applied communities, about the nature of computation itself (Turing 1936).

The Encyclopedia of Computer Science describes computer science as "the systematic study of algorithmic processes that describe and transform information: their theory, analysis, design, efficiency, implementation, and application." The core skills of a computer scientist, therefore, are "algorithmic thinking, representation, programming, and design," though "it is a mistake to equate computer science with any one of them" (Denning 2000). Design and engineering are crucial, as is scientific methodology. We can reasonably view every computer as a laboratory that tests and validates theories of algorithmics, language design, hardware–software interaction, and so on. Every time a piece of code runs, it generates data points that confirm or disconfirm hypotheses. Computer science is no more and no less a science than any other natural science.

The Scientific Practice of Computer Science

The philosophy of science draws heavily on actual scientific practice in a mutually informing relationship: conceptual claims about idealized visions of science are tempered by empirical evidence of historical and current practices and, so modified, inform scientific practice. Such a philosophical investigation, when part of a critical inspection, turns scientific standards on the discipline, seeking to illuminate weaknesses in its application of scientific methodology. Weaknesses uncovered in this fashion are typically rooted in the social structures — often political and economic — supporting the practice of that science. Ideally, these critiques, when fully developed, act to bring about a corrective reform of the sciences. The standards applied in such analyses must, if computer science is truly a science, apply equally well to it.

Objectivity

The most ambitious claim made for science, in the arena of competing epistemologies, is that it is objective and truth-tropic. This claim carries hefty normative implications: subjectivity contaminates scientific results, and particular scientific methodologies and practices are the best preventive measures against subjectivity (Scheffler 1982). According to this view, the proper separation of observer and observed, and the proper employment of nonarbitrary, nonsubjective, non–ad hoc techniques place science on a path toward a Peircean convergence to truth. While this notion of convergence is now abandoned by all but the most optimistic scientists and philosophers, science still claims an epistemological pride of place.

The most vigorous defenses of the scientific method are launched when the objectivity of science is questioned, as evinced by the cottage industry of responses to Thomas Kuhn's analysis of scientific revolutions in the mid-1960s (Kuhn 1962) and in the "science wars" of the late 1990s (Sokal and Bricmont 1999). Kuhn's and Paul Feyerabend's (Feyerabend 1975) analyses directly affected positivists' claims that objectivity depends solely on individual scientists' ability to develop an unmediated view of the world (Ayer 1966). The critical challenges to these claims forced an extensive reexamination of science's conceptual foundations, leading to more sophisticated reformulations of the objectivity thesis as well as sharper defenses of scientific realism (Laudan 1984, 1981).

Post-positivist notions of objectivity, confronted with a crumbling dichotomy between theory and observation, found their grounding in the public nature of the scientific enterprise. Thus, "Objectivity . . . is a characteristic of a community's practice of science rather than of an individual's . . . the practice of science is understood in a much broader sense than most discussions of the logic of scientific method suggest" (Longino 1990, 62). The fallibility of individual scientists is corrected through a social process of criticism and introspection: "It is the possibility of intersubjective criticism . . . that permits objectivity" (Longino 1990, 71). Or, "Objectivity in science is owing not to its practice by individuals but to the mutual critiquing that decreases subjectivity" (Bauer 1992). The result of this process is not undiluted objectivity but evolutionary progress toward it: the critical conversation about scientific "truth" is an environment in which ideas emerge, mutate, and struggle for selection. Science, then, is a "public possession or property in that it is produced for the most part by public resources," and is "itself a public resource" (Longino 1990, 69–70).

In order for a science to achieve the necessary level of public "transformative criticism," its social structures must demonstrate four characteristics: recognized avenues for criticism, peer review in particular, as well as a high valuation of critical activity; shared standards, the principles and epistemic values that undergird meaningful discourse, such as accuracy, consistency, scope, simplicity, and fruitfulness (Kuhn 1998); community response, a discipline-wide awareness of critical activity; and equality of intellectual authority, the structural protection of viewpoints regardless of their authorship (Longino 1990, 76). These structures cooperate to produce scientific knowledge, "the product of many individuals working in (acknowledged or unacknowledged) concert . . . produced through a process of critical emendation and modification of those individual products by the rest of the scientific community . . . [transcending] the contributions of any individual or even any subcommunity within the larger community" (Longino 1990, 67–68). This public situation, this openness, becomes definitive of science, for "the states of affairs to which theoretical explanations are pegged are public in the sense that they are intersubjectively ascertainable" (Longino 1990, 70). It also ensures a meritocracy, as "theoretical assertions, hypotheses, and background assumptions" are publicly available, accessible by those who are interested and suitably trained (Longino 1990, 70).

Thus, the question of why dominant scientific views are not hegemonically asserted is resolved by the implicit requirement of shared power. The diverse cacophony of voices, jostling for attention to ensure the acceptance of their corrective inputs, is the guarantor of objectivity and epistemic fidelity: "[O]nly if the products of inquiry are understood to be formed by the kind of critical discussion that is possible among a plurality of individuals about a commonly accessible phenomenon, can we see how they count as knowledge rather than opinion" (Longino 1990,

74). This valorization of the public nature of science also finds expression in the importance of the community to scientific practice. Practitioners of a science constitute a community embedded in society: the individual members of the community are dependent on one another for the conditions under which they practice (Grene 1985). Initiation into scientific inquiry, then, requires education in the "form-of-life" of the community, in what Kuhn might have termed "paradigm-familiarization."

Philosophical takes on scientific objectivity were foreshadowed in Robert Merton's sociological investigations into the characteristic norms of scientific activity which, he concluded, are universalism ("truth claims, whatever their source, are to be subjected to *pre-established impersonal criteria*: consonant with observation and with previously confirmed knowledge"); communism ("the substantive findings of science are a product of social collaboration and are assigned to the community. . . . The institutional conception of science as part of the public domain is linked with the imperative for communication of findings. Secrecy is the antithesis of this norm"); disinterestedness, the demand for which "has a firm basis in the public and testable character of science" and is "effectively supported by the ultimate accountability of scientists to their compeers"; and organized skepticism ("the temporary suspension of judgment and the detached scrutiny of beliefs in terms of empirical and logical criteria") (Merton 1979, 270–78).

These norms provide structural protection of the mechanisms of the discipline to preserve the objective quality of its investigations. Disinterestedness, therefore, means scientists are subject to demands only from their peers, and not from any institution. Similarly, scientific skepticism carries the potential to invalidate dogma, not only religious but also economic and political, thereby upending existing forms of power. Communism, the antithesis of secrecy, mandates "full and open communication" by which "property rights in science are whittled down to a bare minimum," preventing the hoarding of scientific knowledge for personal gain.

An intellectual enterprise aspiring to the status of science must demonstrate a conformance to methodological norms that confer the stamp of objectivity on the knowledge it creates. Rather than uncritically accepting a priori claims about the nature of a science, critical inquiry must be directed toward its community-wide practices. Given the public nature of the enterprise, our circumscription of the community must err on the side of inclusion. Science is practiced not by individuals but by social groups; it is the set of practices of these groups that constitute that discipline's "scientific method," and that must be the focus of any evaluative critique.

The Political Economy of Science

The disciplinary practice of computer science plays out within a framework of political economy: political economies and scientific objectivity are interwoven. Economies of reputation are well understood to be essential in upholding objectivity, but if [science] is to be paid for, by governments, rich people or corporations, it is probably required to contribute to their agenda somehow. In a representative democratic society this means that the funding of science is done on condition that it contributes to "progress" . . . scarce resources must be effectively distributed or the value of the whole enterprise collapses. (Kelty 2005, 416)

Most scientific methodologies exist to maintain an "ideological separation" between the discipline's mechanisms for allocating scarce resources and society's contributions to, and attempts to control, this allocation. This both requires systems for compensating individual scientists based on the principles of "peer review, open access, experimental verification, and the reduction of conflicts of interest" and prevents science from being "sold to the highest bidder" (Kelty 2005, 416). Reward systems in science may then be understood as strategies to ensure solvency, with citation indexing, for example, acting both as currency and as an informal registration of ideas in order to establish priority. As Merton points out in his preface to Eugene Garfield's *Citation Indexing*:

the more widely scientists make their [research results] available to others, the more securely it becomes identified as their property. For science is public not private knowledge. Only by publishing their work can scientists make their contribution. . . . [O]nly when it thus becomes part of the public domain of science can they truly lay claim to it as theirs. For the claim resides only in the recognition of the source of the contribution by peers. (Garfield 1979, vii–viii, cited in Kelty 2005)

The primary motivation for proprietary science is to gain competitive advantage. A privatized science must use the force of law to defend this advantage. Within such a regime, the scientist must constantly choose between private ownership and public dissemination, with most decisions tending to the former: "In designing an experiment it is no longer a process of simply finding and using the relevant data but of either licensing or purchasing it and of hiring a lawyer to make sure its uses are properly circumscribed" (Kelty 2005, 424).

A science's political economy and its epistemology are directly related: the way a science chooses to finance itself significantly affects its inquiry. The birth of "open science" provides an excellent illustration of this relationship (David 2005). In pre-Enlightenment models of science, medieval science withheld from the vulgar multitude knowledge that granted control over material things: craftsmen held on to technological recipes, trade routes were closely guarded secrets, alchemists shared their knowledge only reluctantly. Such retention ensured both the hoarding of knowledge and the maximization of rent collection from the existing stock of knowledge. This collection of practices changed with the arrival of the scientific patronage system and the reputation-building model it brought in its wake. Scientists, once affiliated with patrons, began to guard their reputations carefully so as to continue to qualify for patronage. But the increasing esotericism of science, due largely to its increasing deployment of mathematical techniques, altered the flow of information between scientists and their patrons. As the language of science tended toward the incomprehensible, the dangers of charlatanism necessitated the emergence of a community-wide internal review system:

> The norms of co-operation and information disclosure within the community of scientists, and their institutionalization through the activities of formal scientific organization emerged at least in part as a response to the informational requirements of a system of patronage in which the competition among noble patrons for prestigious clients was crucial. (David 2005)

Scientists, then, were driven by self-interest to evolve a system by which the community itself could evaluate proposals for patronage, so that cloaking a proposal in mathematical language no longer provided sufficient cover for scam artists. The community-wide evaluation of any claims of scientific knowledge reassured patrons that their generosity was not misdirected. Thus, "the methods of science themselves are not sufficient to induce and sustain the peculiar institutional infrastructures and organizational conditions of the open science regime . . . the institutions of open science are . . . fortuitous social and political constructs" (David 2005, 100).

So, the open-science regime is a contingent fact, a "radical social innovation" (David 2005, 100), which continues to underwrite science's claim to epistemic primacy. If the institutions of science are indeed so contingent on circumstance of political economy, then it should not be surprising to find that changes in these circumstances induce new variances in scientific methodology, possibly threatening the objectivity of the enterprise.

Contemporary Computer Science

Computer science is unique as a scientific discipline, with such a large engineering component that the community continues to debate whether the engineering aspects overshadow the science. Because of its technological nature, computer science became industrialized extremely rapidly — industrialized to the extent that its funding is primarily drawn from commercial interests (National Research Council et al. 1999; Markoff 2005), the practice of the science quickly became subject to the standards of the industrial domain. Although computing has always had a strong business-related component, its emergence as a true industry, one indispensable to the rest of the world's political economy, was an incremental, if rapid, process. This evolution followed a trajectory similar to the industrialization of science in the early twentieth century, which was driven by the twin mandates to turn patent law to industrial advantage and to ensure a steady supply of skilled science workers: "As they worked to standardize scientific and industrial processes and secure corporate command over the patent system, the engineers strove also to direct the human process of scientific research and to create an educational apparatus which could meet the demand for research manpower" (Noble 1979, 167).

Beginning with IBM's provision of discounted machines from its 650 series to universities in exchange for specific curricular changes (Ceruzzi 2003, 44), the relationship of the computing industry to academia through its influence on university curricula has only deepened. Corporations fund university computer science research, and computer science pedagogy is ever increasingly focused on training employees for the computing industry. Corporations use the products of research conducted in universities; university-trained students go to work for companies in which they develop software that is sold back to universities to use for the training and familiarization of future employees. Microsoft Research's University Relations sums up this symbiosis in its statement on "Curriculum Innovation":

> Given rapid and continuous innovation, industry requirements sometimes outpace the current state of the art computing curriculum and related education programs. To meet the demands in the academic world and to increase the prominence and quality of computer curriculum in the education of all students who aspire to careers in the software industry, Microsoft seeks to encourage the advancement of computer science, computer engineering and electronic engineering curricula in conjunction with the use of its corresponding technologies. (Microsoft Research)

This relationship parallels developments in turn-of-the-century engineering: "[T]he transformation of engineering education into a unit of the industrial system demanded the creation of an educational apparatus for the production, selection, and distribution of higher technical manpower, according to changing industrial specifications" (Noble 1979, 169).

The political economy of science requires a workforce trained in its objectives and familiar with its paradigms. A science with a strong industrial component seeks to create a renewable source of workers that will continue to create wealth for the industry: thus, the economy of the corporation is inextricably bound to the economy of the university. This close relationship is a conduit for influence: as industry demands both skilled workers and new knowledge, and provides resources toward the satisfaction of these demands, the university's practices, particularly those relating to the conduct of science, change in response. It is plausible, then, that sciences with large corporate components adopt the corporate model in their practices.

Computer Science, Political Economy, and "Intellectual Property"

Most broadly, the dominant model for the financial upkeep of science in the twentieth and twenty-first centuries is a particular rent maximization scheme. The patent system, in particular, has been a part of the political economy of industrialized science since its birth:

> The novel American patent system, designed to protect the inventor by granting him a monopoly over his creations, had by the turn of the century fostered the development of "institutions" that demanded a controlled promotion of the "progress of science and the useful arts," one that conformed to the exigencies of corporate stability and prosperity. The science-based industries, based upon patent monopolies from the outset, thus sought to redefine the patent system as yet another means to corporate ends. (Noble 1979, 88)

This is a significant departure from the role of publication in science explicated by Merton; rather than extracting intangible rent in the form of reputation and dissemination, scientists and their employers are engaged in monetary rent-seeking. The patenting of parts of the human genome sequence and of genetically modified seeds are but two controversial examples — as the U.S. Department of Energy's Human Genome Program acknowledges, over three million genome-related applications have been filed, and the "the scope and number of claims has generated controversy" (Human Genome Program 2006).

In computer science as well, patents contribute heavily to the monetization of scientific knowledge. The ENIAC itself, as we saw in Chapter 1, was the focus of a patent dispute between its inventors and their employer. The most famous patent in computer hardware, awarded for the integrated circuit, was the subject of a bitter legal dispute between Texas Instruments and Fairchild Semiconductors, the respective employers of Jack Kilby and Robert Noyce, who invented the idea and applied for patents within months of each other. Both companies recognized the financial and innovative potential of the device, spawning a court battle over the patent that lasted from 1961, when Noyce's patent was granted, until 1970, when the Supreme Court denied Kilby's appeal — though by then, both men had agreed to share credit, and the companies developed a mutually agreeable licensing scheme (Gibson 2006). The notion of patenting computer hardware is nothing new: patents historically have been granted for "machines, processes or compositions of matter." The extension of these categories to include software innovations and algorithmic techniques is a recent development, one that enhances the financial well-being of computer science's industrial and academic components while simultaneously posing a threat to the much-vaunted openness of computer science qua science.

In 1968, Martin Goetz, of Applied Data Research (ADR), received what is arguably the first software patent, on a "Sorting System" (US Patent #3,380,029). The patent described a new algorithm for sorting large datasets stored on magnetic tapes — it describes not only "pure" algorithmic processes but also the actions of the coordinated tape drives. It is unclear, in light of later events in the history of software patents, whether this patent was legitimate with respect to the standards in effect at the time, but the patent was neither implemented nor legally defended by ADR. (Also in 1968, as we noted in Chapter 1, Calvin Mooers and Bernie Galler engaged in a highly visible exchange, about the appropriateness of extending trademark protections to programming languages, in the pages of the flagship computer science journal, the *Communications of the ACM*. Galler's response, arguing that progress in the design and implementation of programming languages would be accelerated by the active participation of users, can be read as a claim for the public practice of science [Galler 1968]; Mooers's rejoinder, that the absence of some sort of protection would result in version proliferation and pernicious mutual incompatibility, is an argument for the partial enclosure of science [Mooers 1968].)

For the next several years, commercial attempts to apply patent law to software failed. In 1972, the Supreme Court, in *Gottschalk v. Benson*, ruled that "a method for converting numerical information from binary-coded decimal numbers into pure binary numbers, for use in programming conventional general-purpose digital computers is merely a series of mathematical calculations or mental steps and does not constitute a patentable "process" within the meaning of the Patent Act" (Douglas 1972). That is, algorithms were ruled to be unpatentable. In 1978, the Court again ruled, in *Parker v. Flook*, that a modification to an industrial process, in which the only innovation was the introduction of a mathematical formula implemented in a computerized controller, was unpatentable precisely because the only innovation was the formula itself. Noting in its decision that, "The line between a patentable 'process' and an unpatentable 'principle' is not always clear," the Court observed that "[I]t is equally clear that a process is not unpatentable simply because it contains a law of nature or a mathematical algorithm. . . . The process itself, not merely the mathematical algorithm, must be new and useful. Indeed, the novelty of the mathematical algorithm is not a determining factor at all" (Stevens 1978).

The Court's trajectory of increasing tolerance for the patentability of algorithms continued with the 1981 decision of *Diamond v. Diehr*:

> [T]he respondents here do not seek to patent a mathematical formula. . . . Their process admittedly employs a well-known mathematical equation, but they do not seek to pre-empt the use of that equation. Rather, they seek only to foreclose from others the use of that equation in conjunction with all of the other steps in their claimed process. (Rehnquist 1981)

Here, the Court clarifies that processes that incorporate implementations of equations or algorithms may be patentable despite including such abstract entities — but still, it is the entire process, not the algorithm, to which standards of novelty must be applied, and for which the patent is granted. But

> [e]ven this distinction was gradually eroded. Any real difference in the treatment of software and other inventions was essentially eliminated after a 1994 appeals court decision (*in re Alappat*) upheld the patentability of a computer program that smoothes digital data before displaying it as a waveform on a computer monitor. Shortly after that decision, the Patent and Trademark Office issued a comprehensive

revision to examination guidelines for computer related inventions. Thereafter, the number of software patents granted increased dramatically. (Bessen and Hunt 2004, 4)

Meanwhile, university research had become part of corporate science's quest for the privatization of knowledge through patents:

> The increasingly close link between industries and universities has pragmatic advantages for both sides, namely more research money for universities and higher profits for companies. But it is important to recognize the extent to which they are complemented by a growing *political* unity. . . . [T]hrough united efforts on issues such as patent and tax reform, both have joined forces in helping to concentrate ultimate control of science and its application in the hands of private capital, and to fight off all claims for the social control of knowledge, whether at its point of production or application. (Dickson 1993, 86)

Though universities had historically been reluctant to patent the fruits of their research efforts, these joint efforts toward patent reform resulted in amendments to the Patents and Trademarks Act in 1980 that, for government-sponsored research, automatically assigned any patents to the university (or business) recipient of the funds. This not only created new streams of funding for universities and industry via patent-licensing fees, but also enabled scientific knowledge to be privatized and monetized.

Industrialized computer science thus chose legal mechanisms to sustain its political economy, mechanisms that remain viable today. In this context, we can read Bill Gates's letter to the Homebrew Computer Club as an argument that the viability of computer science, not only as an industry but also as a scientific practice, depends on a particular notion of property as applied to software. Proprietary-software licenses would assert property rights to code, thus supporting high prices for commodity software and ensuring the "continued production of value." This legal and economic arrangement underwrites the practice of computer science: programmers' salaries rise, university enrollments increase as more students study computer science, academic departments expand and flourish, and corporations increase their research budgets, some of which flows to universities. Without the high value of software, this fragile structure collapses. The argument for proprietary software thus becomes an argument for the viability of the entire science.

Intellectual Property and the Closing of Computer Science

Arguments supporting patent protection typically invoke some vision of the humble, impoverished inventor whose ideas are co-opted by a corporate monopolist. Patents, the argument goes, are structured to protect individual innovation and to reward scientists for developing applications of scientific knowledge that are economically productive and socially useful. But the effect of patent law, and its application by individual and corporate patent-holders, has been to constrain the public, open, and critical nature of scientific practice:

> [T]here is no longer (if there ever was) any institutional guarantee of the public nature of science . . . precisely the opposite is true today: the openness or public nature of knowledge cannot be assumed, but must be asserted in order to be assured. Where scientists once raced each other to publish data, they now race to patent it. Science remains "public" in the sense of "not secret," but it also enters a stage of being [private property] first, public scientific research second. . . . Science and its results are now property, and the returns on this property are not subject to peer review. . . . The result has been a sometimes profitable, but always extraordinarily expensive system of pervasive licensing and cross-licensing of [patents]. (Kelty 2001)

Moreover, the domain of patentable knowledge has itself expanded, with the cumulative effect of significantly shrinking the public pool of shared scientific knowledge. This knowledge, when patented and thereby monetized, becomes a means to the end of further investment in scientific research, rather than being a freely shared end in and of itself. As scientific practices shift, so do normative standards, as the antecedent ethic of common access comes to be replaced by the community's acceptance of restrictions on sharing and public criticism: "Scientists are forced to explicitly consider the trade-off between the ownership of data, information, or results and the legal availability of them" (Kelty 2005, 424).

Patents

The concept of "ownership of data" in computer science has particularly far-reaching implications, for when patents are issued for computer-related processes, they are issued not for specific computer programs but either for computer-enabled physical processes or, more controversially, for algorithmic techniques:

> Software patents do not cover entire programs; instead, they cover algorithms and techniques. . . . But whereas the unique combination of algorithms and techniques in a program is considered an "expression" (like a book or a song) and is covered by copyright law, the algorithms and techniques themselves are treated as procedures eligible for patenting. (Garfinkel, Stallman, and Kapor 1991, 51)

Understood as engineering or business processes, these techniques seem intuitively patentable, but viewed as building blocks for scientific innovation, the application of patent law to them is problematic. Because these patents cover all possible implementations of the technique, what is effectively being patented is the abstract algorithm — the idea. Legally sanctioned restrictions on trafficking in these ideas are direct restrictions on scientific discourse, with profound implications for the openness of the science. A patent regime designed to protect investments in mass-manufactured goods is inappropriate for a field that more closely resembles literature or mathematics (Stallman 2005). Contemporary mathematicians prove theorems drawing on many ancient and modern proof techniques: it would be absurd for mathematicians to patent new proof techniques they develop.[2] In analogy with other creative fields, the absurdity becomes especially clear: a claim by David Lynch to patent the use of small American towns as incongruous settings for urban pathology, or by Thomas Pynchon to patent nonlinear narratives, would be not ridiculous but offensive. Regardless of discipline, freely available building blocks are essential for public discourse and the creativity and innovation it brings in its wake (Baxi et al. 1993).

> The changes in the applicability of patent law to software in the mid-1980s resulted in a dramatic patent "land grab." The largest share of these patents was obtained not by software companies, but by hardware companies building large portfolios — so-called patent thickets. Many leading software companies expressed the view that patents were undesirable, although many of these same companies have since been forced to acquire patent portfolios for defensive purposes. Predictably, the number of patent lawsuits has also begun to soar. (Bessen 2002, 27–28)

There is little reason to believe that software patents make a positive contribution to innovation in the computing industry. Most software patents are not held by software firms; the firms that are actively acquiring software patents are not primarily research-oriented (Bessen and Hunt 2004, 3). Thus, it seems that an aggressive stance on patents and a focus on research and development may often be orthogonal to each other. Large firms such as IBM stock their patent portfolios not only as a way of monetizing innovation but also as protection against lawsuits that claim patent violation.

That is, firms use patents, especially portfolios of patents, as bargaining chips. Many of these patents are never used commercially. This behavior arises when technologies are complex, cumulative, and overlapping so that any single product may potentially infringe hundreds or thousands of patents. That's why semiconductor firms regularly engage in strategic cross-licensing of whole portfolios of patents. (Bessen 2002, 17)

The contemporary interpretation of patent law allows computer scientists and corporations to patent algorithms, such as the LZW compression algorithm (League for Programming Freedom 2004), programmable "business processes" such as Amazon's "One-Click" checkout system (Anderson 2006) and Friendster's "social networking" (Gannes 2006). Any sufficiently useful program necessarily relies on hundreds of algorithms and techniques, many of which may have been already used in dozens of other programs, and many of which may be patented:

> [S]oftware involves complex systems and is fundamentally cumulative. Advances in software are, moreover, more often innovative. Improvements are incremental rather than inventive in the patent sense of nonobvious. Few of the daily, valuable

improvements in programs pass the relatively high threshold of inventiveness demanded of patents. (Davis et al. 1996, 24)

An aggressive patenting regime entails that large programs only escape disruptive and expensive lawsuits at the discretion of patent holders. The Linux kernel itself was found, in a 2004 study, potentially to infringe 283 patents held by a variety of firms, including Microsoft, though none of these had yet been litigated (Open Source Risk Management 2004). By way of protection against similar litigation, universities regularly require their faculty to sign agreements that clarify the ownership of research discoveries and provide guidelines for the sharing of any potential revenue.

The reform of patent law did not usher in a new era of software innovation (Bessen and Maskin 1999; Clements 2003): the history of computing shows that software developers have never needed incentive to innovate (Bessen 2002). Instead, patent law, far from fulfilling its primary task of encouraging innovation, stifles it:

> In April 1991, software developer Ross Williams began publishing a series of data compression programs using new algorithms of his own devising. . . . [T]hat September . . . use of these programs in the United States was halted by a newly issued patent, number 5,049,881. . . . [U]nder the patent system's rules, whether the public is allowed to use these programs . . . depends on whether there is "prior art": whether the basic idea was published before the patent application, which was on June 18, 1990. Williams' publication in April 1991 came after that date, so it does not count. . . . A student described a similar algorithm in 1988–1989 . . . but the paper was not published. So it does not count as prior art. . . . [R]eforms to make the patent system work "properly" would not have prevented this problem. Under the rules of the patent system, this patent seems valid. There was no prior art. . . . It is not close to obvious, as the patent system interprets the term. . . . The fault is in the rules themselves, not their execution. . . . [P]atents are intended as a bargain between society and individuals; society is supposed to gain through the disclosure of techniques that would otherwise never be available. . . . [S]ociety has gained nothing by issuing patent number 5,049,881. (Stallman 2001)

The patent system does not work because it is inefficient, because it stifles the very thing it is supposed to protect.

Concerns about the applicability of patent law to software innovation aside, inherent structural problems can be found in the patent system: patents might be inappropriately issued even when prior art exists, or when the vagueness of the nonobviousness condition is exploited to patent processes that are not sufficiently distinctive. Procedures for issuing patents are expensive, time-consuming, and inefficient (Stallman 2001). Thus, on grounds of inefficiency of intent and of execution, the system stands broken.

Copyright

The Copyright Act of 1976, as amended in 1980 after lengthy hearings before the National Commission on New Technological Uses of Copyrighted Works (CONTU), extended copyright protection, initially applied only to literary and artistic works, to software by clarifying that software itself is a literary work (Hollaar 2002). Noting in its final report that

> The United States . . . [is] facing a challenge . . . in the development of policies concerned with information. Forces of economic and technological development are leading to . . . [a] post-industrial society; one in which the source of wealth lies not only in the production and distribution of goods but also in the creation and dissemination of information. The ownership and control of information and the means of disseminating it are emerging as national and international policy issues. (National Commission on New Technological Uses of Copyrighted Works 1980, 2)

CONTU recommended, "The new copyright law should be amended to make it explicit that computer programs, to the extent that they embody an author's original creation, are proper subject matter of copyright" (National Commission on New Technological Uses of Copyrighted Works 1980, 2). Because the 1976 Act also eliminated the requirement that copyrighted works be published, it became possible for software developers to treat source code as a trade secret while simultaneously seeking copyright protection for both source and executable code.

The contemporary legal environment was fashioned to meet the needs of the software industry circa 1980. As Martin Goetz, then a senior vice president of ADR, explained to CONTU in 1977, "Software companies and commercial organizations, in particular, require protection for their property. They want legal protection in two specific areas: One, protection against their competitors and, two, protection against illegal use by users" (National Commission on New Technological Uses of Copyrighted Works 1977, 55–56). But the application of copyright law to software is flawed, for in order for copyright law to work as intended,

> it's crucial that the valuable ideas in the work, be they literary, mathematical, or scientific, are disclosed. . . . [I]f I scribble on a napkin then tuck it into my pocket and claim copyright on it, I've neither added nor taken away from the public's collective knowledge. The Statute of Anne's intent was to *prevent* brilliant authors from doing exactly that. . . . Society . . . gains from publication of these ideas, where they are free to be used at will. . . . [F]or copyright to be truly a "bargain" between authors and society, there has to be some value imparted to society by an author's expression of his work. It makes little sense to grant a monopoly on a work's publication when the work has no value. (Swann and Turner 2004)

That is, the purpose of copyright is not only to incentivize their creators individually but also to provide a social good by making their works public. Binary code is often copyrighted, but no social bargain can be forged by its publication, as the ideas and innovation inherent in it — expressed in the corresponding source code — are not published. This source code therefore does not fall under the umbrella of copyright at all; indeed, concealing source code is an extralegal strategy for maintaining competitive advantage (Weber 2004, 4).

As in the case of software patents, the mismatch between copyright and software is made clear through analogy with other creative genres. The copyright on Howard Shore's soundtrack to *Lord of the Rings: Return of the King* grants the publisher rights to control the distribution of both the movie and the original soundtrack recordings. It also permits the control of the distribution of the soundtrack's musical score, so that the publisher may obtain rent when the Boston Pops performs favorites from the movie. But if the publisher asserted its right not to release the score at all, not only would performance be curtailed, but also would the ability of the musical community to engage in critical conversation about, study of, and creation of derivative works from the composer's expression. Notions of copyright as a protective regime, one whose primary purpose is to afford exclusive rent collection, jeopardize the public imperative:

> For companies investing heavily in software research and development in the hopes of gaining a competitive advantage over others in their market, copyright affords nearly perfect protection against losing their advantage. Not only does copyright allow them to publicly release their object code without the fruits of their research being revealed, it lasts far beyond the time at which their software ceases to provide any new income. (Swann and Turner 2004)

During the CONTU hearings of 1978 it had become clear that the computing industry wanted to be able to apply both copyright and trade secret law to software. For distributors of proprietary software to come under the purview of trade secret law, they must demonstrate efforts to protect the confidentiality of their trade secrets. This is achieved by employing both nondisclosure agreements, which are signed by programmers and prohibit disclosing any details of a particular software project, and license agreements for users, which block copying and sharing of executables. Using trade secret law to deny access to source code denies access to that part of the creators' innovation that could be the focus of public scrutiny and criticism.

Proprietary software poses another fundamental problem for computer science. Computer science is the first physical science whose experimental apparatus and knowledge is substantially nonrival. The practice of physics and chemistry depends on the use of goods ranging from glass flasks to mass spectrometers to particle accelerators. While computer science employs goods such as computer workstations and incorporates subfields that study only hardware, its experiments and experimental apparatus are the programs employed by computer scientists. If running programs are part of the experimental infrastructure, then restrictions on copying executables are constraints on the propagation of scientific knowledge. Physicists may be unable to duplicate their colleagues' laboratory configuration easily, but this limitation is fundamentally a material one. In computer science, the constraints are not logistic or physical but legal and economic.

In sum, the application of proprietary notions to software suffers from systemic incoherence. Not only are these ideas damaging to the current practice of science, they, like all ideologies, function to preserve their own power and to counteract any reformatory imperative. Current applications of patent law pose a clear threat to FOSS, which by its practice and accompanying philosophy not only opposes proprietary software but is able to provide a coherent alternative through its creative licensing policies. This potential is countered by the threat of punitive action: the Linux kernel, for example, is known to be vulnerable to patent litigation, as is any other large FOSS project.[3] If these were to be embroiled in expensive, time-consuming lawsuits, the potential of FOSS to serve as a model for reform of computer science would be severely curtailed.

But most fundamentally, these notions in computer science have implications for the scientific norms identified by Merton. The contemporary application of patent and copyright law clashes most directly with the norm of "communism," which expects scientific findings to "constitute a common heritage in which the equity of the individual producer is severely limited." This limitation should arise because "property rights in science are whittled down to a bare minimum." This sort of communism is "incompatible with the definition of technology as 'private property' in a capitalistic economy." A regime of privatized knowledge, in which scientists' loyalties are divided between their commitment to the public dissemination of their discoveries and the economic compulsions of their employers, conflicts with the norm of disinterestedness, which requires the "ultimate accountability of scientists to their compeers." The closure and monetization of knowledge, institutionalized in the practice of computer science, challenges the norm of organized skepticism, for it adversely affects the ability of scientists to subject their colleagues' investigations to impartial empirical scrutiny (Merton 1979, 270–78). Such policies fail to promote innovation, encourage the "enclosure" of scientific knowledge, and constrain community-wide scientific discourse; they pose a threat not only to future scientific progress, but also to computer science's viability as an objective epistemology.

The Failure of Computer Science

Science is truth-tropic because of open criticism. In the realm of computing, free software provides and protects openness, not only through community-wide criticism but also through its challenge to the very idea of "intellectual property." These practices, contrary to the constraints of proprietary software, have the effect of making public the scientific knowledge embedded in software. Contemporary computer science fails to meet most standards for objectivity in the sciences (Longino 1990), yet it carries the potential to become a strongly objective science, the publicly practiced discipline exemplified by the free software community.

The requirement that an objective science must provide recognized avenues of criticism is only partially met by a world in which proprietary code is so prevalent. While the discipline of computer science is equipped with all the requisite institutions for public criticism, such as peer-reviewed conferences and journals, practitioners who trade in closed code only participate in limited fashion. There is no avenue of criticism for closed code other than private code review among a small group of developers. Corporations or university researchers who work with or produce proprietary software may release research reports, but they provide little knowledge of the inner workings of their code: problem-solving techniques implemented in closed code are not subject to the critique of the entire community. Using closed code is akin to the deliberate obfuscation of research so as to avoid critique, emendation, or poaching: there is no scope for the collective improvement afforded by intersubjective criticism.

Scientific objectivity requires shared principles and values to undergird meaningful discipline-wide discourse. Much of computer science is done in corporate settings, which have their own norms — not necessarily congruent with those of the academy — about the practice of science. If the products of one group within a discipline are not available to the rest, this impoverishes any notion of "scientific community." Google's refusal to publish the code of its proprietary search and indexing algorithms means computer science cannot advance via the study of these algorithms. Indeed, if so little of the knowledge produced within corporate walls is available to the broader scientific community, it may not be accurate to say commercial computing enterprises truly practice the community-wide discipline of "computer science." A discipline is not just a subject matter but also the social structures that sustain it. The distinction could be made explicit by speaking of, for example, Google-CS. Furthermore, communication between universities and corporations is largely devoted to discussions of how universities can keep industry viable by supplying manpower, serving as incubators for projects to be commercialized later, and implementing curricula that will serve industry (Ceruzzi 2003; Noble 1979; Tompkins 1963). It is less clear that corporations respond in any way to academic inputs, calling into question the proposition that corporations and universities meaningfully share norms or values.

Scientific objectivity requires, too, a discipline-wide awareness of critical activity, and, further, that the community inculcate sensitivity to its importance and implement structures to support it. But this requirement seems particularly difficult to satisfy in the computer science community, which is splintered along the corporate-university border. This fracturing of computer science results in a commercial "mission" replacing the discipline's scientific focus. Suggestions for healing this divide are usually restricted to appeals for universities to become more like corporations. In 2006, Association for Computing Machinery (ACM) President Dennis Patterson commented, "There is a huge disconnect between the experience of most professors, who have never worked as professional programmers . . . and the way in which cutting-edge software is written today." In response, a letter to the *Communications of the ACM* titled "To Make CS Relevant, Give It an Industrial Focus" suggested, "Perhaps the profession would help itself eliminate the inbreeding sometimes seen in universities, insisting instead that new faculty be drawn exclusively from industry" (Lozes 2006).

The "Habermasian" requirement for sharing scientific authority among its practitioners suggests a way to "disqualify a community in which a set of assumptions dominates by virtue of the political power of its adherents" (Longino 1990, 78). In computer science, the political power to determine the scientific direction of the discipline flows from the technical and economic power wielded by its dominant commercial members; one significant way in which this power is retained is through the mechanisms of closed code. All authority on closed code rests with its writers and anyone else who has agreed not to disclose its contents. All authority in the matter of Microsoft Word, a software package that must incorporate a vast amount of knowledge in its algorithms, programming techniques, and data structures, rests solely in the hands of its developers, designers, and owners. The determination of which software packages are able to interface with Word is a decision over which Microsoft has sole authority. For the rest of the community, nuanced critiques of Word are only possible at the user level, as we can only observe its features, external form, interface, and behavior. But we have no basis for criticism of flaws in the particulars of its implementation. It is a holy text, beyond reproach and beyond modification. The technical expertise manifest in Word is not disseminated sufficiently for practitioners of the field to learn how it solves technical problems. The closed model thus encourages the creation of an intellectual monopoly in computer science, an artificial scarcity of code that may become the basis of an economic monopoly for its owner. Monopolistic owners of proprietary code then exercise power derived from their domination of the market, introducing inertia by setting impossibly high economic barriers for potential competitors to breach, and forcing conformance by users to their technical standards.

In contrast, free software's structural characteristics imbue it with the potential to dispel authority. In the free software world, authority emerges from merit: the recognition of Richard Stallman's abilities as a programmer is the basis of the respect accorded him; Linus Torvalds remains the final authority on changes to Linux source because of his continued technical prowess. Either of these "wizards" could be displaced, though, as the structures of their community provide no means for them to block the path of a potential usurper.

Closed code adversely affects, too, the objective evaluation of rival hypotheses in computer science. Even if such evaluation were entirely objective, if nonscientific values partly determine the candidacy of these hypotheses, they will play a role in determining which hypotheses are adopted (Okruhlik 1998). We would evaluate scientific theories, then, not against all possible competitors, but against a small number of rival possibilities. If bias or prejudice has prevented some possibilities from being considered at all, then an apparently well-confirmed theory may just be the best of a bad lot. If closed code restricts the evaluation of competitors in the ecology of computer science epistemology, then not all theories compete equally against selection pressures. Closed code, if understood as a hypothesis for a possible solution to a problem, is not subject to refutationist or falsificationist pressures (Popper 1962). When the level of detail for "full disclosure," a standard of "normal" science, is not acceptable, concerns about the decline of objectivity invariably follow.

In discussions of scientific objectivity, "standards" refers to universal epistemic norms. In computer science, "standards" has a precise technical meaning: requirements that undergird some form of interoperation, whether for hardware manufacturing, networked communication or interprogram data exchange. The value of the openness of such standards to the development of computing infrastructure is well documented (Lessig 2000), and is best demonstrated by the Internet, which relies heavily on such standards to codify its fundamental design decisions. Perhaps even more than closed code, proprietary standards can grant disproportionate power to corporations that are able to drive their adoption. When a corporate closed standard is implemented, computing platforms not equipped with it struggle to communicate with machines that are, necessitating time-consuming reverse engineering and reimplementation of the standard. For example, Microsoft's SMB file-sharing protocol was reimplemented, with considerable effort, as the Samba free software package, in order for GNU/Linux machines to able to share files with Windows systems.

Even a supposedly open standard can become effectively closed by deliberate obfuscation: the Microsoft Win32 Applications Programming Interface (API), the public description of how applications must be written to access services provided by the Windows operating systems, "is extraordinarily complex, incompletely specified (indeed, there are numerous inconsistencies between Microsoft's own implementations), poorly documented, and subject to rapid change. As a consequence, the Wine project (an attempt to implement the Win32 API within Linux) has found it very rough going" (Levien 1998).

Closed standards limit the interoperability of diverse computing platforms and protocols. In order for OpenOffice — a free software cross-platform office productivity suite — to be able to open Word documents, developers needed to reverse-engineer the document format used by Microsoft Word. Had the standards describing this file format been openly available, not only would this reduplication of programming effort have been prevented, but a much richer suite of competing and complementary applications might have been available to users. Closed standards create and then conceal incongruence among platforms and systems, analogous to scientific experiments that cannot be verified by independent researchers because their data format is laboratory-specific.

While the Internet community may treat widely used proprietary specifications, "not generally developed in an open fashion . . . and . . . controlled by the vendor, vendors, or organization that produced [them]," as standards, they contrast starkly with Internet Standards, which emerge from a public process applied to "all protocols, procedures, and conventions that are used in or by the Internet" (Bradner 1996). This process, overseen by the Internet Engineering Task Force (IETF), is self-consciously open, encouraging maximum meaningful criticism from a broadly defined community of interest, with the long-term viability of the Internet paramount. There is no barrier to participation; emphasis is placed on garnering comment from all interested parties. Attempting to balance the sometimes-conflicting needs for open discussion and timely adoption, the process is "intended to provide a fair, open, and objective basis for developing, evaluating, and adopting Internet Standards." Draft documents detailing the proposed standard are circulated openly and widely for comments, criticisms, and amendments; any entity, whether an individual, a corporation, or a governmental agency, who identifies as part of "the community" may comment on the proposals. Indeed, "[e]ach distinct version of an Internet standards-related specification" is published as a plain-text document called a "Request For Comments," or RFC; their names speak to the openness of the process. For example, the specification for the formatting of text-only e-mail messages is given in RFC 2822, while specifications for other aspects of the e-mail system, such as transmission, delivery, and other data formats, are given in other RFCs.

In 1997, Microsoft announced that its NT 5.0 operating system (later renamed Windows 2000) would include an implementation of the Kerberos protocol, a network-security protocol developed at MIT in the late 1980s that has seen widespread commercial and academic deployment. The Kerberos specification was published in 1993 as RFC 1910, thus becoming an informal standard.[4] As Ted Ts'o, then leader of Kerberos development at MIT, wrote,

> A lot of excitement was generated by Microsoft's announcement that NT 5.0 would use Kerberos, followed by a lot of controversy when Microsoft announced that it would be adding proprietary extensions to the Kerberos V5 protocol. . . . The original intent of RFC-1510 prohibited what Microsoft was trying to do, but Microsoft found what it claimed to be a loophole in RFC-1510 specification. (Ts'o 1997)

Microsoft had taken advantage of an "optional field" in one of the specified data formats, extending their implementation of the specification in a way that limited interoperability between Windows and non-Windows computers — a result "diametrically contrary to the purpose for which standards, even with optional fields, are developed" (LaSala et al. 2002).

Microsoft drew ire from both commercial and academic sectors. While there was some difference of opinion about Microsoft's intentions regarding the Kerberos protocol — some commentators saw it as an example of Microsoft's strategy to "embrace, extend, and extinguish" competing standards; others saw a legitimate extension of the protocol that took advantage of additional security services provided by Windows servers — the vehemence and duration of the public discussion of these actions illustrate the critical importance of standards and the processes that create them. In 2002, Novell, Inc., commenting on the settlement of the U.S. Department of Justice's 1998 antitrust suit against Microsoft, filed because of the "bundling" of Internet Explorer with Windows, wrote, "by polluting industry standards, such as Java and Kerberos . . . Microsoft can further impede the use and development of competing middleware. Any calls encrypted with Kerberos sent by Microsoft Windows can be read only by other Microsoft Middleware [sic] and not by Novell's middleware. Similarly, Novell's middleware cannot send calls encrypted with Kerberos (the industry standard), because Windows will reject them" (LaSala et al. 2002). Scott Bradner, a technical consultant working with Harvard University, pointed out,

> Now Microsoft has included what it calls Kerberos V5 in Windows 2000. But it is not quite the same as what MIT or the IETF call Kerberos V5, and this is creating a problem. . . . Windows Kerberos clients can only work with Microsoft Kerberos servers and not, for example, the freely available MIT Kerberos server. . . . [T]his would not be a serious issue if Microsoft would openly publish the details of how it is using this field so that MIT and others could add it to their implementations. . . . But the information has not been forthcoming. (Bradner 2000)

Microsoft eventually agreed to publish its standards, but only to readers who agreed to treat them as Microsoft trade secrets. Readers of the Slashdot.org technical forum did not take kindly to this restriction; an anonymous reader posted the Microsoft specifications, resulting in legal threats against Slashdot from Microsoft.

Computer Science Pedagogy

The relationship between the university and the corporation contributes to the financial viability of the university while serving corporate ends: corporations support universities by funding both the production of well-trained personnel for the corporation, where this training involves both content and socialization into corporate paradigms, and the production of scientific knowledge to be monetized by the corporate sector. This relationship is a fundamentally asymmetrical one: "academic" computer science remains open to the corporate sector, while "corporate" computer science is closed off to the academic community. Corporations exert pressure on curricular and pedagogical decision-making, but they steadfastly refuse to make the fruits of their innovation and knowledge available for pedagogical purposes. This has two pernicious effects: damage is done to the teaching of computer science, and, through the increasingly close interweaving between computer science and other sciences, the character of these other sciences alters for the worse.

In this context, the prevalence of commercial computer science exerts particular pressures on the academy: when investors are optimistic about technology, computer science departments see increases in both public and private funding, in undergraduate and graduate enrollment, and in faculty hiring. Sciences such as physics, which continue to be practiced primarily in university and government labs, are much less sensitive to corporate fortunes. Student enrollment trends provide an illustration of this contrast: the number of first-year graduate students studying physics at U.S. universities peaked at over 4,000 in 1965, and since 1970 has slowly fluctuated around 3,000 (Mulvey and Nicholson 2005); graduate enrollment in the computer sciences more than doubled from 1983 to 2001, with a dramatic increase in the late 1990s, most likely because of the explosion of the Internet and the economic opportunities it presented (National Science Board 2004); after the dot-com bust, enrollment fell off.

These market forces also feature in the determination of computer science curricula: if traffic on the ACM's Special Interest Group on Computer Science Education mailing lists is an accurate indicator, computer science departments in the United States spend much time debating curricular changes that might reflect the changing job market. What corporations find valuable in conducting their business invariably becomes hot technology, the critical need-to-know material: computer scientists spend considerable hours developing and teaching classes to train new users of successful commercial software.

More important, sensitivity to the corporate presence in computer science engenders a particular discursive model about the structure of the discipline, creating an artificial dichotomy between theory and application: theoretical computer science, with little obvious application in the workplace, often has to defend its position in undergraduate curricula. This pressure creates a sensibility within computer science departments that their primary mission is vocational, rather than scientific, training. By contrast, there is little question among physicists of the utility of requiring a two-semester sequence in statics and dynamics, despite the scarcity of jobs involving rolling balls down inclined planes.

The close relationship between computer science and industry is grounded in the structure of the long association between industrialized science and the academy:

> The content of the education had to provide the training necessary for technical work, especially for the early years of employment; it had to instill in the student a sense of corporate responsibility, teamwork, service, and loyalty; and it had to provide the fundamental training in the social sciences and humanities which was increasingly being perceived as the key to effective management. . . . In effect [corporate education programs such as GE's Test Course] were the pilot programs in personnel development and management which would transform American higher education in the decades to follow. (Noble 1979, 170, 174)

Students entering a computer science program are often already aware — and quickly become so if they are not — of the significance of commercialized computer science, not only as a career destination but also as a quality that infuses the educational experience. Labs named after corporate donors remind the student that money flows from industry to fund research; business incubator projects remind her that scientific projects often reach maturity only in the corporate sector; the roll call of computer science luminaries is populated equally by individual giants and corporate heavyweights; internships at corporate software houses provide all the socialization of an apprenticeship; "the problem of software piracy" is treated extensively in professional ethics courses; the student comes to learn that "the real world" is synonymous with the corporate sector.

The student accepts the political economy of computer science and the industrial compulsions for the lack of objectivity in his science. Corporate paradigms make their way back into the university; underlying them is the traditional corporate approach to making software proprietary. Most simply, closed code is treated as the norm; free software may not even appear in the undergraduate sequence. Many applications, such as Microsoft's Visual Studio, used specifically by computer science students, are closed; the student becomes familiarized with the idea that these products are "black boxes" whose innards cannot be the subject of investigation and study, much less modification and improvement. It becomes a matter of fact that industrial codebases — some of the highest accomplishments of the discipline — are not available to be taught and learned from. Many computer scientists are thus educated into the proprietary paradigm — it is how they learn to stop worrying and love closed code.

The impoverishment of computer science pedagogy by closed code is most apparent when we consider source code corpora as the textbook of computer science. Studying the works of past masters is a crucial element of learning any craft:

> Benjamin Franklin learned to write by summarizing the points in the essays of Addison and Steele and then trying to reproduce them. . . . Hackers, likewise, can learn to program by looking at good programs—not just at what they do, but at the source code. One of the less publicized benefits of the open source movement is that it has made it easier to learn to program. When I learned to program, we had to rely mostly on examples in books. The one big chunk of code available then was Unix, but even this was not open source. Most of the people who read the source read it in illicit photocopies of John Lions' book. (Graham 2000, 26–27)

Lions's famous commentary on Unix source code follows an ancient tradition of making difficult texts accessible: the book contains the source code of the sixth version of the Unix kernel, organized for presentation and accompanied by Lions's annotations, which have the intent of making the code-reading experience pedagogically useful (Lions 1977). This utility is reflected by its place in computer science legend, which holds it is the most-copied book in computer science.

Lions's book became illegal when AT&T changed the licensing terms of Version 7 of Unix; this change of license had a direct impact on curriculum as well.

> When AT&T released Version 7, it began to realize that UNIX was a valuable commercial product, so it issued Version 7 with a license that prohibited the source code from being studied in courses, in order to avoid endangering its status as a trade

secret. Many universities complied by simply dropping the study of UNIX, and teaching only theory. (Tanenbaum 1987)

Andrew Tanenbaum's response to this was to develop and release a stripped-down form of Unix, called Minix, which quickly became a staple of many operating-systems courses and served as the foundation for the embryonic Linux project (Tanenbaum 1987). One of the particular advantages of Tanenbaum's Minix code is that it is distributed not only as text but also on disks, allowing students the easy opportunity to experiment with modifying the code: by manipulating concrete implementations of abstract data structures, algorithms, and design philosophies, students are able to participate in one of the most important relationships in computer science — that between abstraction and implementation.

But perhaps writing code is just the engineering aspect of computer science with no relevance to it qua science; perhaps what is important is simply the functional characteristics of the code along with the highest-level implementation details. The problem with this perspective is that writing software is not exclusive of solving scientific problems. While the scientific community might have access to high-level descriptions of proprietary solutions to these problems, prospects for further scientific innovation are severely limited by the lack of implementation details. Corporate white papers might, in the best case, describe the data structures, algorithms, and programming languages used, the hardware platform employed, and the testing and debugging techniques and tools that ensure the quality of the final product. But without the means to replicate the experiment, these details are only nominally useful. Source code is a fundamental requirement of scientific study and communication, as was made clear in the *amicus curiae* brief in the DeCSS case. The *amici*, discussing Ronald Rivest's published description of his MD5 cryptographic algorithm, observed that,

> Dr. Rivest uses a mixture of code and English to describe the algorithm and what it does. Then, at the end, he sets forth the full source code for the algorithm. The reason is simple: Dr. Rivest could have spoken forever about the algorithm, but obviously the best way to see if it does what he believed to be the case is to run the code, test it, probe for weaknesses, determine if strengths can be added and so forth. This simply cannot be done without access to the full code. Further, for those who can read code fluently, the code itself is a precise description of what is intended, more than any amount of English. Whether the code is for a cryptographic algorithm or a macroeconomics model, the ability to communicate in code helps to best promote the progress of science and the useful arts. Interfering with the ability of academics and professionals to speak freely in code will chill scientific discourse and force the risk-averse to communicate in a less-preferred form. (Tyre 2001)

Codebases for commercial products, then, are plausibly viewed as elements of the corpus of scientific knowledge, and their inaccessibility via proprietary control ensures that students of the discipline cannot benefit from them.

The structure of the academic research project RoboCup[5] further exemplifies the importance of source code to scientific inquiry. The RoboCup Federation is an international effort to solve many challenging problems of robotics through a focus on the goal of creating, by 2050, a team of robots capable of defeating a team of humans in a soccer match. Researchers test their implementations at highly competitive RoboCup tournaments; on the completion of each tournament, all teams make their source code publicly available. The sharing of source facilitates innovation by ensuring that every detail of every solution is openly shared.

Peer Review

Free software and current scientific practice share a reliance on peer review to help ensure that results are of the highest possible objective quality. Peer review's role in science was formalized in the eighteenth century, when the Royal Society of London's "Committee on Papers" was granted the power to "solicit expert opinions." Peer review became an indispensable part of scientific practice due to the sharp increase in scientific work after the Second World War (Drummond 2003). Just as the increased complexity of science, due to its increasingly mathematical nature, required scientists to conduct peer review in the era of patron-funded science during the Renaissance, the increase in both variety of disciplines and volume of submissions drove formerly self-reliant journal editorial boards to seek larger pools of reviewers.

But peer review, especially its anonymous variant, might not improve the rigor of the review process and thus not adequately facilitate objectivity (van Rooyen et al. 1999). Instead, anonymous peer review might act as a damper on innovation, by placing guardians at the gates to science: paradigms remain unchallenged as the authority of powerful scientists remains unquestioned (Horrobin 1990). The discipline of computer science is not immune to these problems; anecdotal evidence seems to suggest that practitioners are disgruntled about this process. Anonymous critique of papers, they point out, results in a familiar attendance list at premier academic conferences.

But a more serious charge can be leveled against anonymous peer review: it provides no guarantee of the quality of published work (Horrobin 1990, 1996, 1981). An examination (Rothwell and Martyn 2000) of the correlation among reviewers' evaluations of submissions to neuroscience journals and conferences revealed that

> For one journal, the relationships among the reviewers' opinions were no better than that obtained by chance. For the other journal, the relationship was only fractionally better. For the meeting abstracts, the content of the abstract accounted for only about 10 to 20 percent of the variance in opinion of referees, and other factors accounted for 80 to 90 percent of the variance. (Horrobin 2001)

It is difficult to value this form of peer review when little distinguishes it from arbitrary selection.

Responding to these concerns, several eminent journals, such as the *British Medical Journal* and *Nature*, are moving toward systems of "open peer review," with the identity of reviewers made available to authors. More ambitious is the notion that the entire scientific community participate in peer review. The *arxiv* digital repository at Cornell University makes available preprints of scientific papers (Ginsparg 2003) and potentially undergirds open systems of peer review, such as the "dynamical peer review" system implemented at naboj.com.

Similarly, free software is open for review by any interested programmer; code archives such as sourceforge.net and freshmeat.net facilitate this process. At these sites, frequency of downloads suggests the software's breadth of use, in turn a measure of its acceptance by the community. This acceptance is also indicated by the active improvement of the code by its development community. The free software model meets the normative expectations of open peer review facilitated by ubiquitous communication:

> [A]uthors should be free to publish their results and conclusions provided that they are presented in a technically correct manner . . . colleagues should be free to pub-lish their criticisms and derive any credit that may be due for innovative comments, and for exposing themselves to debate. The introduction of electronic means of communication makes possible this ideal of free exchange of scientific informa-tion. (Henneberg 1997)

The content-neutral, end-to-end nature of the Internet's protocols facilitates trans-parent peer review within the free software community and is integral to the objectivity of the review process.

The concerns about the breakdown of peer review in science represent not a failure of scientific objectivity but rather an introspective examination by sci-entists of the soundness of their disciplinary protocols. A good peer-review sys-tem is one that contributes to the right kind of ecology of ideas: one in which good ideas flourish. In the context of code, such an ecology should eventually and purposefully drive out bad code. Yet bad code does persist in free software projects: for example, the code in Linux's Address Resolution Protocol (ARP) modules, which is crucial networking code, is poorly designed and implemented, and similar failures have been identified in the Linux kernel (Rusovan, Lawford, and Parnas 2005; Hissam et al.). Other systematic studies of free software suggest that free software may be significantly better with respect to some metrics (Delio 2004). These studies illuminate the most salient difference between free and pro-prietary software: free software can be openly inspected and criticized, espe-cially by academics conducting comparative analyses of software development models. While most of us are unable to inspect the quality of proprietary code, we are nonetheless exposed to its failings in the forms of code bloat, poor usability, and unexpected terminations. Proponents of proprietary-software models claim that it is exactly their latitude to ignore desires of the community, which may be based on old paradigms, that allows them to innovate rapidly and effectively (Graham 2000). But free software thrives because user needs are not met by proprietary applications: privileging innovation over the satisfaction of user needs is a double-edged sword.

Peer review in free software is akin to the critical commentary to which alert readers subject newly published work. While many academics are content simply to have their papers published, many others eagerly await comments from peers and students, frequently engaging in correspondence that often results in clarification, further innovation, and new collaboration. Such exchanges are commonplaces in, if not constitutive of, the free software development model. Free software peer review is often much more than passive critical commentary: it can be proactive bug-fixing, suggestions for new features, or even draft implementations of these features. Furthermore, because software has a functional aspect, it is possible to use objective benchmarks to assess software quality with respect to desired capabilities and tractability requirements. It is implausible that working code — free of major bugs, not error-prone, functional, tested and substantially correct — could be rejected. When "working" code is rejected, it is typically due to its failure to meet its specifications.

The free software peer-review model unavoidably holds the potential that, just as in science, "guardians of the gate" may come to abuse their power either by ignoring suggestions and improvements to their code or by publicly castigating projects or their developers. But they in turn may be subject to such castigation; the openness goes both ways. Due to the very nature of free software, the original designer is free to "drop the patches on the floor," but if someone disagrees with the direction of a particular project, or is unhappy with its management, they are free to start their own fork of the project. As the short-lived VGER fork of Linux and the experimental EGCS fork of GCC show, reputation is transient, and depends not only on the continual production of good code but also on steady responsiveness to the concerns of the community.

Free Software and Science

The institutional practices of free software are not only significant for computer science but also crucial for science as a whole. As science becomes increasingly "informationalized," the products of computer science come to play an increasingly important role in its inquiries. Much experimental data is stored on computers; many investigations proceed by writing programs for simulations, equipment control, and mining of large data sets; scientific publication utilizes computerized facilities for writing, editing, and dissemination; many disciplines have specialized applications such as mathematical automated proof techniques or robotic spacecraft. As science relies increasingly on computing to underwrite its activities, scientific practice increasingly depends on the conduct of computer science.[6]

As computer science is compromised by closed software, standards, and proto-cols, computing-intensive sciences become cluttered with tools that cannot be adapted by their users.

The threat to scientific institutions from proprietary pressures is part of the folklore of free software: MIT's AI Lab was gutted to provide commercial-soft-ware companies with assets in the form of personnel, while Richard Stallman's struggles with the MIT AI lab printer are easily understood as those of a scientist stymied in his efforts to extend the functionality of lab equipment. Free-software programmers then realized their community needed protection, such as that pro-vided by the GPL, in order to ensure that the fruits of their labors could not be arbitrarily monetized. Unfortunately, "There are very few scientists who realize something similar about science. There is as of yet no such thing as 'Free Science'" (Kelty 2001). Free software is both staffed and funded significantly by institutions of scientific research, including "national science funding agencies, university operating budgets, royal academies, government funding agencies and research labs, industrial R&D labs and non-profit research organizations, governmental and non-governmental science agencies, and private research and development institutes" (Kelty 2001). Thus, the prescription that free software come to under-write science today, that it nourish scientific institutions, is a logical closure of the circle: "If we ask where free software flourished in the period from 1984 to the present, then the answer is: as part of the institutions of science" (Kelty 2001).

The closing of information in response to commercial pressures is not unique to computer science, though computer science is the bellwether. The case of genet-ically modified seeds — a commercial imperative touted as a scientific advance — provides a close analogy to the opposition between free and proprietary soft-ware (Lewontin 1991). Hybrid corn is advertised as having brought inexpensive nourishment to vast portions of the world population through enormous gains in agricultural productivity. The grain, however, lacks a feature traditionally crucial to farmers' economic viability: it is not self-reproducing. Seeds harvested from the hybrid crop have much lower yields than the parents' seeds; hence, the farmer must purchase a new batch of hybrid seeds every year. This characteristic is a deliberate design decision by the seed producers: it is a copy-protection scheme. Shull and East described the significance of this genetic modification in terms of political economy:

> It is the first time in agricultural history that a seedsman is enabled to gain the full
> benefit from a desirable origination of his own or something that he has purchased.
> . . . [T]he man who originates a new plant which may be of incalculable benefit to
> the country gets nothing — not even fame — for his pains and the plant can be
> propagated by anyone. (East and Jones 1919) quoted in (Lewontin 1991)

This sentiment is precisely that expressed by Bill Gates in his letter to the Homebrew Club: the "natural" state is not conducive to the industry's economic viability, and new ways must be, and are being, found. Lewontin makes this analogy explicit:

This is the problem of copy protection that also exists for computer software programs. The developer of computer software will be unwilling to devote time, energy and money to developing a new program, if the first purchasers can copy it and pass it around to their friends for virtually nothing. (Lewontin 1991, 55)

Toward "Open Computer Science"

A computer science based on open code, protocols, and standards promises a reconfiguration of research, industry, and pedagogy, ameliorating the effects of the current entanglement of the academic and corporate sectors on the practice of the science. Universities and commercial vendors could become true partners, with the innovative capabilities of both equally available to the other. Universities dream of being technology incubators; these could take the shape of consortia modeled on the Apache Software Foundation, drawing partners from multiple sources. The availability of previously closed code could infuse teaching and research with new knowledge, as huge bodies of code, currently hidden from the curious, became available for inspection and modification. As a previously closed science opened its textbooks, experimental manuals, and lab notes, we would gain access to new facts, practices, theories, paradigms, and epistemologies. The resulting wave of innovation would benefit not only computer science but also scientists in other disciplines, commercial users, and citizens: the creative expression of closed-code programmers would finally be on display.[7]

Open computer science would bring the discipline closer to meeting the requirements for an objective science (Longino 1990). Opportunities for public intersubjective criticism would be much broader as open code is predicated on vigorous critical activity: "the greater the number of different points of view included in a given community, the more likely it is that its scientific practice will be objective" (Longino 1990, 184). The very act of merging open and formerly closed code would require the development of shared technical standards and norms. This sharing of standards and values and, thereby the reworking of the university–industrial relationship, would give meaning to talk of "the community of computer scientists." The meritocratic structure so familiar to the free software development world would support a more equitable distribution of intellectual authority. The opening of code would bring with it a greater role for the Internet in distributing results and facilitating communication among computer scientists as "Heterogenous computer networks . . . provide the possibility for a kind of peer-review that precedes, and occasionally bypasses . . . the existing, trusted, and well-known peer-review of scientific journals and societies" (Kelty 2001). In this setting, knowledge, no longer under exclusive control to support the extraction of monopoly rent, would gain in value with its increasing availability.

The discipline we describe resembles the fledgling computer science of the 1950s and 1960s, which, because of a dramatic change in its political economy during the 1970s, moved toward a proprietary economy that free software counters. The safeguarding of this potentially objective sphere for the practice of computer science might take inspiration from strong free-software licensing schemes such as the GPL, as its practitioners' endeavors would be available to all under conditions of reciprocity.

Closed software is a fundamental negation of the social character of computer science. Free software reminds us that the political economy of science must not be limited only to the consideration of efficient allocation of scarce resources; it must also address the fundamental principles by which a technologized society should be organized (Kelty 2005). For economic reasons, computer science is currently looking past — indeed, defending — practices that stifle innovation. If economic arguments are used to support bad science and attack potentially reformatory practices, then the science is not easily distinguished from an astrology whose practitioners concoct fantasies for a fee.

Computer science is a young science fumbling toward maturity. But it is a science whose importance, both to other sciences and to society, cannot be overstated. At this juncture, it must undergo the reformation that the natural sciences underwent in the Enlightenment. The proponents of the proprietary software system claim an economic imperative for its indispensability. Were this imperative to be disobeyed, the claim goes, the industry would not survive in its current form. The discipline's wholesale acceptance of this argument points to an alarming indifference to the loss of objectivity that it entails.

A science's claims to objectivity ring hollow if commercial viability is a more desirable objective, as industrialized science ultimately must leave its mark on the academy: "A purely commercial interest has so successfully clothed itself in the claims of pure science that those claims are now taught as scientific gospel. . . . [W]hat appears under the mystical guise of pure science and objective knowledge about nature turns out, underneath, to be political, economic and social ideology (Lewontin 1991, 57)."

Computer science increasingly relies on its private corporate patrons who apply their own closed systems of peer review and criticism, with occasional results thrown over the wall. The closed walls of Redmond or Mountain View enable old-fashioned patronage of nature's secrets. The objectivity and scientific status of computer science is a chimera: we cannot stand on the shoulders of giants in computer science, for they simply refuse to let us.

5

Free Software and the Political Philosophy of the Cyborg World

"We are all chimeras, theorized and fabricated hybrids of machine and organism . . . we are cyborgs. This cyborg is our ontology; it gives us our politics."

— Donna Haraway (Haraway 1991, 151)

"What are the terms for living together in the New World Order? Who will find which terms to be livable? And What is to be done?"

— Donna Haraway (Haraway 1995, xii)

Software's philosophical implications are not only social and political but also metaphysical. Code channels human ingenuity and intention to produce a new, hybrid world — the cyborg world. It both creates and destroys distinctions, reworking our ontologies and therefore necessitating a revision of our politics. Code may both advance and counteract political imperatives: in this context, free software is not just a question of managing technology but of determining the contours of our selves and the politics we choose. Technology and politics become inseparable when technologized entities are political actors and objects of our political philosophy. A new political philosophy for this technological age must reflect the blurring of boundaries, and the new obscurities, that technology induces. The liberatory potential of free software lies in its potential to address both these effects.

Implicit in our discussions of business and science, ethics and politics, is another realm:

A science fiction writer coined the useful term "cyberspace" in 1982. But the territory in question, the electronic frontier, is about a hundred and thirty years old. Cyberspace is the "place" where a telephone conversation appears to occur. Not inside your actual phone, the plastic device on your desk. Not inside the other person's phone, in some other city. *The place between* the phones. The indefinite place *out there*, where the two of you, two human beings, actually meet and communicate. (Sterling 1994)

The elsewhereness of cyberspace promises escape; its lack of essential nature or telos inspires wistful theorizing, speculation about the form and nature of its culture, laws, and politics. To wit, it is "a new frontier of civilization, a digital domain that could and would bring down big business, foster democratic participation, and end economic and social inequities" (Silver 2000). Most of all, the projections of desired states onto this space reflect a weariness with political struggle and an optimism about technology's ability to create new political spaces, impervious to "outside" pressures, for the exercise of individual freedom. Cyberspace is, however, a plastic space: while its original design arguably facilitated this freedom, there is no reason to believe these features will exist in perpetuity. Other spaces — physical, economic, technical, social, historical — supervene on cyberspace; its independence is a mirage. The denizens of this hybrid realm are hybrid creatures, assemblages of biological and technological organization: cyborgs.

Cyborgs, Cyberspace, and the Cyborg World

A cyborg is a creature "of social reality as well as a creature of fiction" (Haraway 1991, 150). A term coined in the early days of the space race, with an eye toward manned exploration of alien terrain, "cyborg" describes a biological entity that "deliberately incorporates exogenous components extending the self-regulating control function of the organism in order to adapt it to new environments" (Clynes and Kline 1960). While the term originally referred to supplementing human astronauts with life-support and communication systems, today its application is more ubiquitous. Cyborgs wear glasses, use electronic pacemakers, communicate wirelessly, shop online, have credit card applications evaluated by software agents, are policed by digital eyes, and write code to change the behavior of machines that work with, for, and against them. Cyborgs are a "melding of the organic and the mechanic, or the engineering of a union between separate organic systems . . . human cyborgs range from the quadriplegic patient totally dependent on a vast array of high-tech equipment to a small child with one immunization" (Gray, Mentor, and Figueroa-Sarriera 1995, 2–4). Their world is populated with technology and flesh, demarcated by the inevitably porous boundary of organic and machinic. Cyborgs offer one avenue for theorizing the relationship between the bodies and digitality, for exploring the extent of the cleavage between our bodies and our environment. Neither our mental nor our physical aspects carve out a unique niche for us: as Marvin Minsky suggested, we may well be meat machines.

But, more broadly, our increasingly technologized understanding of ourselves provokes theoretical challenges to the notion of machines as distinct from humans and nature. In these, the human, the machinic, and the natural unify: "There is no such thing as either man or nature now, only a process . . . that . . . couples the machines together. . . . [M]an and nature are not like two opposite terms confronting each other . . . rather, they are one and the same essential reality" (Deleuze and Guattari 1983, 2–5). Machines, then, are, "indissociable human extensions (an extended phenotype)" (Haraway 1995, xvii), demonstrating that humans and nature are one.

Haraway and Deleuze and Guattari stress the sociopolitical, potentially dystopic, implications of the breakdown of the mechanic/organic boundary. This theorizing implicitly critiques celebrations of the irrelevance of the materiality of information. These "regime[s] of computation" (Wolfram 2002; Fredkin 2001; Morowitz 2002) provide

> a narrative that accounts for the evolution of the universe, life, mind and mind reflecting on mind by connecting these emergences with computational processes that operate both in human-created simulations and in the universe understood as software running on the "Universal Computer" we call reality. This is the larger context in which code acquires special, indeed universal significance. In the Regime of Computation, code is understood as the discourse system that mirrors what happens in nature and that generates nature itself. (Hayles 2005, 33)

In such a picture, "code is elevated to the lingua franca not only of computers but of all physical reality" (Hayles 2005, 15). Code comes to play a constitutive role of "subjectivity through bits," allowing us to anticipate a future in which "code (a synecdoche for information) has become so fundamental that it may be regarded as ontological" (Hayles 2005, 21). While such triumphalism predicts the ascendance of code, the cyborg future requires us to investigate how this code is controlled.

The "Regime of Computation," cyborg theory, artificial intelligence, Deleuze and Guattari's machinic thesis, and Lovelock's Gaia thesis (Lovelock 1979) all seek to break down boundaries between the biological and the technological, between the organic and the synthetic: they are fundamentally concerned with the relationship between organization and physical substrate. Rather than stop at superficial differences in physicality, we can investigate commonalities or discontinuities in the code: the substrate becomes irrelevant and the informational architecture becomes the object of scrutiny. The historiography of theories of personal identity reveals a strong intuition for the irrelevance of the physical body, with the informational content of the self, occasionally called soul or ego, located in memory or personality. Artificial intelligence reinforces such notions: the multiple realizability thesis of mind, that cognition is independent of its material substrate, entails that to "make a brain," we need only instantiate the right kind of code.

The materiality of computers is animated by, filled with information by, the running code of programs. Early talk of "electronic brains" both reflected and prompted optimism about the project of "artificial intelligence." When machines and tools only approximated or augmented human functions, our felt connections to them remained superficial; their animation by code sparked dreams not only of machine intelligence but also of brotherhood. The line from the cybernetic imagination of Norbert Wiener to speculations of humans' postbiological future is direct. Computers signify that we may regain unity with that from which we were sundered by our insistence on a uniquely human consciousness. In this Hegelian self-realization, when we know we are not the center of the universe, do not live in absolute space and time, do not know our own minds, we understand our bodies as just one kind of physical entity that may be animated (Mazlish 1993). The wheel has come full circle — once humans were called computers (Grier 2005), and now computers meld with humans.

The hypothesis of the extended mind, inspired by the Vygotskian idea that thinking is not confined to the individual brain, posits human cognition as distributed over and through its environment (Clark and Chalmers 1998). The description of humans as "natural-born cyborgs" (Clark 2003) suggests that the extension and enhancement of the physical body by tools and prosthetic devices renders vague the boundaries of the body. Together, these theses displace the notion of persons confined by bags of skin; instead we merge with the external world through technology. The self, then, is a "coalition of biological and non-biological elements, whose membership shifts and alters over time and between contexts" (Clark 2006).

The dominant form of technological augmentation is the computing device: our cyborg selves are not just any old man–machine hybrid but a new entity that blends the physical and the informational. Human behavior emerges from the interaction of different components of its technologically enhanced cognitive environment. While human agency still exists, it is "distributed and largely unconscious, or at least a-conscious." This perspective of the human as intelligent machine allows us to view the human self as just one of many "easily spliced . . . distributed cognitive systems" in which intelligence inheres equally in the human, in the machinic infrastructure, and in the interface between the two (Borgmann and Hayles 1999). The human use of any sufficiently advanced technology must rely on cyborgian decision-making. The experimental X-29 fighter jet, for example, used for experimental verification of advanced aeronautical engineering designs that created aerodynamic instability, was unsuitable for operation by a human alone and relied on supplemental operation by computer: thus, human agency and decision-making were blurred by nonhuman agents.[1]

These distributed environments for cognition, while enhancing human cognitive function, raise the possibility that we might not control the parameters of our interactions with them. If cyborg intelligence resides partially in its human component and partially in the machine component, then code becomes a subject of inquiry into the distributed self, and provokes questions about its control. The worry that we surrender decision making to our cognitive extensions is not idle Luddite speculation. It is the real fear of becoming passive recipients of opaque technology. Questions of technology are no longer external to us: to inquire into the nature, shape, form and control of technology is to inquire into our selves. Those to whom we grant this control are those to whom we vouchsafe control of our selves.

While the cyborg can be understood literally as the prosthetic enhancement of the body, it is also a useful metaphor for the transformation of human activity by technology. Spaces formerly partitioned by the organic/synthetic distinction are now populated by "hybrid objects produced by a collaboration between nature and culture — genetically engineered plants and animals, . . . humans with cybernetic implants and explants" (Borgmann and Hayles 1999). But because human production of hybrids and hybridized environments is not new, we need to recast old questions of their ecology in the context of new technologies (Borgmann and Hayles 1999).

In a world in which computer technology infiltrates all interactions with the physical world, when its prosthetic enhancements become ubiquitous, our world is no longer a physical one populated by cyborgs, but is itself a cyborg world. In the cyborg world, humans and machines commingle, a merger enabled and governed by software. This interaction, ranging from mundane uses of computers for personal productivity to networking, from e-government to computer prosthetics, to our saturation by the informational content of media, is in part determined and limited by the abilities of the machine, which are in turn determined by its software. Software, the machines on which it runs, and the humans that use it, create the cyborg world.

As the cyborg displaces man/machine dualism, the cyborg world dissolves the dichotomy of physical space and cyberspace. Cyberspace is sometimes treated as vastly different in both its being and its attributes:

> It is . . . more volatile and less stable than our physical world, reflecting a different sense of time and duration. . . . A different relationship with time and space is at the heart of what is novel about cyberspace. . . . The role of software . . . is to remove constraints of time and space. . . . [T]he computer goes far beyond any other technology in removing such limits . . . in cyberspace the principles of ordinary space and time, can . . . be violated with impunity. . . . [W]hy have cyberspace if we cannot (apparently) bend nature's rules there? (Katsh 1996)

The projected separateness of cyberspace enables optimistic theoretical views of it as beyond requiring full social and political protection. But,

> Although it is not exactly "real," "cyberspace" is a genuine place. Things happen there that have very genuine consequences. This "place" is not "real," but it is serious, it is earnest. . . .

> Politics has entered cyberspace. Where people go, politics follow. (Sterling 1994)

But when we *are* machines rather than only their users, when our interactions with others are modulated by this shared space, when all is interface, cyberspace is not elsewhere. As cyberspace fully interpenetrates the real world, questions about a suitable politics for cyberspace, and its relationship to the politics of physical space, are replaced by questions of the politics of the cyborg world. To devise an appropriate normative political philosophy for the cyborg world, we need not turn away from the physical world to study cyberspace; rather, we must focus on the world in which man and machine have blended. The political philosopher's first task is to uncover the roots of power in this world.

The Cyborg Body Politic

[The] real, non-corporeal soul is not a substance; it is the element in which are articulated the effects of a certain type of power and the reference of a certain type of knowledge, the machinery by which the power relations give rise to a possible corpus of knowledge, and knowledge extends and reinforces the effects of this power. . . . The soul is the effect and instrument of a political anatomy. (Foucault 1977, 29–30) cited by (Gray and Mentor 1995)

Today, the "effect" and the political "instrument" are the control system — cybernetic, informatic, defining, determining. Information, impatterned and wild, is the very context of life as well as the simulacra of essence, whether it is called consciousness, personality, individuality or a unique cognitive system. Having machines, or seeing oneself as a machine, is one thing. Controlling machines, and oneself is another. . . . [T]he machine was triumphant for awhile, before giving way to the system. It is a whole system we are caught in and are part of, organic and machinic. We cannot destroy it without destroying ourselves, but we can reconfigure it, if we understand it, and if we try. (Gray and Mentor 1995, 221)

In the cyborg world, the nature and mode of politics is cyborgian, as political institutions such as nation-states are complex assemblages of human and nonhuman actors, both technological and natural, linked by material and social networks to "the rest of the polities and other forms of life of the Earth." We live in control societies, where "networked bodies are inscribed by . . . bio-informatic networks producing the conditions of experience" (Thacker 2004, xix–xx).

The key to unlocking the modern nation-state, this vast assemblage of political and technical power, lies in its code:

The burden of Hobbes' introduction to Leviathan is to show how to read the text of the body politic. Hobbes chides those whose notion of political reading consists of gossip and censure; instead, he advises, "*Nosce teipsum*; Read thy self." . . . The only way to understand this strange machine-body of the State is to read the actual machine-body of the human being. . . . How can or ought the state work? What controls the automaton or machine and how might one decipher this control? (Gray and Mentor 1995, 221)

The act of reading such a machine-body enables us to understand the constitution of the machinic state. When the state resides in machines, we may decipher its meanings by reading its code. As legal and machine architectures mutually inscribe each other, "the invasion of the body [both human, corporate and that of the state] by discourses of science and politics . . . accelerate[s] beyond all imagination" (Gray and Mentor 1995, 222).

The film *Tron* is not just a cult classic; it illustrates, literally and metaphorically, the merger of man, machine, and politics:

> FLYNN: It's time I levelled with you, Tron. I'm a — well, I'm what you guys call a User.
>
> TRON: But — if you're a User — then everything you've done has been part of a plan . . .
>
> FLYNN: You wish . . . Look, you guys know how it is. You just keep doin' what it looks like you're supposed to, even if it seems crazy, and you hope to hell your User knows what's goin' on.
>
> TRON: Well — that's how it is for programs, yes, but —
>
> FLYNN: I hate to disappoint you, pal, most-the-time, that's how it is for Users, too. (Thacker 2004)

This dialogue highlights the isomorphism of the technological to the sociopolitical. Technical specifications determine not only machine functionality but also our ontological and political view; trajectories of technology are inseparable from those of politics. In this setting, the technopolitical system's control structures become society's code, for "Code is a set of procedures, actions and practices, designed in particular ways to achieve particular ends in particular contexts. Code = Praxis" (Thacker 2004). Code enables protocols for the dissemination and control of information, mechanisms for ensuring the financial and political viability of power structures. In this world, in this age, in this control society, power relationships remain incomprehensible "unless you have understood 'how it works' and 'who it works for'" (Thacker 2004), a comprehension only possible when the system is made to function transparently.

Reading the "text of the body politic" (Gray and Mentor 1995, 221) becomes the decoding of the system's structures of control, as it always has. In the political institutions of days gone by, priests and kings derived authority from texts both sacred and profane. To interrogate these texts and decipher their meanings was to question the grounds of authority and uncover pathways for political change.

Code, Networks, and Forms of Life

Methodologically, the significance of protocols in the cyborg world can be illustrated effectively through example, considering the protocols that drive the Internet, and the software that implements and interacts with them. The fundamental protocols of the Internet are open: their specifications are openly available in the form of Internet Standards. But the applications that depend on these protocols, through which we actually use the Internet, have equal impact on the character of the spaces created by the Internet. They may close off or enhance the freedoms enabled by the lower protocols. "The Internet is not 'open' or 'closed' but above

all a form that is modulated" (Thacker 2004, xx) by protocol and code. By analogy, as political theorists never tire of pointing out, the mere freedom to choose
leaders once every four years means little if other freedoms are traded away. In
the nominally democratic society, one kind of protocol, say, the organization of
elections, can be free, but if other layers are restrained and restricted (e.g., a regulated media or a judiciary hampered by the legislature), the freedom facilitated by
the more fundamental protocol may be dissipated.

The physical structure of the Internet presents a suggestive story about the
concentration of power — it contains "backbones" and "hubs" — but power on the
Internet is not spatial but informational; power inheres in protocol. The techno-
libertarian utopianism associated with the Internet, in the gee-whiz articulations
of the *Wired* crowd, is grounded in an assumption that the novelty of governance
by computer protocols precludes control by corporation or state. But those entities merely needed to understand the residence of power in protocol and to craft
political and technical strategies to exert it. In 2006, U.S. telecommunications
providers sought to impose differential pricing on the provision of Internet services. The coalition of diverse political interests that formed in opposition — to
preserve "Net Neutrality" — demonstrated a widespread awareness that control
over the Net's architecture is control of its politics (The SavetheInternet.com
Coalition 2006).

Code, Sovereignty, and Cyberspace

> But . . . we have the . . . emergence or rather the invention of a new mechanism
> of power possessed of highly specific procedural techniques . . . which is. . . .
> absolutely incompatible with the relations of sovereignty . . . It is a type of power
> which is constantly exercised by means of surveillance rather than in a discontinu-
> ous manner by means of a system of levies or obligations distributed over time.
> . . . It presupposes a tightly knit grid of material coercions rather than the physical
> existence of a sovereign . . . This non-sovereign power, which lies outside the form
> of sovereignty, is disciplinary power. (Foucault 1980)

Adherents of a "catechism of Net inviolability" (Boyle 1997) believe that the
basic architecture of the Net conveys an invisibility that insulates it from traditional applications of state and corporate power. But, as Foucault points out, there
is a difference between a politics that views the relationship of sovereign and citizen as mediated by the sovereign's exertion of state power through the imposition
of rules, and one in which systemic power could be delivered through a diversity
of material or technological pressure points (Boyle 1997). In the latter, the effect
of such "a tightly knit grid of material coercions" (Foucault 1980) is an opaqueness that makes this immanent power more subtle and thus harder to counteract:
"[T]he theory of sovereignty, and the organisation of a legal code centered upon
it, have allowed a system of right to be superimposed upon the mechanism of

discipline in such a way as to conceal its actual procedures" (Foucault 1980, 105). This Foucauldian perspective is especially relevant as an antidote to relentless optimism about the Net; the Net may be invulnerable to traditional modes of control and enforcement, but its architecture provides plenty of avenues for the exertion of state and corporate power.

As the Internet became a trading zone in the mid-1990s, governments were faced with crises of policy induced by the inadequacy of contemporary legal structures and enforcement mechanisms to contend with "[t]he treatment of content, the treatment of personal information, and the preservation of ownership rights" (Reidenberg 1998) within and across national borders that straddled the Internet. This crisis was resolved by the deployment of technological solutions that functioned as legal proxies, as states increasingly called upon the technical power and flexibility of the Net (Rustad 2004). That is, "law and governmental regulation are not the only source of law-making" (Reidenberg 1998).

Code in cyberspace is functionally equivalent to law in society (Lessig 2000). Our personal and social freedoms in this domain are precisely the freedoms granted by software and the protocols it implements. Lessig unpacks this equivalence via a fourfold taxonomy of constraints on human behavior: norms and conventions (social), physical restrictions (architectural), market restrictions (financial), and punitive restrictions (legal). These constraints originated in the physical world, but are now to be found as well on the Internet. Newsgroup members may consider some kinds of dialogue offensive and shun those that indulge in them; software may prevent us from using offensive language in the IRC channel #family; we may not be able to afford broadband Internet access; we may be subject to legal sanction for online exchanges of copyrighted material.

The constraint of law has multiple modalities: it can levy financial penalties, construct norms through the approbation often attached to illegal behaviors, and regulate architecture by, for example, mandating physical access for the disabled. In cyberspace, fundamentally a "software world," reconstruction is a matter of rewriting code:

> If a comparison to the physical world is necessary, one might say that the software designer is the architect, the builder, and the contractor, as well as the interior decorator. Software determines structure as well as appearance. . . . [N]etworks really are what software allows them to be. The Internet is not a network but a set of communications protocols [—software—] that allows information to flow among many different networks. (Katsh 1996)

Because software determines interaction between user and machine, cyberspace is plastic, and is equally amenable to change by governments, criminals, law-abiding citizens, or corporations. Thus, code can function as law even when the laws of the physical world lag behind.

Regulation on the Internet is implemented in both software and hardware, and modulated by local policies: content-filtering software may block child pornography; hardware firewalls may block intruders; the absence of effective legislation against spam is compensated by spam-filtering software and practices (Post 2000). As we will see, the Platform for Internet Content Selection (PICS) was an abortive attempt to use technical means to achieve a socially desirable end, restricting minors' access to pornography, unattainable even through the passage of legislation like the Communications Decency Act (CDA). As the Digital Millennium Copyright Act (DMCA) shows, however, legal and technical policy-making and enforcement can act in concert. Law has merged with architecture.

Thus, through its technological capability, government can impose rules on its citizens; the design choices it makes determine the spaces its citizens inhabit. Governmental policy imperatives are embedded in network designs, standards, and system configurations: the structure of the technical system reveals the exertion of governmental power:

> The creation and implementation of information policy are embedded in network designs and standards as well as in system configurations . . . the set of rules for information flows imposed by technology and communication networks form a *Lex Informatica*. (Reidenberg 1998, 554)

No longer are issues of diplomacy or jurisdictional reach barriers to enforcing the law. States may simply use the "long arm of the code" to implement decisions and policies that can have impact even outside their borders. The infrastructure of the Internet

> empowers the automatic enforcement of policies and decisions. Infrastructure design offers the state an *ex ante* means to assure that policy decisions are enforced. States can require that rules for the treatment of information be embedded within the technical system architecture. By "hard-wiring" particular rules within the infrastructure, states preclude violations and automate the enforcement of public decisions. (Reidenberg 2003–2004, 218)

Much as user interfaces prompt task modifications by users, the government's design can modify its citizens' behaviors as it admonishes, directs, prohibits, and monitors (Katsh 1996). Online instruments such as "electronic borders, electronic blockades and electronic sanctions," built using code and protocols such as "packet interception, viral email, filters and denial of service attacks," might be used by governments to enforce state decisions (Reidenberg 1998, 554). The state may exert its power through technological proxies: attempts to legislate, such as the unsuccessful CDA and the successful DMCA, include language pertaining to enforcement through technology; attempts to impose technical standards, such as the Clipper chip for cryptography and the V-chip for content filtering, burn enforcement regimes into the technology. Through these measures, the government modifies the architectures of cyberspace, of both infrastructure and applications: "The exercise of power is much more a matter of the quotidian shaping and surveillance of activity than of imposing sanctions after the fact" (Boyle 1997).

The government can attempt to "shape code" through regulatory methods such as prohibitions, taxes, liability and copyright law, and disclosure requirements, while leaving "safe harbors" for technology that does not clash with its imperatives (Kesan and Shah 2005). The DMCA provides a new layer of protections for digital content: under its terms, the technical measures taken by content providers to protect copyrighted material are backed up by governmental prohibitions on their circumvention. These provisions, which make it illegal to devise technologies that could bypass or disable content protections, turn the "code is law" metaphor into reality (Lessig 1999). A programmer who writes code capable of decrypting the Content Scramble System is in violation of the law. Even if the program's application is perfectly legitimate, such as the fair use of a legally purchased DVD, the act of writing the program is illegal. This combination of legislation and technology can extend the reach of protective regimes, taking away even those freedoms explicitly provided in copyright law:

> Content providers build code that gives them more control than the law of copyright does over their content. Any effect to disable that control is a crime. Thus the law backs up the content holders' power to control their content more firmly than copyright does. Copyright law gets privatized in code; the law backs this privatized law up; and the result is a radical increase in the control that the content holder has over his content. (Lessig 1999)

The code of a content protection system like CSS is no longer software code but has become legal code as well: "If you build code to crack code then you have violated the US code. . . . Cracking code is to break the law. Code is law" (Lessig 1999). This code grants to its owner the power to control the dissemination and distribution of culture: who gets it and how, who plays it, who hears it, who can share it and how. In the hypertechnical world, control passes to those who wield technical power. This power, if closed off by technological obfuscation, is opaque and beyond challenge. Our only chance for autonomous reactions rests in our ability to view this power. As the hacker's quarterly *2600* pointed out in its editorial on the DeCSS case, "Selling a pirated movie is nothing to them. But telling people how technology works is the real threat" (*2600* 2000).

The story of PICS provides a cautionary tale about the lack of transparency in technological solutions for law enforcement. Responding to the failure of the CDA, "a broad cross-section of companies from the computer, communications, and content industries, as well as trade associations and public interest groups" (Boyle 1997) suggested the architecture of the Net, the application space, could be modified to vacate the need for the CDA. Where bad law, in the shape of the poorly framed CDA, failed, the technical precision of PICS would, they thought, succeed. PICS, which required a filtering system built on top of HTML, reflected the group's conception of "technical solutions as intrinsically more desirable than the exercise of state power by a sovereign, as facilitators of private choice rather than threats of public sanction" (Boyle 1997). PICS specified a language for describing content, such as pornographic images. This language specified the format of content-rating tags that could be embedded within the meta-information provided by a page. Third-party organizations could establish ratings based on these tags, and users could then select which organization's rating scheme they wanted their browser to apply.

The promise of PICS is the provision of a technological fix that does away with the need for legislation that might constrain free speech. But this promise fails for several reasons: content providers may not provide accurate tags, rating organizations become private arbiters of acceptable speech, browsers may come with default ratings settings that could be adjusted only by knowledgeable users. Most important, this technology does not displace regulation but rather provides a new target: where before there was only undifferentiated speech, the regulation of which would quickly clash with the First Amendment, now there are tags and filters, each of which may be independently subject to further regulation. The initial optimism about PICS waned when it became clear it could be "disproportionately used to favour a particular set of ideas and values and exclude others . . . despite the fact that [it is] . . . on its face . . . value neutral" (Boyle 1997).

While PICS offered a solution for the regulation of content at the content-provider end, other means were available at the consumer end. These solutions called for browsers to be equipped with content filters, which could be adjusted by users for sensitivity, by checklists of forbidden words, and so on. But these filters provoke the same questions about control: what if they were hardwired with default values and not easily modifiable? What if government simply made these the target for new regulatory legislation? The usage of content filters revealed a lack of transparency in their application:

> [S]ome programs ban access to newsgroups discussing gay and lesbian issues or topics such as feminism . . . Entire domains are restricted, such as HotWired. Even a web site dedicated to the safe use of fireworks is blocked. All this might be reasonable . . . if parents were actually aware of what the programs banned. But . . . each company holds its database of blocked sites in the highest security. Companies fight for market share based on how well they upgrade and maintain that blocking database. All encrypt that list to protect it from prying eyes. (Boyle 1997)

Though the technologies of the Internet still pose challenges to the exertion of corporate or governmental power, their particular uses may reinforce such power. As illustrated by the Net Neutrality controversy, the political economy of the networked world also locates power in corporations; control of the net can therefore be merely a reinforcement of their corporate imperatives. The control of cyberspace with restrictions implemented in code promises a world in which near-perfect control is possible: the logistic and financial costs associated with legal controls are greatly reduced, and fine-grained tracking ensures effortless supervision. The issue is no longer whether code should regulate. What matters now is a different set of questions: "Does it do so in the open? Is it transparent about its means? Does it advance values that we believe are fundamental?" (Lessig 1999). A political philosophy that will do cyberspace justice must be cognizant of its unique population and the composition, structure, and organization of its politics and communities.

Language in the Cyborg World

The cyborg world is bound together not only by a web of technological artifacts but also by the network of communication linkages within and among cyborgs. The tools that extend our minds are not just technological artifacts but also intangibles such as language, which "provides a manipulative arena which allows operations which complement those of the basic biological brain . . . [making] available concepts, strategies and learning trajectories which are simply not available to individual, un-augmented brains" (Clark 1996). The public nature of language makes possible its use as a cognitive scaffold for individuals and groups alike:

> [T]he expressive power of natural language has been molded by its role as a medium of public, interpersonal exchange. . . . [I]nterpersonal criticism is . . . an integral part of the cooperative use of language to promote so-called collaborative learning. . . . [O]nly a code developed so as to facilitate interpersonal criticism and cooperation would be likely to exhibit the powers of expression, reification and abstraction which subsequently enable the kinds of more sophisticated supra-communicative use. (Clark 1996)

In particular, the use of public language enhances and enriches an individual agent's cognition via interaction with other agents:

> [L]anguage allows ideas to be preserved and to migrate between individuals . . . [which] may allow the communal construction of extremely delicate and difficult intellectual trajectories. . . . [T]he . . . intellectual niches available within a linguistically linked community provides a stunning matrix of possible inter-agent trajectories. . . . [P]ublic language allows human cognition to be collective. (Clark 1996)

This enhancement is dependent on language facilitating the exchange of ideas in a community of intellects capable of inspecting and critiquing them. Language is the medium through which we may represent our own thoughts, making them available for reflection and manipulation (Clark 1998). The ideas generated by an individual agent then become "fixed points capable of attracting and positioning additional intellectual matter" (Clark 1998).

The cognitive development of our extended mind similarly depends on the public language it employs. This language of the cyborg mind is composed of natural and programming languages. Its machine component can be taught to process natural language (Jurafsky and Martin 2000); similarly, biological components of cognition must be able to speak the language of the machine. Software is the determinant of our linguistic interaction with our extended selves, a feature it possesses because *"Code is the only language that is executable . . . .* Code is the first language that actually does what it says — it is a machine for converting meaning into action" (Galloway 2004, 165 emphasis in original).

Whether a particular computing device counts as part of my extended mind depends in part on how the software mediates my interaction with it. If my cell phone is available as a memory store, then the software that regulates my interactions with it is a language I use to integrate my distributed mind. This software determines whether my interactions are pleasing, productive, or infuriating. When we say, "I know the time" as shorthand for "My cell phone has the time and I can retrieve it," we effectively say, "This information is easily accessible in my extended memory." But if it takes three key presses to tell the time, we might not be so inclined to assert this knowledge claim. The options our distributed mind's components provide us not only structure our approach to solving problems, but also sometimes select the problems themselves. The power of the machine to affect what we do is not limited to how we perform a task; it also constrains our abilities.

The functionality of the machines that augment our minds determines the contours of the extended mind as well as the intentional qualities that we attribute it. Very little of the extended mind model would survive if software were poorly designed or otherwise flawed. Dreams of perfect interfaces, through ubiquitous or wearable computing, or seamless spoken or tactile interaction, are aspirations toward a better integration of the organic and machinic elements of the cyborg. It is not the mere presence of technological augmentation that gives rise to the extended mind, but that it meshes and melds with our cognitive styles in co-determining relationships. Thus, to place conditions on software to achieve effective augmentation of the mind is to determine the language of the cyborg self. Software not only integrates our cyborg selves but also facilitates communication among them.

Software affects our expressive potential in two ways. First, it allows us to express algorithmic ideas as programs written, typically, in high-level programming languages. Although any general-purpose language can express any algorithmic idea, computer scientists nonetheless can make fine distinctions in terms of which concepts are more easily expressed in them and in terms of which languages map more closely to individual programmers' cognitive styles. The artificial intelligence language Prolog facilitates the expression and manipulation of relationships among objects; Perl is the language of choice for complex text manipulation. Individual programmers also express preferences for languages based on how well the language's syntax and semantics map to their cognitive and expressive styles: Lisp's endless parenthesized recursion is anathema to some and supremely elegant to others.

Second, as executing code, software constrains the ways in which we may interact with a computing device. The grammar of this language of interaction is the set of constraints that my software places on me — the structure within which I must operate if it is to understand me. Sequences of actions I take constitute utterances in this language; the software instantiates rules that determine which utterances carry meaning. If we want to alter the nature of our interaction with the machine, we must modify the rules that govern this interaction, which are encoded in software. Thus, we only modify our interactions with a computer if we can modify the code that it runs: the only solution to a frustrating interaction with an inflexible interface is to change the interface.

But if the software running on a machine is unavailable for inspection and modification, the expressiveness of our language of interaction is severely restricted. Consider a language with a finite number of unalterable sentences. The restrictions on this language preclude the coining of new words or sentences. The full ramifications of such restrictions are hinted at by a consideration of cognitive development without access to written language:

> Joseph [a deaf eleven-year old with minimal linguistic experience], saw, distin-
> guished, categorized, used; he had no problems with perceptual categorization or
> generalization, but he could not, it seemed, go much beyond this, hold abstract
> ideas in mind, reflect, play, plan . . . he seemed, like an animal or infant, to be stuck
> in the present, to be confined to literal and immediate perception. (Sacks 1990,
> cited in Clark 2003)

Restrictions on the cyborg world's languages would entail that their expressive power and communicative capacity would be severely curtailed, limiting their ability to augment cyborg cognition. Thus, the languages of the cyborg world must afford creative extension, modification, and recombination. We depend on such flexibility in public natural language: our notions of creativity in the verbal cultures of prose and poetry are linked to a facility for exploiting this tailorability, for as we speak and write, we deploy a diverse array of communicational tropes, robustly accommodated by our language.

The expressive modalities of software are closely linked to the contours of our relationship with our machinic selves: restrictions on programmatic expressions in source code would circumscribe our ability to modify the language through which we interact with computing devices. But a great deal of the communication underlying our current interactions in the cyborg world is not under our control, for in a world undergirded by closed software the cyborg has no access to the language of its computing component. These limitations are easily illustrated by the most mundane of examples. A user frustrated by awkward style handling in both Microsoft Word and OpenOffice is provided with different options to resolve this difficulty. While Word allows some tailoring of its interface, these superficial adjustments do not affect the fundamental functionality of the program. But with sufficient determination, the frustrated user could alter OpenOffice's style handling facility to his liking. The user that desires flexibility in his relationship with the machine must change its software; closed software denies him this ability.

The ability to customize, critique, and query our interactions with machines is an important aspect of normative takes on the cognitive properties of human-computer interfaces (Schneiderman and Plaisant 2004; Turoff et al. 1990). The design specifications for the Tailorable Electronic Information Exchange System (TEIES) (Turoff et al. 1990) required interface screens to be modifiable by the user. These screens were implemented in the Standardized General Markup Language (SGML, the direct progenitor of HTML), which produced a variety of forms for handling user input. The user could, with a keystroke, pull up the source code for the screen she was using and modify it, altering the interface to suit her cognitive style. As the nature of the user's work changed, she could continue to change the interface to accommodate a variety of subjects and problem-solving styles. Similarly, Tim Berners-Lee's original specifications for the World Wide Web stressed the need for users to be able to edit the Web — to support collaborative research — as well as browse it (Lawson 2005).

The significance of public language to cognition imposes a normative requirement on the language of the cyborg world. It must facilitate cognition and collaboration within and among cyborgs in the way public natural language does; this language must be flexible and modifiable, carrying arbitrary potential for expressiveness; it must permit the unrestricted flow of ideas among individuals, and support the resulting amplification and enrichment of these ideas. In short, the software that structures this language must be free.

Language, Free Speech, and Free Software

Richard Stallman has described the meaning of free software with the slogan, "Think 'free' as in 'free speech' not 'free beer.'" This slogan suggests that in the cyborg world, the relationship between free software and free speech is not an analogy but an identity. The "free" in "free speech" refers to absence of restriction on expression. The freedoms of free software entail the absence of restrictions on use and modification of the software. These freedoms apply to different modalities of software: Freedoms 0 and 2 guarantee the freedom to use software by protecting the availability of its executable; Freedoms 1 and 3 guarantee the freedom to access and modify the source code. If we consider both modalities of software — source code and executable — then the true resonance for "free" as in "free speech" is the freedom to use the software for any purpose: I am free to use the executables for any task and for distribution, while I am free to use the source code for the purpose of making derivative works. Therefore, software is not free when it is subject to restrictions on the availability of its source, the functionality it provides, the applications in which it is used, or the field of endeavor in which it is deployed.

These restrictions should be rejected just as upholders of free speech reject restrictions on free speech, for the ramifications of these restrictions, in both contexts, are enormous both now and for our future polity. Yet restrictions are placed on speech in most democratic polities. In deciding what restrictions are appropriate, we confront three questions: "[G]iven that it is speech, what does it do, do we want it to be done, and is more to be gained or lost by moving to curtail it?" (Fish 1994). Most commonly, speech is regulated when it can be shown to cause harm.

From the early phases of the commodification of software, opponents of free software and its precursors have asserted that it might be harmful to both programmers and users (Libervis.com 2006). These claims have centered on three themes: economic viability, security, and liability. Echoes of Bill Gates's original fulmination against software copying in his letter to the Homebrew Computer Club persist in Microsoft's claims that its proprietary-software model is part of its stewardship of the "software ecosystem"[2] (Matusow 2005). The proliferation of business models in the FOSS world, the continual provision of employment in FOSS positions, and the commercial success of the GNU/Linux operating system point to the implausibility of these claims.

Critics also assert that free software may be less secure than closed source for a variety of reasons, the most prominent of which is that the vulnerabilities of open source code are much more visible. Eric Raymond argues to the contrary, restating Kerckhoffs's Law (Kerckhoffs 1883) as, "Any security software design that doesn't assume the enemy possesses the source code is already untrustworthy; therefore, *never trust closed source*" (Raymond 2004, emphasis in original). Under simplifying assumptions about the distribution of security vulnerabilities, open and closed source software may be equivalently secure, where particular deviations from the ideal may give the edge to one or the other. That is, the security of open and closed source fails in different ways (Anderson 2005). But fundamentally, "The points [that] are critical are [the] ability to review the code for myself and . . . to fix it myself when it is broken. By 'myself' I do, of course, include 'or anyone of my choice'" (Laurie 2006, 70).

The heavily collaborative nature of free software development is often cast as one of its weaknesses: the "problem of many hands" makes it difficult to assign liability to a legally liable entity. This problem is endemic to any software created collectively, whether proprietary or open (Nissenbaum 1996). Yet "many hands" may be an asset in the free software context: while there may not be a single legally liable entity, the FOSS community's emphases on developer responsibility and reciprocity may result in a larger pool of developers who feel vested and accountable to users.

Most commonly, software is deemed to be harmful when it facilitates the breaking of law, as in the DeCSS case, which was the first to test the enforceability of the DMCA's anticircumvention provisions. In this case, the First Amendment was invoked in defense of the creation and distribution of the "guilty" software: the defendants sought to portray software as a medium for the expression and communication of ideas, not only between humans and machines but also among computer scientists. Implicit in the defendant's brief is the concern that restrictions on such "speech" have broad and complex implications in technologized society.

DeCSS

In 1999, Jon Lech Johansen, a Norwegian student, wrote and published source code for software intended to circumvent DVD access control mechanisms. As part of the movie industry's technical protection of intellectual property, DVDs were encrypted using the proprietary Content Scramble System (CSS), which is intended to allow only licensed players to play DVDs. At the time, the only computers with licensed players were Windows- and Macintosh-based; Linux users could not play DVDs — even if legally purchased — on their machines. Called DeCSS because it reverses the operation of CSS, Johansen's software, circumventing the protective encryption, allowed DVDs to be played on Linux computers.[3] As far as Linux users were concerned, this software merely enabled the fair use of their legally purchased DVDs, though the movie industry had a different perspective. In 2000 American authorities contacted Norwegian police, who raided Johansen's home; arrested and tried in Norwegian court, he was fully acquitted in 2003.

In the United States, Universal Studios filed suit under the terms of the DMCA against Eric Corley, Shawn C. Reimerdes, and Roman Kazan, Americans who had posted a copy of the DeCSS code on the Web site 2600.com. In the ensuing legal proceedings, the defense argued that source code is subject to First Amendment protections, citing the landmark decision in *Bernstein v. US Dept. of Justice*, which had found that "the particular language one chooses [does not] change the nature of language for First Amendment purposes. This court can find no meaningful difference between computer language, particularly high-level languages as defined above, and German or French."[4] The Court agreed to an extent, saying

> It cannot seriously be argued that any form of computer code may be regulated without reference to First Amendment doctrine. The path from idea to human language to source code to object code is a continuum. As one moves from one to the other, the levels of precision and, arguably, abstraction increase, as does the level of training necessary to discern the idea from the expression. Not everyone can understand each of these forms. . . . Only English speakers will understand English formulations. Principally those familiar with the particular programming language will understand the source code expression. And only a relatively small number of skilled programmers and computer scientists will understand the machine readable object code.

But the Court, as a preamble for its finding in favor of placing restrictions on code, continued, "the long history of First Amendment jurisprudence makes equally clear that the fact that words, symbols and even actions convey ideas and evoke emotions does not inevitably place them beyond the power of government." While this has never been contested, even by First Amendment proponents, the Court seemed to be failing to confront the question of whose rights would be protected, and whose infringed, by such restrictions.

The Court concluded that the functional nature of code overshadows its expressive, speechlike aspects:

> The computer code at issue in this case, however, does more than express the programmers' concepts. It does more, in other words, than convey a message. DeCSS, like any other computer program, is a series of instructions that causes a computer to perform a particular sequence of tasks which, in the aggregate, decrypt CSS-protected files. Thus, it has a distinctly functional, non-speech aspect in addition to reflecting the thoughts of the programmers. It enables anyone who receives it and who has a modicum of computer skills to circumvent plaintiffs' access control system.[5]

The Court, after weighing the relative importance of consumers' fair use rights and content providers' protection, ruled that DeCSS code was entitled only to a weak form of First Amendment protection, and found for the motion picture industry. Stripped of the veneer of a copyright debate, at its essence, this ruling reflects and reinscribes an old chauvinism that stresses the mechanic/organic, natural/synthetic, and biological/technological dichotomies. We suspect the issue is not ultimately one of functionality outweighing speech; it is simply that the Court cannot conceive of human–machine communication as speech.[6]

The finding was appealed, and in an *amicus curiae* brief filed by a group of computer scientists, this defense was further elaborated, contesting the Court's argument about the functionality of code:

> [M]ost computer code does not function in a manner legally different from how a cake recipe or a music score "function," but there can be no doubt that the latter are entitled to full First Amendment protection. . . . but in the absence of human intervention . . . [they] do nothing on their own except to inform the reader. So it is with most computer code: a human must give the command to interpret or compile the source code . . . a human must give the command to execute it . . . [and] a human must operate the device which makes the code functional. . . . The law is clear that the protection afforded to speech is not dependent on whether a device is needed to "execute" the speech. (Tyre 2001)

These arguments seek to establish that software (whether source or object code) is not only an avenue of human expression — "that subset . . . which computers can interpret and execute" (Tyre 2001) — but also one that should be subject to regulation only to the extent it is a form of speech. In their brief, the *amici* point out that code is used not only to communicate with computers but with computer scientists as well. That is, code is an integral part of "a complex system of understood meanings within specific communities" (Tyre 2001). Further, the expressive quality of source code, containing the "ideas, commands, objectives" (Tyre 2001) of the programmer, is carried into the executable code during a translation process. Thus, code has both communicative and expressive aspects. In the context of the cyborg world, the free speech protections for which the *amici* advocate generalize in the broadest sense to communication among its hybrid denizens.

Like any other form of speech, code can challenge power and ideology. The act of writing DeCSS was a fundamentally political one, contesting a particular unjust restriction on freedom. The Court's ruling, implicitly recognizing the political implications of this act, upholds that restriction. While the DeCSS ruling is at one level only about intellectual property protection, the implications for the restrictions on expression extend much further. Without doubt, programmers' expression has been restricted by this ruling's chilling effect on the creation and application of cryptographic code; much more alarming is the prospect of restriction of speech and expressiveness in the cyborg world.

Political Philosophy in the Cyborg World

Cyborg Autonomy

Political philosophies are concerned with autonomy and the distribution of power: to enter political society is to enter into power-sharing relationships that may require the surrender of some autonomy. Comparative political theory measures, among other things, the degrees to which these surrenderings and agreements are employed by different political systems. Individual autonomy, the capacity of a person to alter the circumstances that affect her decision making, is a moral good in classical political philosophy. It is also a political tool used to identify and publicize oppression and injustice: prescriptions to increase individual autonomy in a sociopolitical arrangement are attempts to devise a more just society. In particular, this capacity to resist paternalism is "to be one's own person, to live one's life according to reasons and motives that are taken as one's own and not the product of manipulative or distorting external forces" (Dworkin 1988).

In the cyborg world, the mediation of our extended selves by closed software threatens individual autonomy; the advocacy for, and the provision of, closed software is a form of paternalism, diminishing cyborg autonomy as it controls and regulates the nature of human–machine interaction. The proprietary-software industry makes this paternalism explicit by suggesting the rejection of proprietary software will lead to the collapse of the industry; by using free software we hurt the software industry and its consumers, who will be denied its benefits. Thus, it is in consumers' best interest to continue to adopt closed software.

Autonomy characterizes the processes through which agents identify desires and make decisions. If this process is problematically constrained by external factors then the resulting decision and subsequent actions are not autonomously chosen. While consumers appear to consent to the use of closed software by accepting its licenses, closed software holds an effective monopoly in many application domains, limiting the extent to which consumers can grant their full consent. Subsequently, interactions with the software are determined entirely by the software itself; the user plays a passive role. A human agent functioning in this manner, uncritically accepting the constraints of closed software, is a "happy slave," convinced its desires to regulate its interactions with the machine are mere fantasies, not in accord with pragmatic economic realities. But to imagine that this position of dependence and servitude is one a rational agent would will for itself is incoherent. It is similarly implausible to assert that users desire the constraints imposed on them by software with limited, unalterable functionality. The ability to control one's interactions with the machine is not a specialized, esoteric concern, but is a core freedom in the cyborg world.

Software, treated as constitutionally protected free speech, enables a full range of expression and protects the ability to manipulate technological artifacts; most fundamentally, it protects the autonomy of the individual:

> Certain bodies of code are essential tools of expression, in the same way that pens and paper were for an earlier technological era. It enhances personal autonomy to own those tools, or at least to be sure that no one else owns them in a restrictive way. Would it be good for democracy if newsprint were engineered to dissolve when someone tried to photocopy it? Or if you could only write on it in particular languages? (Weber 2004, 247)

Political and social institutions are legitimate to the extent they are subject to an "endorsement constraint" (Dworkin 2000, 216–18) — that the values of a polity only hold for a person if they can be endorsed by him (Rawls 1993). In democratic polities, such endorsement follows a process of participatory democratic discussion (Bessette 1994). When these institutions depend on software, freedom in both its choice and usage is the key to enabling public discussion and endorsement; a politics underwritten by the constraints of closed software is illegitimate.

Our polity is that of the cyborg world, one in which distinctions between man and machine, natural and computer languages, have been displaced. In this world, governmentality resides in machines; our spaces are constructed by technology; we are hybrids of biology and technology. If not only regulation but also political function devolves to code, then we must place the same normative constraints on the technology that we place on the socio-human-political machinery. The social and political philosophy of such a world must capture the technological inflection of its material forms of life. Our arguments about treating software as free speech, then, amount to a claim that software must be protected as speech in the cyborg world. More generally, the construction of such a philosophy requires the selection of designs and specifications for this hybrid world.

William Mitchell suggests a connection between principles for designing an online virtual community and those for governing any technologically constructed space:

> The rules of governing any computer-constructed microworld — of a video game, your personal desktop . . . are precisely and rigorously defined in the text of the

program that constructs it on your screen. Just as Aristotle in *Politics* contemplated alternative constitutions for city-states . . . so denizens of the digital world should pay the closest of critical attention to programmed polity. Is it just and humane? Does it protect our privacy, our property and our freedoms? Does it constrain us unnecessarily or does it allow us to act as we may wish?

[I]t's all a matter of the software's conditionals — those coded rules that specify if some condition holds, then some action follows . . . you are either embraced by the system or excluded and marginalized by it . . . you cannot argue with it. You cannot ask it to exercise discretion. You cannot plead with it, cajole it, or bribe it. (Mitchell 1996)

As governments exert power through and over code, the "programmed polity" is already with us in the contemporary cyborg world; contemporary "e-government" initiatives provide powerful illustrations of the importance of free software in this world.

E-Government

E-government is one culmination of the process of transferring governmental function to technological proxies. Driven by technocratic imperatives of efficiency and cost-saving, as well as populist imperatives of accessibility, e-government promises to "modernize" government. For example, the German e-government initiative is a comprehensive program aimed at migrating much governmental bureaucracy (such as the management of health benefits) to online services (Engemann 2006). In this situation, where governmental function rests in its technical agents who interact with citizens, the nature, behavior, and motivation of those agents is a natural object of scrutiny.

Evoking the rhetorical disjunction between the free and open source movements, most discussion about FOSS in the context of e-government centers on concerns with cost and technical efficacy. There is, however, occasional "negligible, parenthetical and delphic" (Berry and Moss 2006) mention of using FOSS to promulgate social goals having to do with quality of life, citizen engagement, and social inequality, or, as in German e-government, to preserve "the federal constitution's safeguards against centralization" (Kablenet 2001). Cost is certainly a political issue, especially in the developing world, but more significant is FOSS's political and moral message of transparency; by ignoring this aspect of free software, governments pass over an opportunity to remake their machinery toward a different relationship with the polity (Berry and Moss 2006).

Transparency in government requires open procedures so they may be the subject of public scrutiny and critique toward the ends of accountability and legitimacy. In the context of e-government, the characteristics of government depend on the characteristics of code. A system of e-government built on closed software is itself closed, one whose laws and policies are unknowable; by closing off participation, it denies the public nature of democracy. Indeed, many governmental activities only become trustworthy when the code that runs them is open:

> The electronic calculation and collection of taxes is arguably a case where trust can be built into the system when the software code that runs these systems can be publicly viewed. . . . [A]ny e-government system that involves data storage and sharing raises concerns for individual privacy, which would be better understood if their design was open (Berry and Moss 2006, 28)."

With FOSS, the innards of governments are laid bare. Their conduct becomes a subject of public inquiry and accountability. This transparency is not sufficient for a democratic polity, but is a minimum standard.

The open code of e-government would only be studied by a very few technically competent people, just as laws and legal decisions are largely impenetrable to most of us. As most of us are not able to interpret the texts of Congressional transcripts or legislation, lawyers, with their technical training, serve as proxies for the citizenry in this regard. The mere fact that these documents can be publicly read affects the functioning of the system, and leads to a self-regulation of conduct by political and legislative actors (Berry and Moss 2006, 28).

Technology, if represented merely as an engineering issue, will remain one, providing no opportunity for moral or political critique of its application, and therefore open to abuse by private or even governmental interests. The democratic nature of the cyborg world depends on a public political awareness of technology; here, both the code and the language of the free software movement are engines for moving the discussion to a moral and political plane.

E-government based on closed source carries the potential to create a political subject similar to the user of proprietary software: passive and uncritical. A collective, participatory approach to creating the code of government would mitigate these dangers:

> For one thing, increased public involvement in e-government design would avoid the temptation of creating simplified and standardised models of the "citizen-user." Most e-government models have what has been termed a "crippled model," using a data flow that is unidirectional, from government to the individual. . . . (Berry and Moss 2006, 31)

FOSS, then, provides an opportunity for us to modify the code of government. The FOSS mode of open communication could become a model for political discourse: the populace could actively intervene by "developing," "bug-fixing," and "iterating" true participatory government. Citizens could examine the source code of government to determine how it encodes values important to them, and modify it if they deem it unacceptable. For example, it is possible to modify the source code of open source Web browsers, potentially integral components of e-government apparatus, to support privacy and the user's right to give informed consent (Friedman, Howe, and Felten 2002).

Furthermore, free and open source software necessarily opens the standards of the file formats and protocols it manipulates. This allows for a particular kind of participation through extension of software functionality; for example, it becomes possible to build independent applications that are critical of government:

> Software is being used to critically open up technology and expose its underlying structures, Sometimes referred to as "critical software," this allows competing democratic values to be supported. Critical software could have applications in e-government systems. . . . The website "thepublicwhip.com" . . . locate[s] the details of MPs' voting records, their attendance in debates and so on, giving the user the opportunity to scrutinise or supervise their representative. Should government websites rely on proprietary or closed technologies, such as Flash, critical software would not be able to function. (Berry and Moss 2006, 30)

The interplay of governmentality and technology is particularly visible in the challenges of electronic voting. Oversight of elections, considered by many to be the cornerstone of modern representational democracies, is a governmental function; election commissions are responsible for generating ballots; designing, implementing, and maintaining the voting infrastructure; coordinating the voting process; and generally insuring the integrity and transparency of the election. But modern voting technology, specifically that of the computerized electronic voting machine that utilizes closed software, is not inherently in accord with these norms. In elections supported by these machines, a great mystery takes place. A citizen walks into the booth and "casts a vote." Later, the machine announces the results. The magical transformation from a sequence of votes to an electoral decision is a process obscure to all but the manufacturers of the software. The technical efficiency of the electronic voting process becomes part of a package that includes opacity and the partial relinquishing of citizens' autonomy.

The plethora of problems attributed to the closed nature of electronic voting machines in the 2004 U.S. presidential election illustrates the ramifications of tolerating such an opaque process. For example, 30 percent of the total votes were cast on machines that lacked ballot-based audit trails, making accurate recounts impossible (Open Voting Consortium 2006). Like all closed systems, these machines are vulnerable to security hacks, as they rely in part on obscurity, rather than robust engineering mandated by transparent systems. Analysts of code very similar to that found in these machines reported that the voting system should not be used in elections as it failed to meet even the most minimal of security standards (Kohno et al. 2004, 1). The study went on to advocate for FOSS systems to be used in all e-voting:

> An open process would result in more careful development. . . . [Those] who value their democracy would be paying attention to the quality of the software . . . used in their elections. . . . The model where individual vendors write proprietary code to run our elections appears to be unreliable . . . if we do not change the process of

designing our voting systems, we will have no confidence that our election results will reflect the will of the electorate. (Kohno et al. 2004, 21)

The opaqueness of these machines' design is a secret compact between governments and manufacturers of electronic voting machines, who alone are privy to the details of the voting process. The norms that govern the use of these machines must be encapsulated in citizens' requirements, among which transparency is foremost. The voting process and its infrastructure should be a public enterprise, run by a non-partisan Electoral Commission with its operational procedures and functioning transparent to the citizenry. Citizens' forums demand open code in electoral technology, as in the California Voter Foundation's requirement that vendors "provide election officials with access to their source code" (Alexander 2004). Access to this source code provides the polity an explanation of how voting results are reached, just as publicly available transcripts of congressional sessions illustrate governmental decision-making. The use of FOSS would ensure that, at minimum, technology is held to the same standards of openness.

Free Software as an Anarchist Ideal

The activities, mechanisms, and power of government are constitutive of political systems. In an open polity, the government makes the content of laws available for inspection and debates. To use an anarchist term, this power is transparent: the reasons for a particular interaction are available for any citizen to view. When these are concealed, the polity is subject to a system of opaque power.

In the cyborg world, power is

[T]he ability to change the behavior of computers. If you can't change the behavior of computers, you live within a Skinner box created by the people who can change the behavior of computers. Every artifact around you responds by either handing you a banana pellet or a shock, depending upon which button you push and whether you are "right" from the designer's point of view. (Moglen 2003)

Any arrangement that negates our ability autonomously to affect the material circumstances of the cyborg world, most crucially the behavior of computing devices, is one that creates and sustains opaque power relations. In a system governed by such relations, no identifiable person or institution bears ultimate responsibility for decisions. In the cyborg world, a ring of software agents — the true face of interaction with the polity — surrounds the human core of government. If the software is proprietary, un-free, the relationships it mediates remain opaque. Such a system allows for the concealed, untrammeled growth of governmental and corporate power through exquisite systems of control that make tracking, surveillance, privacy and trespass invasions, and restrictions on sharing of information a matter of course. This co-optation of a supposedly liberatory technology is not inevitable. The potentials for both exquisite control and unfettered freedom lie in the way we choose to use this technology.

Anarchism speaks directly to this need for transparent power, calling for the dismissal of all asymmetrical power relations (Goldman 2005). Anarchist philosophies map onto free software ideals that demand, first, no asymmetry in the relationships among users, developers, and distributors, and second, transparency in decision making, power relations, and other interactions among the troika of machine, user, and developer. While some developers occupy positions of power in the free software community, their relationships to the community exemplify the distinction between having authority and being an authority:

> [C]onsider the relation of a student to an authority in some field of knowledge . . . such an authority might be called transparent or open, because anyone with some time and skill can proceed past the authority to assess the claims made. Contrast these with opaque or closed authorities, who simply stand on their position or station. (Sylvan 1996, 221)

FOSS software projects serve as models for the displacement of opaque power. These communities are devoid of coercion: authority figures emerge at the will of the community, and the ever-present possibility of forking renders their authority contingent. Analogously, in a world where governmental function is implemented via code, free software allows for the assessment of the authority of any governmental structure.

Most important, a cyborg world underwritten by free software renders participation in its political structure as contingent and flexible: because law is implemented as code in cyberspace, the polity can choose to change the extent and character of its acceptance (Lessig 2000). Governmental regulation requires "an unmovable, and unmoving, target of regulation" (Lessig 2000, 106), an entity for whom the cost of obedience is lower than that of disobedience. Government regulation is often applied to intermediaries, such as Internet service providers or television manufacturers, which carry the effect of the regulation to citizens/consumers. Thus, citizens may experience, for example, restrictions on content without direct intervention by the government in their activities. To the extent these manufacturers and service providers — proxies for governmental power — are private entities, citizens have few tools with which to resist this intervention; if these proxies were public, instead, such opacity would be untenable.

In 1998, the French government asked Netscape to ship a version of its browser incorporating a form of cryptography weak enough to permit government monitoring of transactions. If Netscape had done so, users unwilling to accept this restriction could simply have taken advantage of the openness of Netscape's code to build, or acquire, and insert a satisfactory cryptographic module in their browsers. Thus,

> To the extent that code is open code, the power of government is constrained. Government can demand, government can threaten, but when the target of regulation is plastic, it cannot rely on its target remaining where it wants. . . . The government's rules are rules only to the extent that they impose restrictions that adopters would want. . . . This architecture, then, is an important check on the government's regulatory power. Open code means open control — there is control, but the user is aware of it. . . . Closed code is . . . a persistent and unrecognized influence. (Lessig 2000, 107)

Free software carries the potential to place substantive restrictions on the regulatory power of cyborg government, whether state or corporate. The power of governments in the cyborg world is inversely related to the freedom of software: "Open code . . . can be a check on state power" (Lessig 2000, 107). This curtailment and rejection of opaque power is an old anarchist ideal: free software makes power transparent. "[Free software] dissolv[es] the categorical distinction between those who code and those for whom there is a Code" (Truscello 2003). If the code-as-law that regulates us is available for us to change, then it ceases to have a hold on us. If code is architecture, then the spaces created through our interaction with it are modifiable ones:

> If Microsoft makes the Windows Media player so that there's no way to save streaming audio on the hard drive [to prevent illegal ripping], it's almost impossible for the user to unmake that decision. But free software is code that any user can change, and therefore it can't be used to substitute for law. And because free software often replaces proprietary software, it can act subversively, to undo "laws" made by proprietary programs. . . . "Who controls the switches?" That's the most important legal and political question in the Internet society. Free software says that, as individuals, we do. So sometimes "code is law" and sometimes code is freedom. (Moglen 2000)

But if adherence to code as law is voluntary, will not chaos result? The laws that citizens tolerate are laws enforced by coercion, they involve the backup arsenals of punitive restrictions, punishments, incarcerations, fines and the like. But when citizens can opt out of compliance, these laws lose their impact. This provides the opportunity for a creative moment in determining which strictures are relevant to which spheres of activity, whether political or cultural.

The mapping between anarchism and open code, closed code and the state, is revealed by the structural similarity of arguments for the indispensability of proprietary code and for the necessity of the state. Both these arguments rely on creation myths and idealized reconstructions. In the case of the state, the story goes, a Hobbesian state of nature was brought to an end when citizens banded together and submitted to the benevolent yet authoritarian Leviathan, resulting in a safer existence, the protection of property, and dramatically improved standards of living and culture. Similarly, the mythology of the software industry insists that at one time, users struggled with little code, most of it poorly written, only to be rescued by technocratic entrepreneurs who, insisting on technical and business standards, brought truly useful, life-enhancing software to the people and employment to hundreds of thousands of programmers. But, as we have seen, the embryonic software industry drew heavily on, and subsequently depleted, a then-flourishing hacker culture inhabited by hobbyists, master programmers imbued with both social and technical vision. And anarchist history suggests the creation of the modern state came at great societal cost, accompanied by much violence, most notably the destruction of the medieval city and its trade guilds (Kropotkin 1902).

Both the state and proprietary software's proponents rely, too, on promoting a vision of their indispensability to the continued smooth functioning of the systems they respectively regulate. The state in arguing for its necessity need only point to its "indispensability" in staving off the brute existence of the "state of nature" by providing for the maintenance of order, the collective defense, and public health; the argument for proprietary software insists it is indispensable for ensuring the health of the political economy of a technocratic world undergirded by software. The aptly named "Fear, Uncertainty, and Doubt" (FUD) arguments put forward by the proprietary-software camp paint a vision of a chaotic world in which grotesquely buggy, insecure, unsupported free software runs rampant, leaving users at the mercy of malicious hackers, decimating business productivity, and bringing the economy to its knees. The proprietary camp claims that the "anarchic" organization of FOSS will only produce bad software; high-quality, reliable software will only result from the tight organization and legal protections of proprietary software. The implausibility of these claims requires little commentary.

Because the cyborg world brings to life new legal and political structures, as code merges with law, we can see in its fundamentals the glimmerings of a new, transparent society, one that by making participation in it voluntary attains the true meaning of a compact, one achieved without coercion. When code is opened, we have the power to view the machinery of authority. The panopticon is inverted, and we observe the state, or what remains of it:

> Open Source creates an anarchic space for tactical intervention in the surveillance and control society by making the principal means of control, the code, "visible" to the greatest number of subjects. The subject, though participant in its own self-subjugation, is also a participant in its own emancipation. The machinations of surveillance, the operating systems and applications of subject construction, are potentially exposed and reconstructed. (Truscello 2003)

Conclusion

Free software provides a framework for interpreting normative claims about the eventual politics of the cyborg world. The need of the polity of the cyborg world for adequate communication undergirding political participation is met by the extension of free speech protections to software. Cyborg rights such as "freedom of electronic speech," "freedom of consciousness," and "freedom of information," (Gray 2001, 27–28) are all secured by the freedoms of software. More broadly, the empowerment of cyborg citizens rests in their ability to resist the authoritarian pressure by gaining knowledge of, access to, and control over the complex technologies that embed them.

In *1984*, George Orwell depicted the restrictions placed on the polity by the provision of an impoverished language, where words are selectively removed from usage, where meaning is subverted. In Jean-Luc Godard's *Alphaville*, the fascist computer ALPHA-60 maintained control through "The Bible," a dictionary of permissible words amended only by ALPHA-60 itself. When language, and the power to control it, is hidden from us, we are no longer free. When code is opaque, when we behave in unalterable conformance with the machines melded with us, we hand over control just as the denizens of Alphaville did.

Freeing software is of a piece with a tradition of devolving power inherent in text. John Wycliffe's translation in the 1380s of the Latin Vulgate Bible into English, or Tulsidas's translation of the *Ramayan* into Brijbasi in the late 1500s, converted canonical texts, exploited by the priestly classes to uphold particular social norms, into popular texts. Translation into the local lingua franca resulted in not just a new discourse on their contents, but radical criticism of previously existing sociopolitical arrangements. The free software project is nothing less than a translation project, bringing us access to language and ideas previously uninterpretable.

Jacques Ellul imagined an iron cage constructed of technology (Ellul 1967), but never the possibility that the cage could be unlocked by its prisoners. We began with a historical note on hacking: the significance of hacking should now be clear. Hackers set out to discover the workings of technical systems but found themselves doing much more. In the cyborg society, investigating a technical system is not idle tinkering: it uncovers the roots of power. A hacker is a public investigator, a gadfly, a muckraker, a public conscience: the guilty hide while the hacker lays bare. Foucault despaired of the immanence of opaque power, but free software creates a moment in which to make the exertion of power transparent. The technical is political: to free software is to free our selves.

7. See, however, Brandle (2006) for an example of a musician asserting his moral right over the reproducibility of his work, or Anderson Strathern (2002) for a discussion on whether musicians can assert rights over performances of their works.

8. A broad array of licenses meet the Free Software and Open Source Definitions. See http://www.gnu.org/licenses/license-list.html and http://www.opensource.org/licenses/ for overlapping lists of licenses meeting these definitions.

9. There are two BSD licenses: the original and the revised. In the revised version, a clause requiring mention of the University of California as a contributor has been removed. Sometimes "BSD-style licenses" is used as a descriptive term for non-copyleft software licenses. See http://www.opensource.org/licenses/bsd-license.php.

10. See Stallman (2006) for an argument favoring copyleft licensing.

11. http://www.catb.org/~esr/writings/cathedral-bazaar/ is a good source for readings and critique.

12. http://www.opensource.org.

13. http://ask.slashdot.org/comments.pl?sid= 32072&cid=3458695.

14. In Berlin's original formulation, z is a person or some institution.

15. Rob Landley, in a posting on the linux-kernel list; see http://www.uwsg.iu.edu/hypermail/linux/kernel/0210.2/1627.html.

16. The precise technical definition of "combination" — usually, whether it is only incorporation of source code, or whether it also includes incorporation of functionality provided by compiled code — is a contested one. Discussion Draft 2 of the GPLv3 uses this language to try to clarify the matter: "Corresponding Source includes scripts used to control those activities, interface definition files associated with the program source files, and the source code for shared libraries and dynamically linked subprograms that the work is specifically designed to require" (The Free Software Foundation 2006).

17. It seems that this is what used to be referred to as "ideological tub-thumping" in the OSI's FAQ.

18. http://www.opensource.org/.

19. Ironically, the phrase "open source" is itself a source of confusion to most people outside the computer industry — they understand the simple directness of "free software" as opposed to the jargonish "open source."

20. Richard Stallman, writing on the linux-kernel mailing list http://groups.google.com/group/linux.kernel/browse_thread/thread/a98de7edab73f365/f9fdc5696a95e8e3/. This comment, and subsequent comments taken from the linux-kernel mailing list, were made in the context of the bitter dispute that followed Larry McVoy's withdrawal of the noncommercial license for BitKeeper.

21. Richard Stallman at http://groups.google.com/group/linux.kernel/browse_ thread/thread/a98de7edab73f365/f9fdc5696a95e8e3.

22. Rob Landley at http://groups.google.com/group/linux.kernel/ browse_thread/ thread/a98de7edab73f365/f9fdc5696a95e8e3.

23. Larry McVoy at http://groups.google.com/group/linux.kernel/browse_thread/ thread/a98de7edab73f365/f9fdc5696a95e8e3.

24. Richard Stallman at http://groups.google.com/group/linux.kernel/browse_ thread/thread/a98de7edab73f365/f9fdc5696a95e8e3.

25. If truth-telling must be universal, according to Kant, then one must, upon being asked, tell a known murderer the location of his prey. In his response to Constant, in *On a Supposed Right to Tell Lies from Benevolent Motives*, Kant argues that it is one's moral duty to be truthful to a murderer, a result in fundamental conflict with our moral intuitions.

26. A maxim is universalizable if and only if it could be coherently applied in a world where everyone else applied the maxim in similar circumstances.

27. http://groups.google.com/group/linux.kernel/browse_thread/thread/ a98de7eda b73f365/7d68ee9f364e93f6.

28. St. Laurent suggests that the GPL's requirement that licensors "Accompany [the software] with a written offer, valid for at least three years, to give any third party, for a charge no more than your cost of physically performing source distribution, a complete machine-readable copy of the corresponding source code . . ." is onerous as well: "This option furthers the purposes of open source and free software, but does so in a way that imposes additional costs on both licensors and licensees. The licensor must maintain a facility for providing copies of the source code; the licensor interested in creating the derivative work must contract and pay for the copying of the source code." St. Laurent also suggests that such provision is counterproductive: "Moreover this provision is limited to three years, which could result in potentially useful software going closed" as a practical matter (at least for the creation of derivative works) once the licensor ceases making the source code available" (St. Laurent 2004). However, note that given the pace of innovation in the software world, the three-year limit seems adequate.

Chapter Three: Free Software and the Aesthetics of Code

1. See, for example, http://ask.slashdot.org/ar ticle.pl?sid=01/01/25/0230208.

2. See http://ask.slashdot.org/article.pl?sid=01/01/25/0230208.

3. http://www.99-bottles-of-beer.net/.

4. http://www.99-bottles-of-beer.net/language-perl-737.html.

5. http://www.cs.cmu.edu/~dst/DeCSS/Gallery.

6. See http://www.ioccc.org for the International Obfuscated C contest, a whimsical acknowledgment of the potential for bad code.

7. In this chapter, we preferentially quote proprietary-software programmers in order to emphasize the generality of portions of our argument.

8. As Heinrich Hertz said, "They have an intelligence of their own, they are wiser than we are, wiser even than their discoverers, that we get more out of them than was originally put into them" (Bell 1937).

9. The special theory of relativity can be concisely expressed as, "The laws of physics are the same in all inertial frames of reference" and the general theory of relativity as, "All objects move in straight lines."

10. http://www.gnu.org/prep/standards/.

11. See, for example, http://www.itmpi.org/.

12. See, for example, http://cs.iit.edu/courses/cs537.html.

13. See, for example, http://www.sito.org/synergy/gridcosm/ and http://jootoart.stikip ad.com/art/show/Art+Collaboration+Project+in+Montreal.

14. While U.S. copyright law does recognize and protect "Derivative Works," they are nonetheless uncommon in most genres. Japanese *manga*, as Vaidhyanathan notes, is an interesting exception (Vaidyanathan 2003).

15. http://w ww.remixreading.org/.

16. See http://movies.zap2it.com/movies/news/story/0,1259,---6903,00.html and http://en.wikipedia.org/wiki/The_ Phantom_Edit.

17. Apollo 11 astronaut Michael Collins uses this term to describe those test pilots at Edward Air Force Base who did not bail out of their stricken jets in time, imagining that as competent pilots, they would be able to fix any problem that arose (Collins 2001).

18. For example, Richard Stallman is regarded as the author of *emacs*, though it has been substantially reworked by many other programmers after him; similarly, Eric Raymond is regarded as the author of *fetchmail*, and Larry Wall as the author of *perl*.

Chapter Four: Free Software and the Scientific Practice of Computer Science

1. These comments were offered, ironically, on the occasion of Brooks's receiving an award named in honor of Newell.

2. In 1962, mathematician Paul Cohen invented a powerful new proof technique called forcing, a proof technique used without license by thousands of practicing mathematicians in their contributions to the flourishing area of large cardinal research.

3. The Linux kernel is currently the subject of a lawsuit by SCO for alleged copyright infringement in *SCO vs. IBM*; see http://en.wikipedia.org/wiki/SCO_v._IBM.

4. RFC 1910 has since been made obsolete by RFC 4120 as Kerberos moves through the Internet Standards process.

5. See http://www.robocup.org/.

6. See Kelty (2005) for two concrete examples of the way proprietary standards can restrict the dissemination of scientific knowledge.

7. Programmers working on proprietary projects have long been unable to draw on a Mertonian reward system, as so few of their peers have the opportunity to read their code. Placing so-called "Easter eggs" (see http://en.wikipedia.org/wiki/Easter_egg_(virtual)) in software applications, many of which list the names of the programming team, is a common practice that mitigates this anonymity.

Chapter Five: Free Software and the Political Philosophy of the Cyborg World

1. See Latour (1999) for a lengthier discussion of the role of nonhuman actors in a technologically enhanced environment.

2. See http://www.microsoft.com/resources/sharedsource/Articles/Microsoft andOpenSource.mspx.

3. The full story of DeCSS may be found at http://www.cs.cmu.edu/~dst/DeCSS/.

4. Cited in Tyre (2001).

5. Cited in Tyre (2001).

6. Fears about computer code as a kind of communication on par with human languages echo the fear of dehumanization. In his dissent from the findings of CONTU's final report (National Commission on New Technological Uses of Copyrighted Works 1980), Commissioner Hersey wrote:

Here is dramatized, in our view, the central flaw — and the subtle dehumanizing danger — of the Commission's position on programs. To call a machine control element a copy of a literary work flies in the face of common sense. Ask any citizen in the street whether a printed circuit in a microprocessor in the emission control of his or her car is a copy of a literary work, and see what answer you get. But if your government tells the citizens in the street that this is so, and makes it law, what then happens to the citizen's sense of distinction between works that speak to the minds and senses of men and women and works that run machines — or, ultimately, the citizen's sense of the saving distinction between human beings themselves and machines themselves.

Bibliography

2600. 2000. Direction. *2600*.

Albert, Phil. 2004. GPL: Viral Infection or Just Your Imagination? *Linux Insider*, May 25, http://www.linuxinsider.com/story/33968.html.

Alexander, Kim. 2004. The Need for Transparent, Accountable and Verifiable U. S. Elections. In *A Framework for Understanding Electronic Voting*. Menlo Park, CA.

Allison, Jeremy. 2005. A Tale of Two Standards. In *Open Sources 2.0*, edited by C. Dibona, D. Cooper, and M. Stone. Sebastopol: O'Reilly.

Ammerman, Michael. 2006. A Terrific Site of Amazing Code Where BVS Was Utilized. July 13, http://blueverticalstudio.com/go/?p=1627.

Anderson, Nate. 2006. Amazon's 'One-Click' Patent Reconsidered. Ars Technica, May 19, http://arstechnica.com/news.ars/post/20060519-6872.html.

Anderson, Ross. 2005. Open and Closed Systems are Equivalent (That is, in an Ideal World). In *Perspectives on Free and Open Source Software*, edited by J. Feller, B. Fitzgerald, S. Hissam, and K. R. Lakhani. Cambridge: MIT Press.

Anderson Strathern. 2002. Can Musicians Stop Political Parties 'Spinning' Their Discs? http://www.andersonstrathern.co.uk/knowledge/media_area/?content_id=585.

Aristotle. 350 BC/1962. *Nichomachean Ethics*. Translated by M. Ostwald. New York: Prentice-Hall.

————. 1984. Physics. In *The Complete Works of Aristotle*, edited by J. Barnes.

————. 1998. *Politics*. Translated by E. Barker. Edited by R. F. Stalley. New York: Oxford University Press, USA.

Associated Press. 1999. Intel Expected to Buy Stake in Linux Firm. *New York Times*, March 1, http://www.nytimes.com/library/tech/99/03/biztech/articles/01linux.html.

Atwood, Jeff. 2006. Pretty Code, Ugly Code. June 19, http://www.codinghorror.com/blog/archives/000615.html.

Ayer, A. J., ed. 1966. *Logical Positivism*. New York: Free Press.

Bailyn, Bernard, ed. 1993. *The Debate on the Constitution: Federalist and Antifederalist Speeches, Articles, and Letters During the Struggle for Ratification. Part One: September 1787 to February 1788*. New York: Library of America.

————, ed. 1993. *The Debate on the Constitution: Federalist and Antifederalist Speeches, Articles, and Letters During the Struggle for Ratification. Part Two: January to August 1788*. New York: Library of America.

Baker, Mitchell. 2005. The Mozilla Project: Past and Future. In *Open Sources 2.0*, edited by C. Dibona, D. Cooper, and M. Stone. Sebastopol: O'Reilly.

Bauer, H. H. 1992. *Scientific Literacy and the Myth of the Scientific Method*. Urbana and Chicago: University of Illinois Press.

Baxi, Upendra, Jay David Bolter, James D. A. Boyle, and Rosemary Coombe. 1993. The Bellagio Declaration. http://www.case.edu/affil/sce/BellagioDec.html.

Beardsley, Monroe C. 1965. On the Creation of Art. *Journal of Aesthetics and Art Criticism* 23:291–304.

Bell, E. T. 1937. *Men of Mathematics*. New York: Simon and Schuster.

Benjamin, Walter. 1969. The Work of Art in the Age of Mechanical Reproduction. In *Illuminations*, edited by H. Arendt. New York: Schocken.

———. 1992. The Author as Producer. In *Art in Theory 1900–1990: An Anthology of Changing Ideas*, edited by C. Harrison and P. Wood. Oxford, U.K.: Blackwell. Original edition, 1934.

Benkler, Yochai. 2002. Coase's Penguin, or, Linux and the Nature of the Firm. *Yale Law Journal* 112 (3): 369–446.

———. 2006. *The Wealth of Networks: How Social Production Transforms Markets and Freedom*. New Haven: Yale University Press.

Benn, S. I., and R. S. Peters. 1959. *The Principles of Political Thought*. New York: Free Press.

Bennis, Warren G., and Patricia Ward Biederman. 1998. *Organizing Genius: The Secrets of Creative Collaboration*. New York: Perseus Books Group.

Berlin, Isaiah. 1969. *Four Essays on Liberty*. Oxford: Oxford University Press.

Berry, David M. 2004. The Contestation of Code: A Preliminary Investigation into the Discourse of the Free/Libre and Open Source Movements. *Critical Discourse Studies* 1 (1): 65–89.

Berry, David M., and Giles Moss. 2006. Free and Open Source Software: Opening and Democratising E-Government's Black Box. *Information Polity* 11:21–34.

Berry, Josephine. 2002. Bare Code: Net Art and the Free Software Movement. *NetArt Commons*, May 7, http://netartcommons.walkerart.org/article.pl?sid=02/05/08/0615215.

Bessen, James. 2002. What Good Is Free Software? In *Government Policy toward Open Source Software*, edited by R. W. Hahn: American Enterprise Institute-Brookings Joint Center for Regulatory Studies.

Bessen, James, and Robert M. Hunt. 2004. The Software Patent Experiment. March 16, http://www.researchoninnovation.org/softpat.pdf.

Bessen, James, and Eric Maskin. 1999. Sequential Innovation, Patents and Imitation. http://www.researchoninnovation.org/patent.pdf.

Bessette, Joseph. 1994. *The Mild Voice of Reason: Deliberative Democracy and American National Government*. Chicago: University of Chicago Press.

Blakeslee, Melise R., and Brian E. Ferguson. 2006. United States: The Truths and Myths of Open Source Software. May 31, http://www.mondaq.com/article.asp?articleid=40128.

Borgmann, Albert, and N. Katharine Hayles. 1999. An Interview/Dialogue on Humans and Machines. University of Chicago Press, http://www.press.uchicago.edu/Misc/Chicago/borghayl.html.

Boring, Randy. 1998. Open Is Still Much Better Than Closed Source. August 11, http://www.mibsoftware.com/bazdev/0015.htm.

Boston Consulting Group. 2002. The Boston Consulting Group/OSTG Hacker Survey. In *O'Reilly Open Source Conference*.

Bourbakis, Nick. 1998. World History. *Metropolis,* February/March, http://www.metropolismag.com/html/content_0298/fe98wor.htm.

Boyle, James. 1996. *Shamans, Software and Spleens: Law and the Information Society.* Cambridge: Harvard University Press.

————. 1997. Foucault in Cyberspace: Surveillance, Sovereignty, and Hard-Wired Censors. *University of Cincinnati Law Review* 66:177.

————. 2000. The First Amendment and Cyberspace: The Clinton Years. *Law and Contemporary Problems* 63:337.

Bradner, S. 1996. RFC 2026: The Internet Standards Process — Revision 3. http://www.ietf.org/rfc/rfc2026.txt.

————. 2000. A Different Hell? *Network World*, May 8, http://www.networkworld.com/columnists/2000/0508bradner.html.

Brandle, Lars. 2006. Waits Wins Spanish Appeal on Ad Sound-Alike Case. *Billboard*, January 20, http://www.billboard.com/bbcom/news/article_display.jsp?vnu_content_id=1001882361.

Brooks, Frederick. 1995. *The Mythical Man-Month: Essays in Software Engineering.* Boston: Addison-Wesley.

————. 1996. The Computer Scientist as Toolsmith II. *Communications of the ACM* 39 (3): 61–68.

Brooks, R. A. 1991. New Approaches to Robotics. *Science* 253:1227–32.

Brown, Ken Spencer. 2006. Linux Provider Red Hat Reports 38% Rise In Sales. June 28, http://news.yahoo.com/s/ibd/20060628/bs_ibd_ibd/2006628tech01.

Campbell, Donald. 1960. Blind Variation and Selective Retention in Creative Thought as in Other Knowledge Processes. *Psychological Review* 67:380–400.

Carroll, Noel. 2003. Art, Creativity, and Tradition. In *The Creation of Art*, edited by B. Gaut and P. Livingston. Cambridge: Cambridge University Press.

Carver, Brian W. 2005. Share and Share Alike: Understanding and Enforcing and Open Source and Free Software Licenses. *Berkeley Technology Law Journal* 20:443–81.

Caslon Analytics. 2006. Caslon Analytics Intellectual Property Guide. http://www.caslon.com.au/ipguide17.htm#cases (accessed July 25, 2006).

Cavalier, Forest J. III. 1998. Some Implications of Bazaar Size. August 11, http://www.mibsoftware.com/bazdev/.

Century, Michael. 2001. Open Code and Creativity in the Digital Age. Paper read at International Conference on Collaboration and Ownership in the Digital Economy, at Cambridge, U.K.

Ceruzzi, Paul E. 2003. *A History of Modern Computing.* 2nd ed. Cambridge: The MIT Press.

Chance, Tom. 2006. *Free Culture*, February 10, http://blog.cmc.oregonstate.edu/mtblogs/jon/2006/02/conference_paper_1.html#comment-805.

Chandrasekhar, C. P. 2002. The Two Faces of Mr. Gates. *Countercurrents.org*, December 2, http://www.countercurrents.org/glo-sekhar.htm.

Chandrashekhar, Subhramanyam. 1990. *Truth and Beauty: Aesthetics and Motivations in Science* Chicago: University of Chicago Press.

Clark, Andy. 2006. Author's Reply to Symposium on *Natural-Born Cyborgs*. June 28, http://hdl.handle.net/1842/1315.

————. 1996. Linguistic Anchors in the Sea of Thought. *Pragmatics and Cognition* 4 (1): 93–103.

————. 1998. Magic Words: How Language Augments Human Computation. In *Language and Thought: Interdisciplinary Themes*, edited by P. Carruthers and J. Boucher. Cambridge: Cambridge University Press.

————. 2003. *Natural-Born Cyborgs*. New York, NY: Oxford University Press.

Clark, Andy, and David Chalmers. 1998. The Extended Mind. *Analysis* 58 (1): 7–19.

Clements, Douglas. 2003. Creation Myths: Does Innovation Require Intellectual Property Rights? *Reason*, March, http://www.reason.com/0303/fe.dc.creation.shtml.

Clynes, Manfred E., and Nathan S. Kline. 1960. Cyborgs and Space. *Astronautics* 14 (9): 26–27, 74–76.

Cole, M. 1991. Conclusion. In *Perspectives on Socially Shared Cognition*, edited by L. B. Resnick, J. M. Levine and S. D. Teasley. Washington, DC: American Psychological Association.

Coleman, Gabriella. 2005. The Social Construction of Freedom in Free and Open Source Software: Hackers, Ethics, and the Liberal Tradition, Anthropology, University of Chicago, Chicago.

————. 2005. Three Ethical Moments in Debian. September 15, http://ssrn.com/abstract=805287.

Collingwood, R. G. 1938. *The Principles of Art*. New York: Oxford University Press.

Collins, Michael. 2001. *Carrying the Fire: An Astronaut's Journey*. Lanham, MD: Cooper Square Press.

Cox, Geoff, Alex McLean, and Adrian Ward. 2004. Coding Praxis: Reconsidering the Aesthetics of Code. In *READ_ME 2004*. Aarhus, Denmark.

Cranston, Maurice. 1954. *Freedom: A New Analysis*. Longmans, Green, and Co.: New York.

Crease, Robert P. 2004. The Greatest Equations Ever. *Physics World*, October.

Crocker, Lawrence. 1980. *Positive Liberty: An Essay in Normative Political Philosophy*. Boston: Martinus Nijhoff Publishers.

Cusumano, Michael. 2004. Reflections on Free and Open Software. *Communications of the ACM* 47(10): 25–27.

————. 2005. Response to "Free Is Not Open Software." *Communications of the ACM* 48 (7): 13.

Cusumano, Michael, Clay Shirky, Joseph Feller, Brian Fitzgerald, Scott A. Hissam, and Karim R. Lakhani, eds. 2005. *Perspectives on Free and Open Source Software*. Cambridge: MIT Press.

David, Paul. 2005. From Keeping 'Nature's Secrets' to the Institutionalization of 'Open Science.' In *CODE: Collaborative Ownership in the Digital Economy*, edited by R. A. Ghosh. Cambridge: MIT Press.

Davis, Randall, Pamela Samuelson, Mitchell Kapor, and Jerome Reichman. 1996. A New View of Intellectual Property and Software. *Communications of the ACM* 39 (3): 21–30.

Debian Project. 2004. *Debian Social Contract*. April 26, http://www.debian.org/social_contract.

Deleuze, Gilles, and Felix Guattari. 1983. *Anti-Oedipus: Capitalism and Schizophrenia*. Translated by R. Hurley, M. Seem, and H. R. Lane. Minneapolis: University of Minnesota Press.

Delio, Michelle. 2004. Linux: Fewer Bugs than Rivals. *Wired*, December 14, http://www.wired.com/news/linux/0,1411,66022,00.html.

Denning, Peter J. 2000. Computer Science: The Discipline. In *The Encyclopedia of Computer Science*, edited by A. Ralston, E. D. Reilly, and D. Hemmendinger. New York: Grove's Dictionaries.

Dewey, John. 1934. *Art as Experience*. New York: Perigee Trade.

Diamond v. Diehr, 450 U.S. 175 (1981). http://laws.findlaw.com/us/450/175.html.

Dibona, Chris, Danese Cooper, and Mark Stone. 2005. *Open Sources 2.0*. Sebastopol: O'Reilly.

DiBona, Chris, Danese Cooper, and Mark Stone. 2006. Introduction. In *Open Sources 2.0: The Continuing Evolution*, edited by C. DiBona, D. Cooper, and M. Stone. Sebastopol: O'Reilly.

DiBona, Chris, Sam Ockman, and Mark Stone, eds. 1999. *Open Sources: Voices from the Open Source Revolution*. Sebastopol: O'Reilly.

Dickie, George. 1974. *Art and the Aesthetic: An Institutional Analysis*. Ithaca: Cornell University Press.

Dickson, David. 1993. *The New Politics of Science*. Chicago: University of Chicago Press.

Dijkstra, Edsger Wysbe. 1968. Go-to statement considered harmful. *Communications of the ACM* 11(3): 147–48.

_____. 1970. Notes on Structured Programming. Eindhoven: Technological University Eindhoven.

_____. 1980. Some Beautiful Arguments Using Mathematical Induction. *Acta Informatica* 13:1–8.

_____. 1999. EWD1284: Computing Science; Achievements and Challenges. http://www.cs.utexas.edu/users/EWD/transcriptions/EWD12xx/EWD1284.html.

Dixon, Rod. 2003. *Open Source Software Law*. Norwood, MA: Artech House Publishers.

Drepper, Ulrich. 2001. Glibc 2.2.4 Release Notes. http://sources.redhat.com/ml/libc-announce/2001/msg00000.html.

Drummond, Rennie. 2003. Editorial Peer Review: Its Development and Rationale. In *Peer Review in Health Sciences*, edited by F. Godlee and T. Jefferson. London: BMJ Publishing Group.

Dunn, Peter, and Loraine Leeson. 1997. The Aesthetics of Collaboration: Aesthetics and the Body Politic. *Art Journal* 56 (1).

Dupuy, Jean-Pierre. 2000. *The Mechanization of the Mind*. Translated by M. B. DeBevoise. Princeton: Princeton University Press.

Dworkin, Gerald. 1988. *The Theory and Practice of Autonomy*. New York: Cambridge University Press.

Dworkin, Ronald. 2000. *Sovereign Virtue: The Theory and Practice of Equality*. Cambridge, MA: Harvard University Press.

East, E. M., and D. F. Jones. 1919. *Inbreeding and Outbreeeding*. Philadelphia: Lippincott.

Eco, Umberto. 1984. *The Role of the Reader: Explorations in the Semiotics of Texts*. Bloomington: Indiana University Press.

_____. 1989. *The Open Work*. Translated by A. Cancogni. Cambridge: Harvard University Press.

Ellul, Jacques. 1967. *The Technological Society*. London: Vintage.

Elster, Jon. 2000. *Ulysses Unbound: Studies in Rationality, Pre-Commitment, and Constraints*. Cambridge: Cambridge University Press.

Engemann, Christoph. 2006. The Citoyen of Electronic Government, Sociology, University of Bremen, Bremen, Germany.

Eunice, Jonathan. 1998. Beyond the Cathedral, Beyond the Bazaar. http://www.illuminata.com/cgi-local/pub.cgi?docid=cathedral&section=cathedral1.

Europa. 2003. Cases of Official Recognition/Adoption of F/OSS. http://europa.eu.int/information_society/activities/opensource/cases/index_en.htm.

Evans, James. 2006. Horrible Code. http://www.nabble.com/Horrible-code-t1631900.html.

Farmelo, Graham, ed. 2002. *It Must be Beautiful: Great Equations of Modern Science.* London: Granta Books.

Farrell, Nick. 2006. Sun will open source Java 'in months.' *The Inquirer*, June 28, http://www.theinquirer.net/default.aspx?article=32685.

Fells, David. 2004. Writing Clean and Efficient PHP Code. May 26, http://www.devshed.com/c/a/PHP/Writing-Clean-and-Efficient-PHP-Code/.

Feyerabend, Paul. 1975. *Against Method.* London: New Left Books.

Feynman, Richard. 1965. *The Character of Physical Law.* New York: The Modern Library.

Fish, Stanley. 1994. *There's No Such Thing as Free Speech . . . and It's a Good Thing Too.* New York: Oxford University Press.

Fishwick, Paul, Stephan Diehl, Jane Prophet, and Jonas Löwgren. 2003. Aesthetic Computing Manifesto. *Leonardo* 36, no. 4, doi:10.1162/002409403322258556, http://www.mitpressjournals.org/doi/abs/10.1162/002409403322258556.

Fitzgerald, Brian. 2005. Has Open Source Software a Future? In *Perspectives on Free and Open Source Software*, edited by J. Feller, B. Fitzgerald, S. Hissam, and K. R. Lakhani. Cambridge: MIT Press.

Fogel, Karl. 2005. Managing Volunteers. In *Producing Open Source Software: How to Run a Successful Free Software Project.* Sebastopol: O'Reilly.

Forsythe, George. 1967. A University's Education Program in Computer Science. *Communications of the ACM* 10(1): 3–11.

Foucault, Michel. 1977. *Discipline and Punish: The Birth of the Prison.* Translated by A. Sheridan. New York: Vintage.

———. 1980. Two Lectures. In *Power/Knowledge: Selected Interviews and Other Writings, 1972–1977*, edited by C. Gordon. New York: Pantheon.

Fourman, Michael. 2002. Informatics. In *Routledge International Encyclopedia of Information and Library Science*, edited by J. Feather and P. Sturges. New York: Routledge.

Fredkin, Edward. 2001. Introduction to Digital Philosophy. http://www.digitalphilosophy.org/digital_philosophy/toc.htm.

Freud, Sigmund. 1994. Creative Writers and Day-Dreaming. In *Psychoanalytic Explorations in Art*, edited by A. Neill and A. Ridley. New York: McGraw-Hill.

Friedman, B., D. C. Howe, and E. Felten. 2002. Informed Consent in the Mozilla Browser: Implementing Value Sensitive Design. Paper read at 35th Annual Hawaii International Conference on System Sciences (HICSS'02).

Gallaway, Terrel, and Douglas Kinnear. 2004. Open Source Software, the Wrongs of Copyright, and the Rise of Technology. *Journal of Economic Issues* 38 (2): 467–75.

Galler, Bernie. 1968. Language Protection by Trademark Ill-Advised. *Communications of the ACM* 11(3): 148.

Galli, Peter. 2005. Sun Sees Shining Future in Open Source. *eWeek.com*, April 5, http://www.eweek.com/article2/0,1759,1782922,00.asp.

Gallie, W. B. 1956. Essentially Contested Concepts. *Proceedings of the Aristotelean Society* 56:167–88.

Galloway, Alexander R. 2004. *Protocol: How Control Exists after Decentralization.* Cambridge: MIT Press.

Gannes, L. 2006. Friendster Wins Patent. *Red Herring*, July 6, http://www.redherring.com/Article.aspx?a=17498&hed=Friendster+Wins+Patent#.

Garfield, Eugene. 1979. *Citation Indexing: Its Theory and Application in Science, Technology, and Humanities.* New York: Wiley.

Garfinkel, Simson L., Richard M. Stallman, and Mitchell Kapor. 1991. Why Patents are Bad for Software. *Issues in Science & Technology* 8 (1): 50–55.

Gates, William. 1976. An Open Letter to Hobbyists. http://www.digibarn.com/ collections/newsletters/homebrew/V2_01/.

Gatto, James G. 2006. Open Source License Survives Challenge: Doubts About GPL Enforceability Continue to Wane. http://www.pillsburylaw.com/content/portal/ publications/2006/4/20064181257864/Open%20Source_IP%20Vol%201402%20 No%204023%2004-18-06.pdf.

Gaut, Berys, and Paisley Livingston. 2003. The Creation of Art: Issues and Perspectives. In *The Creation of Art: New Essays in Philosophical Aesthetics*, edited by B. Gaut and P. Livingston. Cambridge: Cambridge University Press.

Ghosh, Rishab Aiyer. 1998. Cooking-pot Markets: An Economic Model for the Trade in Free Goods and Services on the Internet. *First Monday* 3(3).

———, ed. 2005. *CODE: Collaborative Ownership in the Digital Economy*. Cambridge: MIT Press.

Ghosh, Rishab Aiyer, and Ruediger Glott. 2002. Free/Libre and Open Source Software: Survey and Study. http://www.infonomics.nl/FLOSS/report/index.htm.

Gibson, Christine. 2006. How Jack Kilby Changed Your Life. *AmericanHeritage.com*, February 6, http://www.americanheritage.com/people/articles/web/20060206-jack-kilby-microchip-integrated-circuit-transistor-vacuum-tube-texas-instruments-robert-noyce-semiconductor-computer-calculator.shtml.

Ginsparg, Paul. 2003. Can Peer Review be Better Focused? March 13, http://people.ccmr. cornell.edu/~ginsparg/blurb/pg02pr.html.

Glass, Robert L. 2005. Standing in Front of the Open Source Steamroller. In *Perspectives on Free and Open Source Software*, edited by J. Feller, B. Fitzgerald, S. Hissam, and K. R. Lakhani. Cambridge: MIT Press.

Goldman, Emma. 2005. *Anarchism and Other Essays*: Filiquarian Publishing.

Gottschalk v. Benson, 409 U.S. 63 (1972).

Graham, Paul. 2000. *Hackers and Painters: Big Ideas from the Computer Age*. Sebastopol: O'Reilly.

Gray, Chris Hables. 2001. *Cyborg Citizen: Politics in the Posthuman Age*. New York: Routledge.

Gray, Chris Hables, S. Mentor, and H. J. Figueroa-Sarriera. 1995. Cyborgology: Constructing the Knowledge of Cybernetic Organisms. In *The Cyborg Handbook*, edited by C. H. Gray. New York: Routledge.

Gray, Chris Hables, and Steven Mentor. 1995. The Cyborg Body Politic and the New World Order. In *Prosthetic Territories: Politics and Hypertechnologies*, edited by G. Brahm and M. Driscoll. Colorado Springs: Westview Press.

Greene, Richard C. 2001. Ballmer: "Linux is a cancer." *The Register*, June 2, http://www. theregister.co.uk/2001/06/02/ballmer_linux_is_a_cancer/.

Grene, Marjorie. 1985. Perception, Interpretation and the Sciences. In *Evolution at a Crossroads*, edited by D. Depew and B. Weber. Cambridge: MIT Press.

Grier, David Alan. 2005. *When Computers Were Human*. Princeton: Princeton University Press.

Gude, Olivia. 1989. An Aesthetics of Collaboration. *Art Journal* 48 (4): 321–23.

Hannemyr, Gisle. 1999. Technology and Pleasure: Considering Hacking Constructive. *First Monday* 2, no. 4 (February 1), http://www.firstmonday.dk/ISSUES/issue4_2/ index.html.

Haraway, Donna. 1991. A Cyborg Manifesto: Science, Technology, and Socialist-Feminism in the Late Twentieth Century. In *Simians, Cyborgs, and Women: The Reinvention of Nature*. New York: Routledge.

———. 1995. Cyborgs and Symbionts: Living Together in the New World Order. In *The Cyborg Handbook*, edited by C. H. Gray, H. J. Figueroa-Sarriera and S. Mentor. New York: Routledge.

Harmon, Amy. 2000. For Many Online Music Fans, Court Ruling Is Call to Arms. *New York Times*, July 28, http://partners.nytimes.com/library/tech/00/07/biztech/articles/28napster.html.

Harvey, David. 1989. *The Condition of Modernity*. Cambridge: Cambridge University Press.

Haskins, Walaika K. 2006. Microsoft and XenSource Team Up on Viridian. *Newsfactor.com*, July 18, http://www.newsfactor.com/story.xhtml?story_id=001000000YIJ.

Hauben, Michael, Ronda Hauben, and Thomas Truscott. 1997. *Netizens: On the History and Impact of Usenet and the Internet*. Los Alamitos, CA: Wiley-IEEE Computer Society Press.

Hausman, Carl. 1981. Criteria for Creativity. In *The Concept of Creativity in Science and Art*, edited by D. Dutton and M. Krausz. The Hague: Martinus Nijhoff.

Hayles, N. Katherine. 2005. *My Mother Was a Computer: Digital Subjects and Literary Texts*. Chicago: University of Chicago Press.

Heisenberg, Werner. 1974. The Meaning of Beauty in the Exact Sciences. In *Across the Frontiers*, edited by R. Nanda. New York: Harper and Row.

Heiss, Janice J. 2002. The Poetry of Programming. http://java.sun.com/features/2002/11/gabriel_qa.html.

Henneberg, Maciej. 1997. Peer Review: The Holy Office of Modern Science. *naturalSCIENCE 2* (February). http://naturalscience.com/ns/articles/01-02/ns_mh.html.

Himanen, Pekka. 2002. *The Hacker Ethic: A Radical Approach to the Philosophy of Business*. New York: Random House.

Hippel, E. von, and G. von Krogh. 2003. Open Source Software and the Private-Collective Innovation Model: Issues for Organization Science. *Organization Science* 14 (2): 209–23.

Hissam, Scott A., Charles B. Weinstock, Daniel Plakosh, and Jayatirtha Asundi. 2001. Perspectives on Open Source Software. Technical Report CMU/SEI-2001-TR-019, Carnegie Mellon Software Engineering Institute, http://www.sei.cmu.edu/publications/documents/01.reports/01tr019.html.

Hollaar, Lee A. 2002. *Legal Protection of Digital Information*. Edison, NJ: BNA Books.

Horrobin, David. 2001. Something Rotten at the Core of Science? *Trends in Pharmacological Sciences* 22 (2): 51–52.

Horrobin, David F. 1981. Peer Review: Is the Good the Enemy of the Best? *Journal of Research in Communication Studies* 3:327–34.

———. 1990. The Philosophical Basis of Peer Review and the Suppression of Innovation. *Journal of the American Medical Association* 263:1438–41.

———. 1996. Peer Review of Grant Applications: A Harbinger for Mediocrity in Clinical Research? *Lancet* 348:1293–95.

Horvath, John. 1998. Freeware Capitalism. Email to nettime mailing list, February 5, http://www.nettime.org/Lists-Archives/nettime-l-9802/msg00026.html.

House, Ron. 1999. Uniting the Open-Source and Commercial Software Worlds. http://www.sci.usq.edu.au/staff/house/ipl/ppunite.htm.

Human Genome Program. 2006. Genetics and Patenting. http://www.ornl.gov/sci/techresources/Human_Genome/elsi/patents.shtml (accessed August 8, 2006).

Hume, David. 1978. *A Treatise of Human Nature*. Edited by L. A. Selby-Bigge and P. H. Nidditch. Oxford: Clarendon Press. Original edition, 1739.

Hylton, Jeremy. 2002. Infuriating ZClass Registry Heisenbug. Email to Zope-dev mailing list, December 16, http://mail.zope.org/pipermail/zope-dev/2002-December/018339.html.

Ignatieff, Michael. 1998. *Isaiah Berlin: A Life*. London: Chatto and Windus.

James, William. 1950. *Principles of Psychology*. New York: Dover. Original edition, 1890.

Jameson, Fredric. 1991. *Postmodernism, or, The Cultural Logic of Late Capitalism*. Durham: Duke University Press.

John-Steiner, Vera. 2000. *Creative Collaboration*. New York: Oxford University Press, USA.

Jones, Pamela. 2003. The GPL Is a License, Not a Contract, Which Is Why the Sky Isn't Falling. *Groklaw*, December 14, http://www.groklaw.net/articlebasic.php?story=20031214210634851.

Jurafsky, Daniel, and James H. Martin. 2000. *Speech and Language Processing: An Introduction to Natural Language Processing, Computational Linguistics, and Speech Recognition*. Upper Saddle River, NJ: Prentice-Hall.

Juris, Jeffrey S. 2005. Youth and the World Social Forum. http://ya.ssrc.org/transnational/Juris/.

Kablenet. 2001. From Father State to Partner State. http://www.staat-modern.de/infos/daten/r140501_1.html (accessed November 10, 2005; article no longer available).

Kaku, Michio. 1994. *Hyperspace*. New York: Oxford University Press.

Kalnichevski, Oleg. 2005. RFC: HttpEntity, HttpIncomingEntity, HttpOutgoingEntity Revisited. Email to jakarta-httpcomponents-dev mailing list, May 1. http://mail-archives.apache.org/mod_mbox/jakarta-httpcomponents-dev/200505.mbox/%3c1114948928.4890.6.camel@localhost.localdomain%3e.

Kant, Immanuel. 1790/1987. *Critique of Judgment*. Translated by W. S. Pluhar. Indianapolis: Hackett.

————. 1991. *A Metaphysics of Morals*. Translated by M. Gregor. Cambridge: Cambridge University Press. Original edition, 1797.

Katsh, M. Ethan. 1996. Software Worlds and the First Amendment: Virtual Doorkeepers in Cyberspace. *University of Chicago Legal Forum*. 335.

Kelty, Christopher. 2001. Free Software/Free Science. *First Monday* 6, no. 12 (December 2001), http://www.firstmonday.org/issues/issue6_12/kelty/.

————. 2002. Hau to Do Things with Words. http://kelty.org/or/papers/Kelty.Hautodothings.2002.rtf.

————. 2005. Free Science. In *Perspectives on Free and Open Source Software*, edited by J. Feller, B. Fitzgerald, S. Hissam and K. R. Lakhani. Cambridge: MIT Press.

Kempf, Karl. 1961. *Electronic Computers Within the Ordnance Corps*: U.S. Army Ordnance Corps.

Kerckhoffs, Auguste. 1883. La Cryptographie Militaire. *Journal des Sciences Militaires* IX:5–83, 161–91.

Kernighan, Brian W., and P. J. Plauger. 1978. *The Elements of Programming Style*. New York: McGraw-Hill.

Kesan, Jay P., and Rajiv C. Shah. 2005. Shaping Code. *Harvard Journal of Law & Technology* 18 (2): 319–99.

Kesteloot, Lawrence. 1998. Thoughts About Bazaars. http://www.teamten.com/lawrence/cathedral-bazaar.html.

Kim, Eugene. 2006. Everything Is Known. In *Open Sources 2.0: The Continuing Evolution*, edited by C. DiBona, D. Cooper and M. Stone. Sebastopol: O'Reilly.

Kludge. http://en.wikipedia.org/wiki/Kludge (accessed August 22, 2006).

Knuth, Donald E. 1972. George Forsythe and the Development of Computer Science. *Communications of the ACM* 15 (8).

———. 1992. *Literate Programming*. Stanford, CA: Center for the Study of Language and Information.

Kohno, Tadayoshi, Adam Stubblefield, Aviel D. Rubin, and Dan S. Wallach. 2004. Analysis of an Electronic Voting System. Paper read at IEEE Symposium on Security and Privacy, at Oakland, CA.

Kollock, Peter. 1997. The Economies of Online Cooperation: Gifts and Public Goods in Computer Communities. In *Communities in Cyberspace*, edited by M. Smith and P. Kollock. Berkeley: University of California Press.

Kragh, H., and R. C. Hovis. 1993. P. A. M. Dirac and the Beauty of Physics. *Scientific American*, 104–09.

Krill, Paul. 2006. Microsoft Executive Lauds Open Source. *InfoWorld*, July 19, http://www.infoworld.com/article/06/07/19/HNkaefer_1.html.

Kropotkin, Peter. 1902. *Mutual Aid*. London: Heinemann.

Kuhn, Thomas. 1962. *The Structure of Scientific Revolutions*. Chicago: University of Chicago Press.

Kuhn, Thomas S. 1998. Objectivity, Value Judgment, and Theory Choice. In *Philosophy of Science: The Central Issues*, edited by M. Curd and J. A. Cover. New York: W. W. Norton & Company.

Laffoon, Eric. 2005. Qt, the GPL, Business and Freedom. *Open for Business*, August 5, http://www.ofb.biz/article.pl?sid=381.

Lakhani, Karim R., and Robert G. Wolf. 2005. Why Hackers Do What They Do: Understanding Motivation and Effort in Free/Open Source Software Projects. In *Perspectives on Free and Open Source Software*, edited by M. Cusumano, C. Shirky, J. Feller, B. Fitzgerald, S. A. Hissam, and K. R. Lakhani. Cambridge: MIT Press.

Lammers, Susan. 1989. *Programmers at Work: Interviews With 19 Programmers Who Shaped the Computer Industry*. Redmond, WA: Tempus Books of Microsoft Press.

Lancashire, David. 2001. The Fading Altruism of Open Source Development. *First Monday* 6.

LaSala, Joseph A., Ryan Richards, Judith L. Harris, and Gary L. Kaplan. 2002. Comments of Novell Inc. http://www.usdoj.gov/atr/cases/ms_tuncom/major/mtc-00029523.htm.

Latour, Bruno. 1999. A Collective of Humans and Nonhumans. In *Pandora's Hope: Essays on the Reality of Science Studies*. Cambridge: Harvard University Press.

Laudan, Larry. 1981. A Confutation of Convergent Realism. *Philosophy of Science* 48:19–49.

———. 1984. *Science and Values: The Aims of Science and Their Role in Scientific Debate*. Berkeley: University of California Press.

Laurent, Andrew M. St. 2004. *Open Source and Free Software Licensing*. Sebastopol: O'Reilly.

Laurie, Ben. 2006. Open Source and Security. In *Open Sources 2.0: The Continuing Evolution*, edited by C. DiBona, D. Cooper and M. Stone. Sebastopol: O'Reilly.

Lawson, Mark. 2005. Berners-Lee on the Read/Write Web. *BBC News*, August 9, http://news.bbc.co.uk/1/hi/technology/4132752.stm.

League for Programming Freedom. 2004. Unisys/CompuServe GIF Controversy. July 2 http://lpf.ai.mit.edu/Patents/Gif/Gif.html.

Leonard, Andrew. 1999. Open Season. *Wired* 7, no. 5 (May), http://www.wirednews.com/wired/ archive/7.05/open_source.html.

_____. 2006. Free Software, Big Oil, and Venezuelan Politics, *Salon.com,* January 12, http://www.salon.com/tech/htww/2006/01/12/venezuela/index_np.html.

Lerner, Josh, and Jean Tirole. 2001. The Open Source Movement: Key Research Questions. *European Economic Review Papers and Proceedings* 35:819–26.

Lessig, Lawrence. 1999. The Code Is the Law. *The Standard*, April 9, http://www.lessig.org/content/standard/0,1902,4165,00.html.

_____. 2000. *Code and Other Laws of Cyberspace*. New York: Basic Books.

Letowska, Ewa. 1997. A Constitution of Possibilities. *East European Constitutional Review* 6 (2 &3).

Levien, Ralph. 1998. The Decommoditization of Protocols. November 4, http://www.levien.com/free/decommoditizing.html.

Levy, Stephen. 1994. *Hackers: Heroes of the Computer Revolution*. New York: Penguin.

Lewontin, Richard. 1991. *Biology as Ideology: The Doctrine of DNA*. New York: Harper Perennial.

Libervis.com. 2006. FUDzilla: Anti-disinformation Project. http://www.libervis.com/x/modules/mylinks/.

Lindquist, Christopher. 2006. Dirty Code, Licenses and Open Source. *CIO Magazine*, July 1, http://www.cio.com/archive/070106/et_main.html.

Lions, John. 1977. *Lions' Commentary on Unix*. 6th ed. Charlottesville, VA: Peer-to-Peer Communications.

Livingston, Paisley. 2003. Pentimento. In *The Creation of Art: New Essays in Philosophical Aesthetics*, edited by B. Gaut and P. Livingston. Cambridge: Cambridge University Press.

Lohr, Steve, and Laurie J. Flynn. 2006. Microsoft announces another delay for Windows Vista. *San Diego Union-Tribune*, March 22. http://www.signonsandiego.com/uniontrib/20060322/news_1b22vista.html.

Longino, Helen. 1990. *Science as Social Knowledge: Values and Objectivity in Scientific Inquiry*. Princeton: Princeton University Press.

Lovelock, J. E. 1979. *Gaia: A New Look at Life on Earth*. New York: Oxford University Press.

Lozes, Richard L. 2006. To Make CS Relevant, Give It an Industrial Focus. *Communications of the ACM* 49 (6): 11.

MacCallum, Gerald. 1967. Negative and Positive Freedom. *Philosophical Review* 76:312–34.

Machan, Tibor. 1998. *Generosity: Virtue in the Civil Society*. Washington, DC: The Cato Institute.

Mahoney, Michael. 1990. Software and the Assembly Line. Paper read at Workshop on Technohistory of Electrical Information Technology, at Deutsches Museum, Munich.

Markoff, John. 2005. Three Technology Companies Join to Finance Research. *New York Times*, December 15, C5.

Matusow, Jason. 2005. Shared Source at Microsoft. In *Perspectives on Free and Open Source Software*, edited by J. Feller, B. Fitzgerald, S. Hissam, and K. R. Lakhani. Cambridge: MIT Press.

Maynard, Patrick. 2003. Drawings as Drawn: An Approach to Creation in an Art. In *The Creation of Art: Issues and Perspectives*, edited by B. Gaut and P. Livingston. New York: Cambridge University Press.

Mazlish, Bruce. 1993. *The Fourth Discontinuity: The Co-evolution of Human and Machines*. New Haven: Yale University Press.

McCullagh, Declan. 1999. Prix Ars Elctronica 1999 Jury-Statement. http://www.aec.at/en/archives/prix_archive/prixjuryStatement.asp?iProjectID=2600.

Merton, Robert. 1979. *The Sociology of Science: Theoretical and Empirical Investigations*. Chicago: University of Chicago Press.

Microsoft Research. 2006. University Relations. http://research.microsoft.com/ur/asia/.

Mill, John Stuart. 1975. *On Liberty*. New York: Penguin Classics.

Miller, David. 2006. Constraints on Freedom. In *The Liberty Reader*, edited by D. Miller. Boulder, Colorado: Paradigm Publishers.

Mills, Harlan D. 1983. *Software Productivity*. Boston: Little, Brown and Company.

Miner, Robert C. 1998. Verum-factum and Practical Wisdom in the Early Writings of Giambattista Vico. *Journal of the History of Ideas* 59 (1): 53–73.

Mirapaul, Matthew. 1999. Lyrics Site in Copyright Dispute May Go Commercial. *New York Times*, July 30, http://www.nytimes.com/library/tech/99/01/cyber/articles/30lyrics.html.

Mitchell, William. 1996. *City of Bits: Space, Place and the Infobahn*. Cambridge: MIT Press.

Moglen, Eben. 2000. When Code Isn't Law, April 3, http://emoglen.law.columbia.edu/publications/lu-01.pdf.

———. 2003. Freeing the Mind: Free Software and the Death of Proprietary Culture. July 29, http://moglen.law.columbia.edu/publications/maine-speech.html.

———. 2003. The dotCommunist Manifesto. http://emoglen.law.columbia.edu/publications/dcm.html.

Moody, Glyn. 2002. *Rebel Code: Linux and the Open Source Revolution*. New York: Basic Books.

Mooers, Calvin N. 1968. Reply to "Language Protection by Trademark Ill-Advised." *Communications of the ACM* 11 (3): 148–49.

Moore, Fred. 1975. The Club is All of Us. *Homebrew Computer Club Newsletter* 1, no. 2 (April 12), http://www.digibarn.com/collections/newsletters/homebrew/V1_02/.

Morowitz, Harold. 2002. *The Emergence of Everything: How the World Become Complex*. New York: Oxford University Press.

Mulvey, Patrick J., and Starr Nicholson. 2005. Enrollment and Degrees Report, 2003: American Institute Physics.

Napoli, Lisa. 1999. Yahoo Angers GeoCities Members With Copyright. *New York Times*, June 30, http://www.nytimes.com/library/tech/99/07/cyber/articles/01yahoo.html.

National Commission on New Technological Uses of Copyrighted Works. 1977. Transcript of Meeting No. 16. http://homepages.nyu.edu/~gmp216/documents/contu/meeting-16.txt.

———. 1980. Final Report http://digital-law-online.info/CONTU/contu1.html.

National Research Council, Committee on Innovations in Computing and Communications: Lessons from History, Computer Science and Telecommunications Board, and Mathematics Commission on Physical Sciences, and Applications. 1999. *Funding a Revolution: Government Support for Computing Research*. Washington, DC: National Academy Press.

National Science Board. 2004. Science and Engineering Indicators 2004.

Newell, A., A.J. Perlis, and H.A Simon. 1967. What Is Computer Science? *Science* 157 (1373–74).

Newell, Allen, and Herbert A. Simon. 1976. Computer Science as Empirical Inquiry: Symbols and Search. *Communications of the ACM* 19 (3): 113–26.

Nissenbaum, Helen. 1996. Accountability in a Computerized Society. *Science and Engineering Ethics* 2:25–42.

Noble, David. 1979. *America by Design : Science, Technology, and the Rise of Corporate Capitalism*. New York: Oxford University Press, USA.

Noble, David F. 1991. *Progress Without People: In Defense of Luddism*. Chicago: Charles H. Kerr.

Novitz, David. 2003. Explanations of Creativity. In *The Creation of Art: New Essays in Philosophical Aesthetics*, edited by B. Gaut and P. Livingston. Cambridge: Cambridge University Press.

O'Reilly, Tim. 2001. Is Open Source Un-American? *OnLAMP.com*, March 8, http://www.onlamp.com/pub/a/onlamp/2001/03/08/unamerican.html.

O'Mara, Margaret Pugh. 2005. *Cities of Knowledge: Cold War Science and the Search For the Next Silicon Valley*. Princeton: Princeton University Press.

Okruhlik, Kathleen. 1998. Gender and the Biological Sciences. In *Philosophy of Science: The Central Issues*, edited by M. Curd and J. A. Cover. New York: W. W. Norton & Company.

Olsen, Stein Haugom. 2003. Culture, Convention, and Creativity. In *The Creation of Art*, edited by B. Gaut and P. Livingston. Cambridge: Cambridge University Press.

Olson, Michael. 2006. Dual Licensing. In *Open Sources 2.0: The Continuing Evolution*, edited by C. DiBona, D. Cooper, and M. Stone. Sebastopol: O'Reilly.

Open Source Initiative. 2006. The Open Source Definition (Annotated), version 1.9. http://www.opensource.org/docs/definition.php.

Open Source Risk Management. 2004. Position Paper: Mitigating Linux Patent Risk. http://www.osriskmanagement.com/pdf_articles/linuxpatentpaper.pdf.

Open Voting Consortium. 2006. Specter of Stolen Elections Creates Crisis. http://www.openvotingconsortium.org/the_problem.

Orlowski, Andrew. 2005. 'Cool it, Linus' — Bruce Perens. *The Register*, April 15, http://www.theregister.co.uk/2005/04/15/perens_on_torvalds/.

———. 2005. Torvalds Knifes Tridgell. *The Register*, April 14, http://www.theregister.co.uk/2005/04/14/torvalds_attacks_tridgell/.

Parker v. Flook, 437 U.S. 584 (1978). http://laws.findlaw.com/us/437/584.html.

PC SOFT. 2006. An Easy and Powerful 5th Generation Language: W-Language. http://www.pcsoft.fr/us/windev/broch9/Export19.htm.

Pepperdine, Kirk. 2006. The Commercialization of Open Source: Is VC Investment a Good Thing for Open Source? *Enterprise Open Source Magazine*, April 5, http://opensource.sys-con.com/read/44367.htm.

Pollock, Lansing. 1981. *The Freedom Principle*. Amherst, New York: Prometheus Books.

Popper, Karl. 1962. *Conjectures and Refutations: The Growth of Scientific Knowledge.*
     New York: Basic Books.
_____. 1966. *The Open Society and its Enemies.* Vol. II. Princeton: Princeton University
     Press. Original edition, 1945.
Post, David G. 2000. Internet: Of Black Holes and Decentralized Law-Making in Cyber-
     space. *2 Vanderbilt Journal of Enterntainment Law and Practice 70.*
Putnam, Hilary. 1995. *Pragmatism: An Open Question.* London: Blackwell Publishers.
Quine, W. V. 2005. *The Ways of Paradox and Other Essays.* Cambridge: Harvard Uni-
     versity Press.
Radack, David V. 1994. Understanding Confidentiality Agreements. *Journal of the Min-
     erals, Metals and Materials Society* 46 (4): 68.
Rawls, John. 1971. *A Theory of Justice.* Cambridge: Harvard University Press.
_____. 1993. *Political Liberalism.* New York: Columbia University Press.
Raymond, Eric S. 1998. The Halloween Documents. http://www.catb.org/~esr/halloween/.
_____. 2001. Freedom, Power, or Confusion. *Linux Today*, August 17, http://www.linux-
     today.com/news_story.php3?ltsn=2001-08-17-016-20-OP-CY.
_____. 2001. *The Cathedral and the Bazaar.* Cambridge: O'Reilly Books.
_____. 2002. Homesteading the Noosphere, version 3.0. http://www.catb.org/~esr/writings/
     cathedral-bazaar/homesteading/ (accessed June 28, 2006).
_____. 2002. The Cathedral and the Bazaar, version 3.0. http://www.catb.org/~esr/writings/
     cathedral-bazaar/cathedral-bazaar/ (accessed June 24, 2006).
_____. 2002. The Magic Cauldron, version 3.0. http://www.catb.org/~esr/writings/cathedral-
     bazaar/magic-cauldron/ (accessed June 28, 2006).
_____. 2001. How to Become a Hacker. http://www.catb.org/~esr/faqs/hacker-howto.
     html (accessed April 23, 2006).
_____. 2000. A Brief History of Hackerdom. http://www.catb.org/~esr/writings/cathedral-
     bazaar/hacker-history/ (accessed June 22, 2006).
_____. 2004. If Cisco Ignored Kerckhoffs's Law, Users Will Pay the Price. *LWN.net*,
     May 17, http://lwn.net/Articles/85958/.
_____. 2002. Software Release Practice HOWTO, version 3.4. http://en.tldp.org/HOWTO/
     Software-Release-Practice-HOWTO/index.html (accessed November 12, 2005).
Rees, Martin. 2006. Dark Materials. *The Guardian*, June 10, http://www.guardian.co.uk/
     commentisfree/story/0,,1794383,00.html.
Reidenberg, Joel E. 1998. Lex Informatica: The Formulation of Information Policy Rules
     Through Technology. *Texas Law Review* 76 (3): 553–84.
_____. 2003–2004. States and Internet Enforcement. *University of Ottawa Law and
     Technology Journal* 1 (1–2): 213–30.
Resnick, L. B., J. M. Levine, and S. D. Teasley, eds. 1991. *Perspectives on Socially Shared
     Cognition.* Washington, DC: American Psychological Association.
Reuters. 1999. Dell Bolsters Support of Windows Rival Linux. *New York Times*, April
     7, http://www.nytimes.com/library/tech/99/04/biztech/articles/07linux.html.
Richtel, Matt. 1999. Share Price More Than Triples in Red Hat's Public Offering. *New
     York Times*, August 12, http://www.nytimes.com/library/tech/99/08/biztech/
     articles/12linux.html.
Rosen, Lawrence. 2004. *Open Source Licensing: Software Freedom and Intellectual
     Property Law.* Upper Saddle River, NJ: Prentice-Hall PTR.

Rothwell, P. M., and C. N. Martyn. 2000. Reproducibility of Peer Review in Clinical Neuroscience: Is Agreement Between Reviewers any Greater Than Would be Expected by Chance Alone? *Brain* 123:1964–69.

Rusovan, Srdjan, Mark Lawford, and David Lorge Parnas. 2005. Open Source Software Development: Future or Fad? In *Perspectives on Free and Open Source Software*, edited by J. Feller, B. Fitzgerald, S. Hissam, and K. R. Lakhani. Cambridge: MIT Press.

Rustad, Roger E., Jr. 2004. Joel Reidenberg on Hack Toolz, Lex Informatica, and Affirming Non-US Democratic Values. March 23, http://grep.law.harvard.edu/articles/04/03/23/1640243.shtml.

Sacks, Oliver. 1990. *Seeing Voices*. New York: Harper Collins.

Salkever, Alex. 2003. For Windows, Less Fat Means Fewer Bugs. *BusinessWeek*, April 29, http://www.businessweek.com/technology/content/apr2003/tc20030429_6540_tc047.htm.

Sawyer, R. Keith. 2003. *Group Creativity : Music, Theater, Collaboration*. Mahwah, NJ: LEA, Inc.

Scheffler, Israel. 1982. *Science and Subjectivity*. Indianapolis: Hackett.

Schneiderman, Ben, and Catherine Plaisant. 2004. *Designing the User Interface: Strategies for Effective Human-Computer Interaction*. 4th ed. Boston: Addison Wesley.

Seiwald, Christopher. 2005. Seven Pillars of Pretty Code. http://www.perforce.com/perforce/papers/prettycode.html.

Shankland, Stephen. 2000. Web Pioneer Andreessen Joins Open-Source Venture. CNET *News.com*, March 27, http://news.com.com/2100-1001-238484.html.

———. 2004. Torvalds: A Solaris Skeptic. *CNET News.com*, December 21, http://news.com.com/Torvalds+A+Solaris+skeptic/2008-1082_3-5498799.html.

Shirky, Clay. 1998. View Source . . . Lessons from the Web's Massively Parallel Development. http://www.shirky.com/writings/view_source.html.

———. 2005. Epilogue: Open Source Outside the Domain of Software. In *Perspectives on Free and Open Source Software*, edited by J. Feller, B. Fitzgerald, S. Hissam, and K. R. Lakhani. Cambridge: MIT Press.

Sidgwick, Henry. 1981. *The Methods of Ethics*. 7th ed. London: Hackett Publishing Company.

Silver, David. 2000. Looking Backwards, Looking Forward: Cyberculture Studies 1990–2000. In *Web.studies: Rewiring Media Studies for the Digital Age*, edited by D. Gauntlett. Oxford: Oxford University Press.

Simonton, D. K. 1988. *Scientific Genius: A Psychology of Science*. New York: Cambridge University Press.

Smyth, Colm. 2004. 'Bazaar' — How Useful is the Right to Fork? November 28, http://blogs.sun.com/roller/page/ColmSmyth?entry=bazaar_how_useful_is_the.

Sokal, Alan, and Jean Bricmont. 1999. *Fashionable Nonsense: Postmodern Intellectuals' Abuse of Science*. New York: Picador.

St. Laurent, Andrew M. 2004. *Understanding Open Source & Free Software Licensing*. Sebastopol: O'Reilly.

Stallman, Richard. 1983. Initial Announcement. Message to newsgroups net.unix-wizards and net.usoft, September 27, http://www.gnu.org/gnu/initial-announcement.html.

———. 1992. Why Software Should Be Free. http://www.gnu.org/philosophy/shouldbe-free.html.

_____. 1994. Why Software Should Not Have Owners. http://www.gnu.org/philosophy/why-free.html.

_____. 1999. The X-Windows Trap. http://www.gnu.org/philosophy/x.html.

_____. 1999. The GNU operating system and the free software movement. In *Open Sources: Voices from the Open Source Revolution*, edited by C. Dibona. Sebastopol: O'Reilly & Associates.

_____. 2000. Qt, the GPL, KDE, and GNOME. *Linux Today*, September 5, http://www.linuxtoday.com/news_story.php3?ltsn=2000-09-05-001-21-OP-LF-KE.

_____. 2001. Patent Reform Is Not Enough. http://www.gnu.org/philosophy/patent-reform-is-not-enough.html.

_____. 2001. The GNU GPL and the American Way. http://www.gnu.org/philosophy/gpl-american-way.html.

_____. 2001. The Danger of Software Patents. http://www.gnu.org/philosophy/stallman-mec-india.html.

_____. 2002. My Lisp Experiences and the Development of GNU Emacs. http://www.gnu.org/gnu/rms-lisp.html.

_____. 2003. Copyleft: Pragmatic Idealism. http://www.gnu.org/philosophy/pragmatic.html.

_____. 2005. BitKeeper Bon Voyage is a Happy Ending. *NewsForge*, April 25, http://software.newsforge.com/article.pl?sid=05/04/25/130207.

_____. 2005. Ethical Analysis of the GPL. Personal communication.

_____. 2005. Patent Absurdity. *Guardian Unlimited*, June 20, http://technology.guardian.co.uk/online/comment/story/0,12449,1510566,00.html

Sterling, Bruce. 1994. *The Hacker Crackdown: Law and Disorder on the Electronic Frontier*. http://www.mit.edu/hacker/hacker.html.

Strathern, Marilyn. 2005. Imagined Collectivities and Multiple Authorship. In *CODE: Collaborative Ownership in the Digital Economy*, edited by R. A. Ghosh. Cambridge: MIT Press.

Sutton, Adrian. 2004. Beautiful Code Is Important. http://www.symphonious.net/2004/11/27/beautiful-code-is-important/.

Swann, Matthew, and Clark Turner. 2004. Executable Code is not the Proper Subject of Copyright Law: Cal Poly State University.

Sweet, David. 2001. *KDE 2.0 Development*. Vol. 2006. Indianapolis: Sams Publishing.

Sylvan, Richard. 1996. Anarchism. In *A Companion to Contemporary Political Philosophy*, edited by R. E. Goodin and P. Pettit. London: Blackwell.

Tanenbaum, Andrew S. 1987. *Operating Systems: Design and Implementations*. Upper Saddle River, NJ: Prentice-Hall.

Tanksley, William, and Neel Krishnaswami. 1999. Be Gentle With Me . . . . Email to python-list mailing list, December 3, http://mail.python.org/pipermail/python-list/1999-December/017213.html.

Taylor, Charles. 1979. What's Wrong with Negative Liberty? In *The Idea of Freedom: Essays in Honour of Isaiah Berlin*, edited by A. Ryan. Oxford Oxford University Press.

Terranova, Tiziana. 2000. Free Labor: Producing Culture for the Digital Economy. *Social Text* 18 (2): 33–58.

Thacker, Eugene. 2004. Foreword: Protocol Is As Protocol Does. In *Protocol: How Control Exists After Decentralization*. Cambridge: MIT Press.

The Canadian Press. 2005. Nationalized Oil Resources, Firms Appeal to Many Canadi-
ans. *Business Edge*, September 15, http://www.businessedge.ca/article.cfm/new-
sID/10433.cfm.

The European Convention. 2003. Draft Treaty Establishing a Constitution for Europe.
http://europa.eu.int/constitution/futurum/constitution/index_en.htm.

The Free Software Foundation. 2005. The Free Software Definition. http://www.fsf.org/
licensing/essays/free-sw.html (accessed June 22, 2006).

———. 2006. Discussion Draft 1 of the GPL, Version 3. http://gplv3.fsf.org/comments/
(accessed July 25, 2006).

———. 2006. Discussion Draft 2 of the GPL, Version 3. http://gplv3.fsf.org/gpl-draft-
2006-07-27.html (accessed August 10, 2006).

The Open Source Initiative. 2006. Frequently Asked Questions. http://www.opensource.
org/advocacy/faq.php (accessed June 22, 2006).

———. 2006. History of the OSI. http://www.opensource.org/history.

The Pugwash Conferences. 2002. Mission Statement. http://www.pugwash.org/about/
mission.htm.

The SavetheInternet.com Coalition. 2006. Save the Internet. http://www.savetheinternet.com/.

Thompson, Ken. 1999. Unix and Beyond: An Interview with Ken Thompson. *IEEE Computer* 5:58–64.

Thomson, Judith Jarvis. 1976. Killing, Letting Die, and the Trolley Problem. *The Monist*
59:204–17.

Tolstoy, Leo. 1960. *What Is Art?* Translated by A. Maude. New York: MacMillan.

Tompkins, Howard E. 1963. Computer Education. In *Advances in Computers*, edited by F.
L. Alt and M. Rubinoff. New York: Academic Press.

Tridgell, Andrew. 2000. Samba-TNG Fork. http://us1.samba.org/samba/tng.html.

Truscello, Michael. 2003. The Architecture of Information: Open Source Software and
Tactical Poststructuralist Anarchism. *Postmodern Culture* 13 (3).

Ts'o, Theodore. 1997. Microsoft "embraces and extends" Kerberos V5. *Usenix*, December
3, https://db.usenix.org/publications/login/1997-11/embraces.html.

Turing, Alan. 1936. On Computable Numbers, with an application to the Entschei-
dungsproblem. *Proceedings of the London Mathematical Society* 2 (42): 230–65.

Turoff, Murray, John Foster, Roxanne Hiltz, and Kenneth Ng. 1990. The TEIES Design
and Objectives: Computer Mediated Communications and Tailorability. Paper
read at 22 Annual Hawaii International Conference on System Sciences, 1989.

Tyre, James. 2001. Brief of Amici Curiae, Universal City Studios, Inc., et al. vs. Eric
Corley, a/k/a Emmanuel Goldstein, 2600 Enterprises, Inc., Shawn C. Reimerdes,
Roman Kazan. http://cryptome.org/mpaa-v-2600-bac.htm.

Vaidyanathan, Siva. 2003. *Copyrights and Copywrongs: The Rise of Copyright and How
It Threatens Creativity*. New York: New York University Press.

van Rooyen, Susan, Fiona Godlee, Stephen Evans, Nick Black, and Richard Smith. 1999.
Effect of Open Peer Review on Quality of Reviews and on Reviewers' Recommen-
dations: a Randomised Trial. *British Medical Journal* 318 (7175): 23–27.

Vaughan-Nichols, Steven J. 2005. Red Hat's Earnings and Stock Soar. *eWeek.com*, September 29, http://www.eweek.com/article2/0,1895,1865193,00.asp.

Vermazen, Bruce. 1991. The Aesthetic Value of Originality. *Midwest Studies in Philosophy* 16:266–79.

Vygotsky, L. S. 1962. *Thought and Language*. Translated by E. Hanfmann and G. Vakar.
Cambridge: MIT Press.

_____. 1978. *Mind in Society: The Development of Higher Psychological Processes.* Cambridge: Harvard University Press.

W3C. 2006. Extensible Markup Language (XML). http://www.w3.org/XML/.

Wacha, Jason B. 2004. Taking The Case: Is the GPL Enforceable. *Santa Clara Computer and High Technology Law Journal* 21:451–88.

Wallace, Daniel. 2004. Why the GPL is Invalid. Email to license-discuss mailing list, February 12, http://www.mail-archive.com/license-discuss@opensource.org/msg07093.html.

Wallas, Graham. 1926. *The Art of Thought.* London: J. Cape.

Warsaw, Barry. 1999. Be Gentle With Me. . . . Email to python-list mailing list, December 6, http://mail.python.org/pipermail/python-list/1999-December/017384.html.

Weber, Steven. 2004. *The Success of Open Source.* Cambridge: Harvard University Press.

Weeks, Stephen. 2005. *Why BSD-style Instead of the GPL?* Posting to web forum, December 5, http://www.codecomments.com/archive269-2005-12-721015.html.

Weik, Martin H. 1961. The ENIAC Story. *ORDNANCE* (January–February), http://ftp.arl.mil/~mike/comphist/eniac-story.html.

Weisberg, Robert W. 2006. *Creativity: Understanding Innovation in Problem Solving, Science, Invention, and the Arts.* New York: Wiley.

Wheeler, David A. 2005. Why Open Source Software / Free Software (OSS/FS, FLOSS, or FOSS)? Look at the Numbers! http://www.dwheeler.com/oss_fs_why.html.

Williams, Sam. 2002. *Free as in Freedom: Richard Stallman's Crusade for Free Software.* Sebastopol, CA: O'Reilly Media.

Wirth, Niklaus. 1995. A Plea for Lean Software. *IEEE Computer* 28 (2).

Wittgenstein, Ludwig. 1953/1999. *Philosophical Investigations.* Translated by G.E.M. Anscombe. Third ed. New York: Prentice-Hall.

Wolfram, Stephan. 2002. *A New Kind of Science.* New York: Wolfram Media.

Wollheim, Richard. 1980. Criticism as Retrieval. In *Art and Its Objects.* Cambridge: Cambridge University Press.

Zawinski, Jamie. 2000. The Lemacs/FSFmacs Schism. http://www.jwz.org/doc/lemacs.html.

Zittrain, Jonathan. 2004. Normative Principles for Evaluating Free and Proprietary Software. *University of Chicago Law Review* 71 (1).

Zymaris, Con. 2003. A Comparison of the GPL and the Microsoft EULA. http://www.cyber.com.au/about/comparing_the_gpl_to_eula.pdf.

Index

For Product Safety Concerns and Information please contact our EU
representative GPSR@taylorandfrancis.com
Taylor & Francis Verlag GmbH, Kaufingerstraße 24, 80331 München, Germany